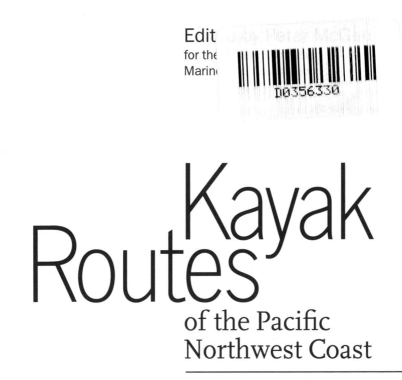

Edit
for the
Marine

D0356330

Kayak Routes

of the Pacific
Northwest Coast

THE
MOUNTAINEERS
SEATTLE

GREYSTONE BOOKS

Douglas & McIntyre
Vancouver/Toronto

99 00 01 02   5 4 3 2

Greystone Books
A division of Douglas & McIntyre Ltd.
1615 Venables Street
Vancouver, British Columbia
V5L 2H1

Canadian Cataloguing in Publication Data

McGee, Peter.
Kayak routes of the Pacific Northwest coast

ISBN 1-55054-615-5

1. Sea kayaking—British Columbia—
Pacific Coast—Guidebooks. 2. Sea kayak-
ing—Washington (State)—Puget
Sound—Guidebooks. 3. Pacific Coast
(B.C.)—Guidebooks. 4. Puget Sound
(Wash.)—Guidebooks. I. Title
GV776.15.B7M33 1998 797.1'224'097111
C97-911100-5

Originated by Greystone Books and
published simultaneously in the
United States of America by
The Mountaineers
1001 S.W. Klickitat Way, Suite 107,
Seattle, WA 98134

**Library of Congress Cataloging-in-
Publication Data**

Kayak Routes of the Pacific Northwest coast
/ edited by Peter McGee for the B.C. Marine
Trail Association.
    p.   cm.
Includes bibliographic references (p.)
and index.
ISBN 00-89886-579-4
1. Kayaking—Northwest Coast of North
America—Guidebooks. 2. Northwest
Coast of North America—Guidebooks.
I. McGee, Peter. II. BC Marine Trail Asso-
ciation.
GV776.5.K39   1998
796.1'224'09795—DC21   97-52684
                                        CIP

Editing by Nancy Pollak
Cover design by Peter Cocking
Cover photograph by Peter McGee
Text design by Val Speidel
Maps by ODIN Graffix
Printed and bound in Canada by Best Book
    Manufacturers
Printed on acid-free paper

The publisher gratefully acknowledges the
support of the Canada Council for the Arts
and of the British Columbia Ministry of
Tourism, Small Business and Culture.

To all those who care for the coast

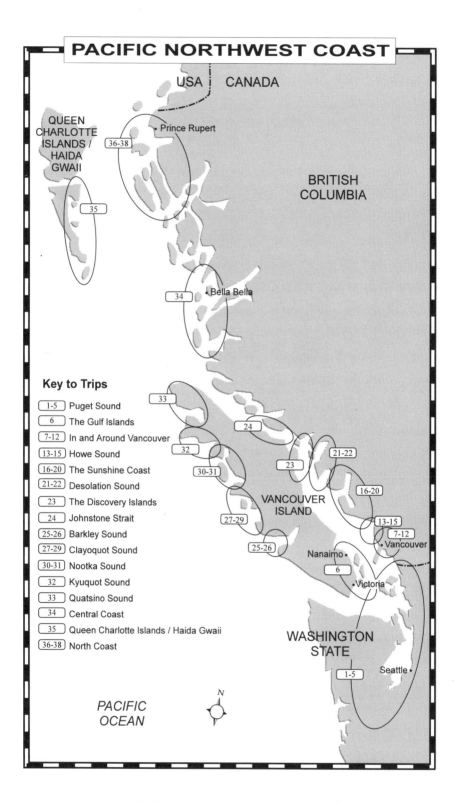

PACIFIC NORTHWEST COAST

USA | CANADA

QUEEN
CHARLOTTE
ISLANDS /
HAIDA
GWAII

Prince Rupert

36-38

35

BRITISH
COLUMBIA

34 Bella Bella

Key to Trips

1-5	Puget Sound
6	The Gulf Islands
7-12	In and Around Vancouver
13-15	Howe Sound
16-20	The Sunshine Coast
21-22	Desolation Sound
23	The Discovery Islands
24	Johnstone Strait
25-26	Barkley Sound
27-29	Clayoquot Sound
30-31	Nootka Sound
32	Kyuquot Sound
33	Quatsino Sound
34	Central Coast
35	Queen Charlotte Islands / Haida Gwaii
36-38	North Coast

33

24

32

23

21-22

30-31

16-20

VANCOUVER
ISLAND

27-29

13-15

7-12

Vancouver

25-26

Nanaimo

6

Victoria

WASHINGTON
STATE

1-5

Seattle

*PACIFIC
OCEAN*

N

Contents

What was once a galaxy of well-guarded secrets for a fairly reclusive bunch of kayakers is now a coastal playground at risk of being loved to death. Not only are thousands of paddlers making increasing demands on the areas earmarked for the Cascadia Marine Trail of the Pacific Northwest coast, so too are yachties, divers, powerboaters, even alas jet-skiers. It is significant that the sea kayaking community has shown the initiative to adopt a custodial role on the West Coast. This is a group with considerable political sting. I remember when B.C. Ferries became annoyed by pesky kayakers in the 1980s and decided to ban roll-on kayak traffic between islands. The response from the rapidly assembled kayak political assault team fairly staggered the public relations department at the ferry corporation, which backed down hastily with the rueful observation that they had never encountered such a formidable response.

Now the sea kayak community is being heard on the matter of a marine trail, and this time there is an encouraging element of maturity as seasoned activists try on their custodial garb. The B.C. Marine Trail Association meetings I attended were full of level-headed, thoughtful people who cared about what was happening to our coast. Few people I know value personal freedom and independence more than these people, yet underlying every meeting was the realization that if we were to preserve wild coastal places, a new approach was needed: we would need to become more proactive about informing our community how best to interact with the sensitive areas we have grown to love, and we would need to work with other interested parties.

Perhaps the main reason I came to support the BCMTA was because its focus is to inform and educate rather than to restrict and control. Implicit is the recognition that the flip side of the coin of freedom is a lofty combination of responsibility and vigilance. That ties in really nicely with kayaking as I know it. This guidebook reflects those values and is a timely work that fills a significant gap in the West Coast kayaker's library.

John Dowd

Preface

It was only after considerable soul-searching that the B.C. Marine Trail Association decided to pursue this project. We knew a site-specific guide would eventually be produced, and we believed it would be best if a group such as the BCMTA could create a book that would actually help mitigate some of the damage brought about by increased public exposure. With this in mind, *Kayak Routes of the Pacific Northwest Coast* has a strong educational component regarding minimum impact camping and cultural impacts. All the contributors live or work in the areas they describe, and each went to great lengths to ensure that local and environmental concerns were addressed in the site-selection process. In addition, all royalties from this book will be used to help with site clean-up and maintenance.

Ultimately, however, responsibility for caring for the coast rests with you. Paddlers are gaining a political voice in the Pacific Northwest, yet our status as a legitimate interest group depends to a large degree on our conduct as individuals. Tread lightly when you visit the areas described in this guide, but always speak loudly for their preservation. Don't be afraid to express your love or concerns for an area. Remember, it is both your actions on and off the water that will help keep the spirit of our coast alive.

Thank you for choosing *Kayak Routes of the Pacific Northwest Coast* as your kayak guide to British Columbia and Washington. Happy paddling.

Peter McGee

Acknowledgements

This book has been a collaborative effort from the very beginning so it is difficult to list everyone who has helped in its creation. To give the authors their appropriate due, small biographies are supplied at the back of the book. All these authors deserve enormous thanks for volunteering their time and local expertise to ensure this guide happened.

For their help with content and editing, thanks also to John Dowd, Paul Chaplow, Rich Brame, Stuart Smith, Glen Harris, Michael Pardy, Chris Ladner, Cathie Findlay-Brook, Nicki Browne, Bob Austad, Wally Priedolins, Meredith Reeve, Dr. Helga Sickert, Pauline Scott, Rueben Weir, Jennifer Carpenter of the Heiltsuk Cultural Education Centre, John Bolton of the Heiltsuk Fisheries Co-Management Program, and the Gwaii Haanas Archipelago Management Board. We are also grateful to David Getchell, Mary Monfort, Sandie Rumble, Jamie Little, Catherine France, Sarah Robertson and all others who have helped with the B.C. Marine Trail Association over the years.

A special thanks goes to Nancy Pollak, Rob Sanders, Nancy Flight, Terri Wershler and Leanne Denis for their incredible patience in dealing with a publishing rookie such as myself. Finally, thanks to my parents who allowed the B.C. Marine Trail Association to evolve in their basement and, at various times, take over every other room in their home.

Marine Trails of the Pacific Northwest Coast

A paddling trail that winds its way along the coast of the Pacific Northwest has, in essence, always existed. For thousands of years people have paddled these waters, travelling from camp to camp and village to village, as they worked their way north or south along the Inside Passage. Times are changing, however, and pressures from industry and private development, as well as from increased recreational use, are putting a strain on the number of suitable camping and resting areas available for the growing paddling community.

In light of this, the B.C. Marine Trail Association (BCMTA) and the Washington Water Trails Association (WWTA) were formed in the early 1990s to establish marine trails in their respective parts of the coast. When connected, these trails will form a marine trail system without political boundaries. The Cascadia Marine Trail, as it is known, will be the longest and most spectacular protected marine corridor in the world.

Currently the Washington State portion of the Cascadia Marine Trail has a permit system, unlike the less official British Columbia portion; however, the BCMTA and WWTA have the same goals and are working hard to preserve areas that are important to paddlers and other small boaters. Both organizations need your help. If you have not already done so, don't wait until it's too late to protect the beauty of the coast. Join your local water trail association today!

British Columbia Marine Trail Association,
Box 36046, 1153 Esquimalt Road,
Victoria, B.C., V9A 3N7
Tel./fax: (250) 383-1100

Members of the B.C. Marine Trail Association and the Washington Water Trails Association meet on the beach at White Rock. PETER McGEE

Washington Water Trails Association,
#305 4649 Sunnyside Avenue North,
Seattle, WA 98103-6900
Tel./fax: (206) 545-9161
Webpage: www.eskimo.com/~wwta

North American Water Trails Network,
24130 Johnson Road NW,
Poulsbo, WA 98370
Tel: (360) 697-3234

The opening chapter of this guide explores issues relating to safety, minimum impact camping, wildlife, cultural impacts, weather, tides and currents, and hazards of the Pacific Northwest. Chapters 2-17 provide descriptions of paddle routes. At the back of the book is the Useful Contacts section with various phone/fax numbers and addresses for weather, camping and travel information as well as First Nations and emergency contacts. Very few phone numbers or addresses have been included in the main text.

This guide is not an instruction manual. For helpful reading on technical and safety aspects of paddling, as well as on natural and local history, see the Recommended Reading list at the back of the book.

Although this is the most complete guide to the Pacific Northwest available, as you adventure along the coast you are bound to discover places that aren't included here. There are a few reasons for this. First, we may not have known about them. Second, due to space limitations we included only the best, most practically located sites. Third, we never intended to put out a book that would take away your sense of discovery, and several sites were left out as little gifts for the more adventuresome paddler to stumble upon—a small reward for those willing to take the path less travelled. Finally, there are spots of local endearment that, in a sense, belong to the communities. While you are free to find and use them, it was simply not appropriate for us to point them out.

The paddle routes are divided by region, and the format for each chapter is roughly as follows:

The **Map** provided in each chapter, while as accurate as possible, is not meant for navigational use; it is only intended to help orient the reader to some of the features discussed in the chapter.

The **Background** section is meant to give you a taste for the history of an area and inform you about some of the issues the local people are facing today. This section is meant to encourage further research and is supplemented by the Recommended Reading list at the back of the book.

Getting to a suitable launch site is half the battle when beginning a kayak trip. We have tried to simplify this process in the **Getting There** section by providing you with up-to-date information on travelling to your destination by car, bus, ferry, plane and sometimes even train.

Only local weather conditions and hazards are discussed in the **Weather and Hazards** section. General principles regarding the prevalent weather conditions and many hazards of the Pacific Northwest can be found in Chapter 1.

Special Considerations deals with any specific issues, aside from weather and hazards, that you need to be aware of before beginning your journey. These can range from the habits of animals that frequent the area to the concerns of local residents regarding the impacts of kayakers.

The **Trip Summaries** are in point form and give suggested trip length, suggested skill level(s), prominent hazards in the area, major access points, and relevant marine charts and tide books. Trip length (for a round trip) and skill level are based on the prevalent paddling conditions of an area. However, it is essential that you make your own assessment as to whether the conditions of a particular day and time of year are compatible with your paddling ability. *Even the most sheltered waters can be hazardous in certain seasons and weather conditions, and a trip labelled Beginner can quickly become challenging to even an expert paddler.* It is up to you to exercise good judgement in selecting your destination and determining your paddling route.

Proper nautical **Charts and Tide Tables** should always be used in conjunction with this book. Depending on the scope of your trip, you may require one, several or all of the charts listed. (Please note: Marine charts, as well as the maps in this book, are based on nautical miles. One nautical mile (nm) is equal to 1.151 stature miles. There is no straightforward metric equivalent to a nautical mile, but 1 stature mile equals 1.61 kilometres.) Marine charts and tide tables for British Columbia are published by the Canadian Hydrographic Service; charts and tables for Washington State are available from the National Oceanic and Atmospheric Administration (see Useful Contacts at the back of the book for addresses).

The **Trip Descriptions** give detailed information on suggested launch sites, campsites and paddle routes in an area. Suggested trip times are based on reasonable paddling conditions and the assumption that most people like to spend between 3–5 hours a day in their boats and travel approximately 2 nautical miles per hour. Thus, it is extremely important that you determine the particular speed and capabilities of your group and plan accordingly.

On the rare occasion that prices are given, the amounts were current in 1997. Prices in Washington State are in U.S. dollars; prices in British Columbia are in Canadian dollars.

Most of the routes in this guide are circle routes contained within a single region, with the same start and end point. **Additional Routes** provides some information for those wanting to travel between regions in a northerly/southerly direction. Descriptions are admittedly brief, and anyone requiring further information or maps should contact either the B.C. Marine Trail Association or the Washington Water Trails Association. These organizations are well prepared to give up-to-date information on camping areas and launch sites for most of the Pacific Northwest.

> Heading out. PETER McGEE

Chapter One

Kayaking the Pacific Northwest Coast

SAFETY FIRST

Safe travel in the Pacific Northwest is entirely dependent on your skill, judgement and common sense. Although the routes listed in this book were selected with the limitation of ocean kayaks in mind, they still have inherent dangers.

You are on your own when paddling in the Pacific Northwest, so be prepared. If you get in a jam, there is not a lot of help out there. If you are injured, the nearest hospital may be many hours away. The following are suggestions to help you head off catastrophe. They are not the only issues a kayaker may face, but they are important bases to cover.

- Be prepared to solve your own problems. For example, pack the necessary supplies to make emergency boat repairs and have extra food in case your paddling schedule is delayed by poor weather.
- Whether paddling solo or in a group, have your techniques for self- and assisted rescues so well learned that you can do them under any conditions. The Eskimo roll is great for a quick recovery but should not be counted on. Be sure to practise alternative exit and re-entry techniques.
- Enhance your boating skills by taking courses or travelling with more experienced boaters who can share their knowledge.
- Do not paddle alone unless you are experienced and have your act well in hand regarding skill, physical condition and mental preparedness. If you are travelling solo, leave yourself a wide margin of safety.
- The greatest single danger to sea kayakers is hypothermia. Cold water kills. Dress appropriately and educate yourself about hypothermia.

- Get a marine weather forecast each day *before* you head out on the water.
- The Canadian and U.S. Coast Guards recommend that all boaters file a float plan with someone. That person should know where you are going and when you are due in port. If you make major changes to your plan during your trip, update your contact party.
- Always carry a compass when paddling and know how to use it. A deck-mounted compass will help you keep your bearings over long distances.
- Carrying a VHF (Very High Frequency) radio aboard is a good idea but will not eliminate the need for any of the above. Keep in mind: electronics do not fare well in small open boats and may fail when you need them most. Small hand-held VHF radios (including weather radios) have a very limited range and work on line of sight. Do not expect to pick up VHF channels (either sending or receiving) while on shore, because the land mass on which you are sitting may be blocking the signal. To reach a VHF channel, you may have to paddle 150–200 m (500–600 ft.) offshore. The same limitations apply when travelling up a steep-sided inlet; you may have to completely leave the inlet to use your VHF radio.
- Always tie your boat when you go ashore, even when it has been pulled well above the high tide line. A sudden squall can toss a lightweight boat right back into the water. As for beaching your boat "for just a minute," you may not realize how fast the tide rises until you turn to see your pride and joy drifting off to sea.
- Always carry a first aid kit. Know exactly what it contains and how to use it. Make sure that others in your group know where to find it. A full equipment checklist can be found at the back of the book.
- Do not try to keep to a tight schedule because doing so may tempt you to take unnecessary chances. Relax, and adjust your schedule to fit the weather and other circumstances. Better to hole up short of a goal than to risk your life and those of your companions.

Remember: Safe travel involves having not only the appropriate knowledge, but a healthy respect for the sea and an ability to expect the unexpected. These are gained through experience and by living according to the rules of the sea.

PRINCIPLES OF MINIMUM IMPACT CAMPING

The purpose of this guidebook is to help people discover the beauty of the Pacific Northwest and the joys of paddling. The authors agreed to voluntarily contribute to this project on condition that the guide also help teach the essentials of minimum impact camping. If we are to preserve the natural beauty of our islands in the face of increasing use, we must all take responsibility to educate ourselves and to become equipped with the skills and habits that enable us to minimize our impacts on the environment. Minimum impact camping is the mark of a skillful camper, yet years of experience are not required to master the simple techniques that make the difference between a mess and a site that blends naturally into its surroundings. If you concentrate on the effort to leave little or no mark on the land, you will find that it works. It's that easy.

Much of the information in this section has been drawn, with permission, from the Maine Island Trail Association Guide and the National Outdoor Leadership School's Leave No Trace brochure on temperate coastal zones. For additional information, contact MITA or NOLS/Leave No Trace Inc.

Plan Ahead and Be Prepared

Unnecessary impact in coastal areas can be avoided by carefully preparing for your trip. For example, if you fail to bring enough fuel and are forced to make fires in areas where wood is scarce, you further deplete an already strained source. Proper preparation includes: knowing what to expect; having the proper equipment; researching the area you plan to visit; adequately planning and packaging food supplies; and having the proper skills to travel safely. Consider the mottos "Leave No Trace" or "Minimum Impact" as inspiration to develop the right attitude and plan appropriately to lessen your presence in the backcountry.

Carefully plan your rations to reduce waste from leftovers, and repackage your food to reduce the amount of potential trash. If possible, visit the backcountry during seasons or days of the week when use levels are low, and limit your group size. This should also be tempered with an effort to avoid travel when the environment is particularly fragile such as during critical waterfowl and marine mammal breeding or hatching periods.

Finally, proper training or experience in paddling the coast is essential both to your safety and to minimizing your impact. Poor decision making, injury or illness can force you into a situation where outside help is needed, at which time minimum impact concerns go out the window. The basis of safe and sensitive paddling is sound judgement, technical competence and self-responsibility. This includes developing skills such as leadership and wilderness first aid.

Select Appropriate Campsites

Selecting an appropriate campsite is perhaps the most important aspect of low impact coastal travel. It requires the greatest use of judgement and often involves making trade-offs between ecological and social impacts. A decision about where to camp should be based on the level and type of use in the area, the fragility of vegetation and soil, the likelihood of wildlife disturbance, an assessment of previous impacts and your party's potential to cause or avoid impact.

Allow enough time and energy at the end of the day to select an appropriate site. Plan ahead to avoid being forced to use a poor or fragile campsite due to tiredness or foul weather. Avoid camping close to trails and fresh water sources: a distance of 90 m (300 ft.) is a good standard. There are four basic principles to selecting a campsite.

Concentrate Impact on Established Sites   It is best to camp on sites that are so highly used that further careful use will cause no additional impact. In popular areas these sites are obvious because they have already lost their vegetation cover. In coastal environments it is usually possible to lessen your impact even more by choosing the established sites that naturally lack vegetation such as gravelly or sandy beaches.

Tents, traffic routes and kitchen areas should be concentrated on already impacted areas. Your objective is to confine impact to places that already show use to avoid enlarging the disturbed areas. When leaving camp, make sure it is clean, attractive and appealing to campers who follow.

Minimize Site Alterations   Good campsites are *found* not made. Do not dig trenches for tents or construct lean-tos, tables, chairs or other rudimentary improvements. If you clear a camp area of surface rocks, driftwood or seaweed, replace these items before leaving. On highly impacted sites, it is appropriate to clean up the site and dismantle inappropriate user-built facilities such as constructed seats or tables. Properly located and legal facilities (e.g., a fire ring or picnic bench) should be left.

Allow others a sense of discovery by leaving rocks, plants, bones, archeological artifacts and other objects of interest as you found them—and avoid damaging live animals and plants.

Avoid Places Where Impact Is Just Beginning   Most campsites can withstand a certain level of use and still recover to a pristine state. However, a threshold is eventually reached where the regenerative power of the vegetation cannot keep pace with the amount of trampling. Once this threshold is reached, the site will deteriorate more rapidly with continued use. This will result in the development of an established campsite with a discernible "barren core."

A general guideline is to avoid all sites that show slight signs of use. If these areas receive no further use, they can revegetate and revert back to their natural appearance. By spreading out while camping on durable surfaces in remote areas and staying on well-established ones in popular areas, it is possible to minimize or prevent the proliferation of many unnecessary campsites and trails.

Spread Use and Impacts in Pristine Areas Pristine areas are typically remote, seldom visited and have few or no obvious impacts from camping. Visit pristine areas only if you are committed to the following specific techniques required to minimize impacts.

When selecting an undisturbed site, look for an area of beach below the highest winter storm tide level and above current high tides. This zone is usually made up of sand, rock or gravel, relatively level and well suited for absorbing impact. If you are able to camp on the beach below the highest tide of the month, all the better, but beware: this can lead to a sleepless night spent with a watch, headlamp and tide table. Whatever site you choose, be sure to camp away from fresh water sources and critical wildlife habitat.

Avoid camping in forests or meadows unless forced to by extenuating circumstances such as extremely foul weather or high tides. If you must resort to these areas, durability of the ground surface is the most important impact consideration. Nonvegetated areas are best but forest duff is acceptable if you can avoid crushing plants or seedlings. Grassy areas are more resilient than woody stemmed forest undergrowth.

On any pristine site, spread out and avoid creating traffic routes over vegetation. This will help to minimize the number of times a given site is trampled. Choose the most durable areas for tents and kitchens. Wear soft-soled shoes around camp. Minimize activity around the kitchen and in places where bags and boats are stashed, and always watch where you walk to avoid crushing vegetation. Use carrying containers to lessen the number of trips to fetch water and take alternative paths to the water source.

When breaking camp, take time to naturalize the site. Covering scuffed-up areas with native materials, replacing moved logs and rocks, and raking matted grassy areas with a stick will help a site recover and make it less obvious as a campsite. This extra effort will help hide the fact that you camped there and make it less likely that others will follow. Remember, regardless of your minimum impact techniques, the less often a pristine campsite is used, the better chance it has of remaining pristine.

Use Fire Responsibly—and Infrequently

Campfires in the backcountry were once necessary for cooking, and their use is steeped in history and tradition. The tradition is so entrenched in our minds that for some, the idea of going on a backcountry trip without having a fire is almost unthinkable. As a direct result of the past misuse of campfires, however, a new attitude is developing. Fires are no longer advisable or even permitted in many areas along the coast. Some of the reasons are the increasing number of backcountry travellers, diminishing firewood supplies, alterations to the ecosystem when dead trees and branches are removed and the chance of an escaped wildfire.

Camp stoves should always be used in areas where fires are prohibited, a fire hazard exists or there is little available dead wood. Keep in mind, however, that even in areas where fires are allowed, a stove is preferable because blackened circles of rocks and charred wood significantly diminish a wilderness experience.

If you must have a fire, use an existing fire ring or a site below the high tide line but above the sensitive intertidal zone. Build fires on rocky or sandy soil away from overhanging trees, dry vegetation or root systems. Use only dry and downed dead wood and collect only what you need, taking it from different locations. Do not break dead branches off live, standing trees as this leaves a discernible and long-lasting impact. Do not burn food scraps or plastic. Driftwood is an ideal source of firewood although you should avoid painted, laminated or creosote-treated wood products because they emit toxic fumes when burned. Small pieces of wood are best: they are much easier to burn thoroughly and will not leave half-burned logs that remain as obvious signs of your fire.

Leave your firewood in natural lengths until you are ready to burn it. If you have any unburned lengths left over when breaking camp, they can easily be scattered around the area and will blend in naturally. Burn wood down to a white ash before extinguishing the fire, then stir and pour water on the site until you feel no hot spots with your bare hand. Collect any remaining refuse, then scatter the ashes and blackened rocks below the tide line so that no sign of your fire is noticeable. Disperse any wood that is left before you leave camp and cover the fire site with a thin layer of sand or gravel.

If you are building a fire below the high tide line, scoop a shallow pit in the sand or gravel. If the beach is made up of larger stones that will scar, you can line the pit with an inch or two of sand or small gravel taken from another suitable location. If you are unable to take advantage of the beach, it is best to forego a fire.

Pack It In, Pack It Out

Pick up and pack out all of your litter. Burying, dumping or leaving trash in the backcountry is unacceptable. On the way out—when your boat space has increased—try to pick up litter left by others.

Reduce litter at the source. When preparing for your trip, repackage food into reusable containers and remove any excess packaging. This simple practice lessens the chance that you will inadvertently leave litter behind and will likely help free up some space in your boat. A few hints: use knots, not twist ties, to secure food bags, and put your garbage bag in a nylon stuff sac to ensure it doesn't tear when pulled in and out of the boat.

Protect Water Quality

Many intestinal diseases are transmitted through water so it is important to be very careful not to contaminate water supplies in wilderness areas. Of particular concern in the Pacific Northwest is giardiasis. This internal infection is caused by the parasite *Giardia lamblia* and is transmitted through water contaminated by the feces of infected animals (including dogs) and people. In order to prevent its spread, you should never urinate or defecate directly into fresh water, either in camp or when travelling. As a general rule, washing and disposing of any waste should be done at least 90 m (300 ft.) from a fresh water source. If a toilet facility is provided, use it; if not, incorporate the disposal techniques listed in the following section.

To be completely safe when collecting drinking water, you should consider *all* water to be contaminated and in need of treatment before drinking. Three common methods are boiling water (minimum one minute at a full boil), water filters and iodine. Regardless of whether you treat water, it is best to collect from a clear and flowing source and away from the shore. The higher up the source of running water, the less likely it is to be contaminated.

Properly Dispose of Human Waste

Visitors to coastal areas create certain types of wastes that are hard to pack out. These include human waste and waste water from cooking and washing. Although often unpleasant to deal with in the absence of a toilet facility, human waste needs to be properly disposed of to maintain your health and the health of others.

Ocean Disposal   The ocean is a vast and dynamic reservoir of bacteria—and the best location for feces decomposition in the absence of a toilet or outhouse. It should not be used, however, in areas of little water movement or areas where people commonly swim.

When disposing of human waste in the ocean, the best option is to use a "honey bucket" or bag and deposit the fecal matter well off-shore by kayak. The container can then be rinsed and reused. If this is neither feasible nor attractive, the next best option is to dispose of your waste from the shore into the ocean. Take the time to assess the shoreline to determine if there is an accessible area with strong water movement such as tidal currents or wave action. Headlands or rocky points are usually good sites for disposal; calm protected bays are not. Take care to avoid tide pools, shellfish beds and other sensitive areas. Once you have chosen your site, do your business directly into the water (preferably at low tide). If this is awkward, you can try the infamous "shit-put." Find something such as a large, flat rock to serve as a platter to launch the feces into the water. Then do your business a comfortable distance from the water, take the rock to the water's edge and throw it as far as you can into the ocean. It may not be pretty but it works.

Cat Holes and Latrines   Cat holes are a widely accepted method of waste disposal in certain situations but are less commonly used in coastal environments and should be viewed as a last resort. Beaches that make good campsites are often too wet or confining, or receive too much use for the cat-hole method to be effective. There are appropriate places, however, to use cat holes, such as when you are camped in a calm bay with no water movement. Cat holes must be located 90 m (300 ft.) from fresh water, trails and camp. Select a site that is inconspicuous and where other people will be unlikely to walk or camp.

With a small garden trowel, dig a hole 10–15 cm (roughly 6 in.), removing the sod intact. Make sure the depth does not exceed the dark-coloured, biologically active layer of top soil where decomposition will occur. Soil removed from the cat hole should be placed nearby in a pile; after each use, spread a light layer of soil back in the hole. After the final use, fill the cat hole with the remaining loose soil and tamp the sod lightly back into place.

One cat hole per group is suggested rather than one per person. When the hole is used for multiple uses, it is typically called a latrine. To make a latrine, dig a trench of similar depth and width as a cat hole but increase its length to accommodate all users. Since the higher concentration of feces will decompose very slowly, location is especially important.

Toilet Paper Use toilet paper sparingly and only the nonperfumed brands. Toilet paper must be disposed of properly: placed in plastic bags and packed out, or completely burned. One way of dealing with toilet paper used for urination is to keep it in a small plastic bag dedicated to this task until the end of the day, when a hot fire can be built to burn the used paper. Burning with matches or lighters has resulted in a number of forest fires, so this technique should only be used on fire-resistant beaches or rocky shores. If you do use matches or a lighter, be sure the paper burns completely. Keep it dry and "fluff it" before you light it or there will be incomplete burning. Burning the paper in a hot campfire is a much better alternative, assuming the site is suitable for a fire.

The low impact camper willing to go the extra mile might consider foregoing toilet paper altogether and using natural alternatives. When used correctly, natural toilet paper is as effective as regular toilet paper. Popular types of natural toilet paper include stones, vegetation and snow. Some experimentation is necessary to make this practice work for you but it is worth a try.

Used tampons and sanitary pads should be also bagged and packed out, or burned in a hot campfire. They should never be buried.

Urination Urination has little direct effect on vegetation or soil. However, urine may draw wildlife, which are attracted to human salts and may then defoliate plants and dig up soil. It is best to urinate directly into the ocean or below the high tide line where the ocean can absorb it; be sure you're at least 90 m (300 ft.) away from a fresh water source. Avoid urinating in dry areas close to campsites that are protected from the elements—they may hold odors.

Grey/Soapy Water Disposal The primary consideration when washing yourself or your clothes is to avoid contamination of fresh water or intertidal life. Without soap, you can bathe directly in the ocean. If you prefer to use fresh water, carry a supply in a pot or jug to a bathing site below the high tide line and well away from fresh water sources.

Bathing with soap is a luxury as opposed to a necessity. Soap is foreign to the coastal environment and can adversely affect local flora and fauna, so its use should be minimized. This includes biodegradable soap; although it breaks down more quickly than other soaps, it still impacts on local life forms in the short term if misused. If you choose to bathe with soap, get wet first and then lather up on shore, far from fresh water and any intertidal life. Rinse off by pouring water over yourself. Avoid lathering up directly in the salt water, as this will probably cause you to use more soap than is necessary. When brushing teeth, spit toothpaste below the high tide line or into the ocean.

Also, limit your use of soap to wash dishes. Try using sand or gravel instead. If you are unable to properly dispose of your grey/dish water in the ocean, consider using a sumphole. To build a sumphole, dig 25–30 cm (10–12 in.) into the soil, a good 90 m (300 ft.) from any fresh water source, and pile the dirt to the side of the hole. Pour in your grey water and, after the final use, replace the soil.

Camping Etiquette

When you are paddling the Northwest Pacific coast in the summer, be prepared to find other people on the site you have chosen for the night. Conversely, don't be surprised if another camping party lands on "your" island before sundown. On most sites, paddlers should have no trouble making room for other visitors. As for the smallest of islands and campsites, there are the traditions of the sea to consider. It is hardly courteous and may even be hazardous to others to tell them to camp elsewhere when there is no place nearby where they can safely or legally do so. Most paddlers will be compatible souls who will also treat the site and others with respect. Accommodate them if you can.

Finally, leave your pets at home—you will do yourself, others and the coast a big favour. On small islands, especially, wildlife is vulnerable to harassment by pets, and in a few spirited seconds a dog can wipe out a bird's progeny for an entire year.

Inquisitive seal, Darwin Sound, Queen Charlotte Islands/Haida Gwaii. PETER McGEE

RESPECTING WILDLIFE

One of the great attractions of the coastal environment is its large variety of wildlife. As visitors to these areas, you must be aware of how your presence affects the animals. Most animals react with alarm when approached by humans and specifically by paddlers: our approach tends to be silent and without warning. Such reactions are stressful and cause the animal to expend energy—to swim, run or fly away—in order to feel safe. Although a single disturbance may not affect an animal to a large degree, multiple or prolonged disturbances may add up to higher energy expenditures than the animal can afford. Repeated disturbance may cause wildlife to completely avoid an area, even one that offers the best food or nesting sites.

Marine Mammals

Marine mammals are an essential concern to sea kayakers, especially when they are in their breeding or nursery areas, sites that they use year after year. Seals and sea lions that are "hauled out" on beaches, rocks or ledges are more vulnerable and therefore more easily frightened. Seals nurse their pups only on shore, so a pup can lose up to a day of valuable nursing time or become separated from its mother when they are frightened into the water by humans. Haul-outs and rookeries should not be approached—use binoculars to observe animals from a distance. Back off if seals or sea lions show signs of disturbance such as stretching their necks or moving towards the water.

Sometimes seals, sea lions and sea otters appear inquisitive and will watch or follow a kayak in the water, where they feel relatively safe. In these situations it is appropriate to observe the animal from whatever distance it chooses; however, you should not approach it. To leave the area, paddle on a course perpendicular or away from the animal, not towards it.

Some marine mammals are discussed in greater detail in Chapters 9 (orcas), 11 (gray whales) and 13 (sea otters).

Finally, don't feed animals. Human food does not provide proper nutrition for wild animals, and eating your food may lead to their eventual starvation or potentially dangerous habituation. (For information about bears, see Other Hazards later in this chapter.)

Seabirds

Seabirds are abundant on the coast. It is important not to disturb birds during their nesting season because you may endanger chicks or eggs by scaring away the parents. Give rookeries a wide berth and observe with binoculars. The biggest danger here is that predatory birds such as eagles will take advantage of the parents' absence to raid the nests. Along beaches, watch for signs such as a "broken wing" distraction display, which will alert you to the presence of nearby nests. When walking, be careful to avoid stepping on camouflaged nests; if you discover one, leave the area quickly and carefully.

Intertidal Life

Marine intertidal areas are home to a host of fascinating animals, each adapted to a particular habitat. Because most of these creatures are so small, they are easily overlooked, and coastal campers must be especially careful to avoid causing them harm. All these animals are susceptible to pollutants in the water such as concentrations of soap, and many are crushed by human traffic and simple tidal exploration. Take advantage of low tides to view these animals in tide pools and along the beaches, but be aware of your potential negative impacts.

CULTURAL IMPACTS

Traditional routes of canoe travel by native peoples cover the entire Northwest Pacific coast, and virtually every area that has appeal to paddlers today has a human history stretching back thousands of years. This puts paddlers in British Columbia and Washington State in a unique and privileged position because the areas we visit are the traditional lands and waters of the First Nations. It is important that we recognize and respect the historical significance and ownership of these areas.

The First Nations have a long history of dealing with the many encroachments on their territories. They have been active, even pro-active participants in some developments; the challenge today is to preserve the values that sustained their ancestors, resources and environment in the face of new developments and encroachments and to ensure a healthy and meaningful lifestyle for future generations. Visitors are encouraged to learn about traditional territories, history and values from the First Nations themselves.

To help you in this regard, we have tried to include the names and numbers of the appropriate First Nations in the Useful Contacts section at the back of the book. Nonetheless, you may have to do some additional research to find the contacts for specific sites or villages you plan to visit. This can take time, and it is best not to leave it until the last minute. Keep in mind that areas marked as Indian Reserve (or Reservation) on nautical charts represent only a portion of the hundreds of native sites along the coast that provide resting and camping opportunities for paddlers. These unofficial spots are important archeological sites that most likely have contemporary significance too, so please treat them with the same respect you do the legally recognized Indian Reserves and Reservations.

It is our hope that you will embrace the following guidelines and do your part to acknowledge the peoples who first paddled the islands and inlets of the Pacific Northwest coast.

Ask Permission Most Indian Reserves are marked with an IR on nautical charts and are private property. If you wish to visit First Nations sites on your paddling trip, call or preferably write the local tribal council well before your trip. Be sure to seek permission from the tribal council, not from individuals, and consider a lack of response from a tribal council to be a negative response. Avoid First Nations sites unless you have been granted permission. Once you have been granted permission, look, photograph and enjoy—but do not disturb.

Ask Your Outfitter If They Have Permission Guides and outfitters make their living from the natural and cultural features of the areas they visit. It doesn't take much effort for an outfitter to show respect by seeking permission from local tribal councils to visit traditional lands and waters. If an outfitter does not seek permission, encourage them to make this their practice.

Leave Artifacts Alone What may appear lost or forgotten to our eyes is often of great significance, and part of that significance is where the object lies. Artifacts, including whale and human bones, are often tied to a specific location and are deliberately left in their natural surroundings rather than removed to a museum or private collection. Once they are removed from context without proper study, they can no longer speak to the past history of the place. If you suspect the artifacts or sites you have found are unknown, then contact the local tribal council and the Archaeology Branch of the B.C. Ministry of Small Business, Tourism and Culture. In Washington State, contact the Governor's Office of Indian Affairs.

Note: It is strictly illegal to remove any object that has heritage value without the appropriate permit(s).

Respect Harvesting Areas Clam beds and other intertidal harvesting areas should be approached as areas of traditional food harvesting that may still be in contemporary use by First Nations and other local residents. Be sure to minimize your impact on these areas. Take no more than you need, eat what you take and avoid harvesting in popular areas. Check with the local tribal councils for advice on this matter.

Avoid Midden Sites Middens are basically refuse heaps: deposits built up over time from discarded material—usually kitchen garbage—associated with past human occupation. The term "shell midden" refers to the middens left by coastal aboriginal occupants, often dating back many hundreds to several thousands of years. These contain large amounts of shell fragments (left over from the consumption of clams) mixed in with rich, dark, greasy soil often containing broken pieces of fire-charred rock. They can be anything from a few centimetres to several metres in depth. The rates of accumulation vary greatly depending on the intensity and duration of resource use. They are as valuable to understanding human history as the pyramids of Egypt or the peat bogs of Northern

Europe—but only if they are protected and investigated in an appropriate manner.

Shell middens are typically found on any reasonably level area above a shoreline with good access to sandy beaches, fresh water and suitable canoe landing places. These are the same types of places paddlers today find desirable to land, camp and picnic on. They are often evident from a distance by the presence of slightly greener, more deciduous vegetation, or even a lack of vegetation. In some cases, middens may be associated with burial or petroglyph sites.

Shell middens in B.C., like other types of archaeological sites, are protected by law under provisions of B.C.'s Heritage Conservation Act. A person must not damage, alter, dig or remove objects from them. This means zero impact camping or visitation—and only after the appropriate permission has been secured.

CLIMATE, WEATHER AND HAZARDS

The Pacific Northwest is a region that intertwines land and sea in a setting that is as dramatic as it is beautiful. When we first planned the section on weather, we intended to keep it separate from the section on paddling hazards. It soon became apparent, however, that like the land and sea, the weather and hazards of this coast are intertwined. Quite simply, if you do not have a basic understanding of the climate and weather you will be paddling in, they will quickly become hazards. Although weather patterns are by no means easy to understand, let alone predict, the following section gives you a brief background to the climate, weather and hazards in the Pacific Northwest and will help get you on the water safely. We strongly recommend that you spend some time researching the topic thoroughly (see the Recommended Reading list at the back of the book). Much of the information in this section has been drawn, with permission, from Environment Canada's *Marine Weather Hazards Manual*. For more information or your own copy, contact Environment Canada (see Useful Contacts).

The Pacific Weather Centre, a part of Environment Canada, issues marine forecasts for all of B.C.; the National Oceanic and Atmospheric Administration in Washington State issues forecasts for Puget Sound. Always have a weather radio or VHF with you and be sure to listen to the weather forecast before you plan your day. For more information on weather services, see Useful Contacts.

The influence of the Pacific Ocean on climate and weather patterns in the Pacific Northwest cannot be understated. Winters are significantly warmer, summers are significantly cooler and it is wetter year round near the Pacific Ocean than in comparable areas farther inland. Generally speaking, June, July, August and September are the most popular months to paddle. If you are prepared for the shorter, wetter days of fall and spring, however, paddling in the off-season has many advantages, including a greater sense of solitude.

Precipitation

Annual rainfall in the Pacific Northwest ranges from less that 1,000 mm to over 5,000 mm (40–196 in.). Much of the rain on the coast is called orographic precipitation: rain caused by warm moist air being forced up over mountains, cooling as it rises, condensing and falling. With this in mind, and the fact that most fronts approach from the west due to winds high in the atmosphere, it is relatively easy to predict the areas of heavy rainfall. Essentially, areas just west of a mountain range receive more rain than areas to the east or in the lee of the range. Barkley Sound, for instance, just west of the Vancouver Island Range, often receives as much as five times the amount of rain as the Gulf Islands even though they lie less than 80 km (48 mi.) to the east. The effect is so dramatic that much of the west coast of Vancouver Island is classified as temperate rainforest while the Gulf Islands, San Juan Islands and much of the Sunshine Coast are said to have a semi-arid, even Mediterranean, climate. Such variations can also be found near the mainland of B.C. and in Washington State as a result of the Coast Mountains. Yet, for all the talk and jokes about the rain in this part of the world (you don't tan in the Pacific Northwest, you rust . . .), summers are typically quite pleasant and precipitation is limited to about a quarter of the days during the prime paddling season.

Temperatures

Summer temperatures typically range from 6–27°C (41–80°F) while the average daytime temperature hovers between 18–24°C (62–74°F). Although this is quite comfortable, visitors to the region are often surprised by the damp chill of foggy days and the brisk, clear nights, so be sure to bring warm clothing any time of year.

Paddlers must also be aware of the cool ocean temperatures, ranging from 5–15°C (40–59°F). No matter how warm the air temperature, the northwest Pacific Ocean remains cool year round, and immersion can lead to numbness in as little as 5 minutes and to hypothermia in 20 minutes. Never head out without practising rescue techniques, and consider wearing a wet suit or dry suit if you are paddling exposed coastal waters, undertaking a major crossing or travelling in areas of unusually cold water.

Wind

As a paddler, winds are one of your most important concerns. While the overall patterns of winds are quite well understood, it is their daily variation—where and how strongly they blow—that remains a problem. This becomes even more difficult as the rugged coastline of B.C. and Washington modifies wind-flow patterns in many different ways.

For the most part, summer winds are predominately from the northwest or west and reach peak velocity during the afternoon. This is a general rule, however, and you should check the weather reports each morning *before leaving camp* to ensure you will not be caught by unusual conditions. In the 1990s alone there have been two huge southeasterly blows in August on the west coast of Vancouver Island, so be prepared for dramatic weather changes any time of year.

In the winter, winds are predominately from the southeast with the strongest winds accompanying intense lows and their associated fronts. Typically, as a low approaches the coast, winds back into the southeast and increase in speed, often reaching gale or storm force. With the passage of the front, winds usually shift to the northwest. Again, these are general patterns. There are also some specific types of winds that you should know about.

Sea and Land Breezes   Sea and land breezes are localized phenomena that occur commonly during the summer. Both kinds of wind are caused by the different rates of heating and cooling between the land and sea. Over the course of a sunny day, the land heats up faster than the water. As the heated air rises, the cooler ocean air flows onshore to replace it. This onshore breeze is known as a sea breeze. Its counterpart is the land breeze that develops at night when the land cools faster than the ocean: it blows from land to sea.

Afternoon sea breezes can develop at any time of year when strong daytime heating occurs, so don't be caught off guard by this predictable phenomenon. For the most part, speeds don't exceed 25 knots, but localized funnelling can increase this to upwards of 40 knots so it is important to be aware of the surrounding topography.

Anabatic and Katabatic Winds Although you may rarely hear the terms anabatic and katabatic winds, they technically describe the local prevailing conditions of most mainland inlets and behave in a very similar way to land and sea breezes. Anabatic and katabatic winds often contribute to land and sea breezes and result in increased wind speeds. To safely paddle many of the inlets in this guide, it is important to have a general understanding of the conditions that cause anabatic and katabatic winds.

During the day, the sides of coastal valleys become warmer than the valley bottoms because they are more exposed to the sun. As a result, the winds blow up the slopes. These daytime, upslope winds are called anabatic winds. At night, the air cools and "avalanches" down the slope and out to sea. These cool night winds are called drainage or katabatic winds and are often quite gusty and strong. This is a simple description of these winds and will help you plan around them; however, bear in mind that other local factors may either intensify or cancel these phenomena.

Outflow Winds Outflow winds differ from katabatic winds in that they are driven by temperature differences as well as large-scale pressure differences. The most famous outflow wind, possibly in the entire world, is the Bute Wind that flows out of Bute Inlet during the winter. Bute Inlet snakes about 50 km (30 mi.) into the mainland and is surrounded by British Columbia's highest mountains, some reaching heights of 4000 m (13,100 ft.). These mountains are besieged by massive glaciers and huge ice fields. All this ice produces cold air that "falls" down the mountainsides and valleys out to the coast. During the winter, the winds are subzero in temperature, and as they travel over any body of water, they create a deadly, freezing spray. A classic outflow condition, where winds reach lethal proportions, occurs when intense high pressure ridges in the interior of the province are accompanied by intense low pressure systems offshore. In 1990, one such condition produced winds estimated at about 200 km per/hr (120 mph), flattening hundreds of hectares of forest on the windward side of Stuart Island (Desolation Sound). Although this was an extreme case, winds exceeding 100 km per/hr (60 mph) are common.

As a general rule when paddling in inlets, start paddling early and finish by lunch time. Sometimes the wind effect is virtually nil or very mild tempered—but don't ever plan on it. The mountains of the inlets rise straight out of the ocean, and it is often necessary to paddle several kilometres to find a safe place to haul out. Of course, when it is overcast and rainy, the heating cycle is interrupted and you can usually rely on smooth, windless paddling conditions.

In closing, it is worth noting that the inlets of this coast are born of mountains, and any climber will tell you that mountains are unpredictable and extreme places to travel. So too are their inlets. Remember to paddle with humility, and keep your eyes and ears open.

Gap and Corner Winds   When winds are forced to flow through a narrow opening or gap, such as through an inlet or between two islands, the wind speed will increase and may even double in strength. This effect, called funnelling, is similar to pinching a water hose to create a faster, denser spray. The coastal topography can also change the direction of the wind by forcing it to flow along the route of a pass or through a strait. This is referred to as channelling.

Winds that are modified by funnelling and channelling are called gap winds. The constricted channels not only increase wind speeds but also strengthen tidal currents. Care is necessary when the increased winds are directed against strong tidal currents. The result is steep, breaking waves and much rougher waters than in more open areas.

The most famous gap wind in B.C. is known as a Qualicum. It occurs when southwesterlies blow into the Alberni Inlet on the west coast of Vancouver Island, through a mountain pass and down over the east coast of the island to Qualicum Beach and the Strait of Georgia. Winds of up to 40 knots can hit the coast in less than an hour creating an extreme local hazard in an area no wider than a few kilometres.

Paddlers should also be aware of corner winds that occur off the points of islands or around a headland. These can be up to 25 per cent stronger than the average wind speed due to a convergence of airstreams, so take note of the wind when passing by "corners" of land.

Fog

Fog is a common companion on the West Coast and can result in sudden and total disorientation. Two types of fog that you are likely to encounter are radiation fog and sea (or advection) fog.

Radiation fog forms when moisture from the ground evaporates into the lower layer of the atmosphere. It tends to develop over land during the early morning and is primarily a problem in harbours and estuaries, rarely spreading far out to sea. After the sun comes up, the fog usually dissipates over the land and then clears more slowly over the water. Radiation fog is quite rare in the summer but becomes more frequent from late autumn to early spring.

Sea (advection) fog, on the other hard, is most frequent during the summer and fall and is formed when warm, moist air moves over colder sea water. Unlike radiation fog, which requires calm or light wind conditions, sea fog may form when winds are moderate and may even persist as winds become strong. In fact, dense fog is often noted in Juan de Fuca Strait with westerly winds up to 30 knots.

The bottom line is that fog can be encountered at any time on the coast, so you need to prepare yourself. Always carry a compass when paddling—navigating by compass is not a hard skill to learn but must be practised when conditions are good. Avoid crossings in the fog. If that is not possible, make your crossings short or try to split a long crossing into two shorter crossings by altering your route. Do not aim for tiny islands and always allow a good margin of error. For example, do not aim for the tip of a peninsula; instead, shoot for the midsection and work your way along the shore until you have reached the point. In addition to the compass, you can gain some orientation from the sounds of beach surf, bells and fog horns as well as from steady wave and wind direction, so stay alert from the time you leave shore until the time you land. A deck-mounted compass will help you keep a bearing over a long distance, and a watch will help you calculate approximate distances travelled. A GPS (Global Positioning System) also helps but will not eliminate the need for any of the above.

If you feel uncomfortable about travelling in the fog or find yourself in an area of high boat traffic, sit it out. Unless you have modified your boat, radar will not pick you up and it is quite likely that ships will not see you until a collision is unavoidable. Finally, try not to rush when navigating in the fog. Fog and speed don't mix, and hurrying can get you lost that much more quickly and thoroughly.

Superstorms

Every now and then the Pacific Northwest coast gets nailed by what locals call superstorms. Similar in strength to hurricanes, these storms develop as low pressure systems far away in the tropics or subtropics and gain strength on their journey north. Although rare, they are frequent enough that it is worth knowing the tell-tale signs. Wind speeds increase dramatically, with gusts exceeding 100 knots, but your best bet is to keep an eye on the barometric pressure for an early warning. Whenever weather radio broadcasts warn of an approaching low that reads 975 millibars or less, pay close attention to all updates. If the barometer reading indicates a 3-hour pressure drop matching or exceeding 6 millibars, be prepared to seek immediate refuge and secure your boat carefully. The low pressure and increased wind speeds will also create what is known as a storm surge, or rise in the normal tide level, so be sure to place your gear and campsite high on the shore or in the trees.

TIDES AND CURRENTS

The tide refers to the daily movement—the rise and fall—of the ocean that is produced by the gravitational forces of the sun and moon. Tides actually move as a long, shallow wave with a period (the time interval between the passage of two wave crests) of around 12 hours. The passing of the wave is gradual, and the result is two high and two low tides in a 24-hour period. Because the wave moves south to north, the tide floods (rises) from south to north and ebbs (falls) from north to south. There are a few exceptions to this trend, however, the most notable being the northeast coast of Vancouver Island where the flooding tide actually wraps around Cape Scott and heads south.

To predict tides, paddlers should always carry a set of tide tables, which are available at most marine stores. Don't forget the time indicated in the tide tables refers to Pacific Standard Time; you will need to add an hour during Pacific Daylight Saving Time (April to October).

On shore, tides are a concern to paddlers because they affect the location of camp and how high boats must be pulled up for the night. The difference between the high and low tides can be up to 7.5 m (24 ft.) on some parts of the coast, so knowing how to use tide tables is critical to selecting a safe, dry camp. The highest and lowest tides occur near the time of a new or full moon and are called spring tides. Tides with the minimum range, known as neap tides, occur when the moon is in the first or third quarter.

On the water, tides are a concern to paddlers because of the tidal streams and currents they create. Although the strength of the flood and ebb tidal streams within the Strait of Georgia and other unrestricted channels and inlets seldom exceed 2 knots, currents frequently can aggravate conditions caused by adverse weather, particularly when current and wind are opposing. In certain cases, currents can actually cause difficult eddy and wave conditions, even on utterly still days, from the sheer force of their flow. When currents exceed 5 knots, you start to get what is commonly called a tidal rapid. Canadian Hydrographic Nautical Charts refer to this hazard as "heavy tidal overfall."

Tidal Rapids

Essentially, a tidal rapid occurs when millions of tons of water are forced through relatively small openings in a fixed period of time. During times of extreme tidal activity, conditions within the boundaries of a rapid are highly turbulent and erratic. Because of the incredible volumes of water, extreme depths and constantly changing flow rates, it is difficult to predict what the water will do. Surface water speeds can exceed 13 knots, standing waves in excess of 2 m (6.5 ft.) are not unusual and there are known whirlpools capable of sucking under large vessels. Clearly, this is no place for a kayak.

Tidal rapids are linked to the movement of the tide and hence are cyclical in nature. Calm periods can be predicted by using the Canadian Tides and Current Tables, NOAA's guides or other independently published current tables. If you do plan on navigating a tidal rapid, read the relevant chart carefully to help identify danger points, use all available information to estimate slack or favourable currents, and time your passage or crossing for that period. As always, exercise caution when the current and wind direction oppose each other. Like paddling in surf, it is best to paddle in currents under controlled conditions to familiarize yourself with the effects on your boat before you head out on a trip.

Surf, Swell and the Open Coast

While the open coast is one of the most scenic areas to paddle, it is not a place for beginners. If you are planning a kayak trip along a stretch of exposed coastline, be sure you have both the necessary paddling skills (including surf skills) and mental preparation. When considering a run down the open coast, remember that ocean swells are generated far away by distant storms. Local winds have no connection to the swell size on a given day; calm winds locally do not generate calm seas. Rather, local winds generate local waves that add to the tops of existing ocean swells; this is what weather radio forecasters mean when they say, "Sea states are combined wind wave and swell height."

Swells also pose a hazard when they break on offshore reefs or shallow rocks, often called boomers. Read your charts carefully and scan the horizon constantly. Be very alert and remember that swell size is random and can change. Do not be lulled into a false sense of security because "the swells are small today."

When landing in surf with a loaded boat, the goal is actually not to surf—the weight of the gear can damage you and your boat quite easily if you capsize. A surf-free landing often can be accomplished by tucking in behind islets or reefs, but if you are forced to land on a surf beach, wait for a window of opportunity and paddle to shore between breaking waves. This takes experience and should be practised with an empty boat and under the watchful eye of a qualified instructor.

OTHER HAZARDS

Aside from the hazards relating to weather and water conditions, there are a number of potential encounters or emergencies that paddlers should be aware of and prepared to deal with on the coast.

Bears

Although it is unlikely that you will encounter bears when paddling in Washington State, British Columbia has about a quarter of all the black bears in Canada and half the grizzly bears. Paddlers must respect the fact that the wilderness is home to bears, and as a visitor you must do your part to help conserve bears and their home.

The best way to avoid an encounter with bears is to keep a clean camp and never leave out food or garbage. When storing food, make sure it is hung at least 5 m (16 ft.) high and 1.5 m (5 ft.) from the trunk. One system that seems to work quite well is stringing a single line between two trees and draping a second line over the middle; the second line holds the food and can be lowered and raised easily.

Do not sleep in the same clothes you cook in, never keep food in your tent and try to camp at least 50 m (164 ft.) from your "kitchen." Finally, do not cache food or garbage in your kayaks when on shore.

All bears can be dangerous, so try to anticipate and avoid encounters. Never approach or attempt to feed a bear. Respect their territory and avoid areas they frequent such as the mouths of streams during spawning season. It is your responsibility to ensure that you do not force bears to leave their habitat, teach them to eat human foods or place them in situations where people or bears get hurt.

Motor Vessel Traffic

One of the most dangerous hazards paddlers must deal with is the presence of other boats and ships. Your best bet is to assume that no matter what the right of way, you will not be seen by other boaters and it is you who must move. As author and kayaker John Dowd writes, when a ship appears to be coming straight for you, you may find it difficult to decide which side to move to in order to get out of the way. It is worth a few seconds' pause to get it right. Resist the common reaction to scuttle across in front of her; instead, watch the line-up of the bow and mast closely to see if she is likely to pass in front of you or astern. Then paddle away from her line of course, taking care to watch the vessel until she is past—just in case she alters course.

In fog, of course, the danger of a collision is heightened. The first question you should ask yourself is, should you be on the water in the first place? If you do take to the water and hear traffic, point your bow to the source of the noise so you can pinpoint the traffic's location and determine your relative position. If the noise becomes louder and remains off your bow, you will likely have to change course. If the source of the sound moves in relation to your bow and compass setting, you are probably safe. In either event, you should avoid getting into such situations if at all possible.

Stay together when travelling in a group across shipping lanes or busy channels. It is much easier for ships to avoid a tightly clustered group than a string of multi-coloured speed bumps. Take your time before setting out on the crossing and make sure everyone involved understands the final destination and compass bearing. Keep in mind that ferries and other ships move extremely quickly and a small speck on the horizon can quickly become a hazard. Also remember that many vessels on the coast have booms or barges in tow—always stay alert for towlines or cables.

Hypothermia

Hypothermia—the loss of body heat, or lowering of the deep body core temperature—is a deadly serious matter. Once cooling begins, a person's body temperature drops very rapidly, and unconsciousness, cardiac arrest and death can result.

Immersion in cold water is the quickest way to get hypothermia—and any immersion in Pacific Northwest waters will be *cold*. You are also susceptible on shore and in your bed, especially on cool, wet and windy days.

Anybody who is exhausted, cold and exposed is at risk. Be alert to your own condition and to others in your group.

Hypothermia can set in quite rapidly at any time of the year. Prevention is the best strategy. Always dress for cold water immersion, regardless of the air temperature, and keep extra warm, dry clothes readily available in a waterproof bag. Eat adequately to replenish your energy stores—aim for 4000 calories a day (regardless of gender). Drink adequately, too—up to 3 l (3 qt.) of water a day. And take sufficient breaks to avoid getting exhausted.

For information about the symptoms and treatment of hypothermia, see the Recommended Reading section at the end of the book. And please take note of this important fact: Hypothermic casualties who have gone into cardiac arrest should not be considered dead until they are "warm" and dead. Hospital treatment may be able to resuscitate severely hypothermic victims who appear to be dead.

Paralytic Shellfish Poisoning

Paralytic Shellfish Poisoning (PSP) is caused by the contamination of bivalve shellfish by microorganisms called dinoflagellates. These microorganisms are always present in the water but when salinity, nutrient and temperature conditions are right, a population explosion or "bloom" occurs. Sometimes the bloom turns the water red, hence the name "red tide," but toxic conditions can exist without any trace of colour. You may hear of people "testing" for red tide by rubbing the shellfish on their lips to see if it causes a tingling sensation or by feeding it to an animal first, but these methods are not reliable. Unfortunately, there really isn't a reliable test for paddlers to use in the field, so skipping the mussel feast is a good idea—particularly in the warm months when a bloom is likely to occur.

If someone experiences symptoms of PSP, paralysis and respiratory failure may occur quickly. Seek medical help immediately.

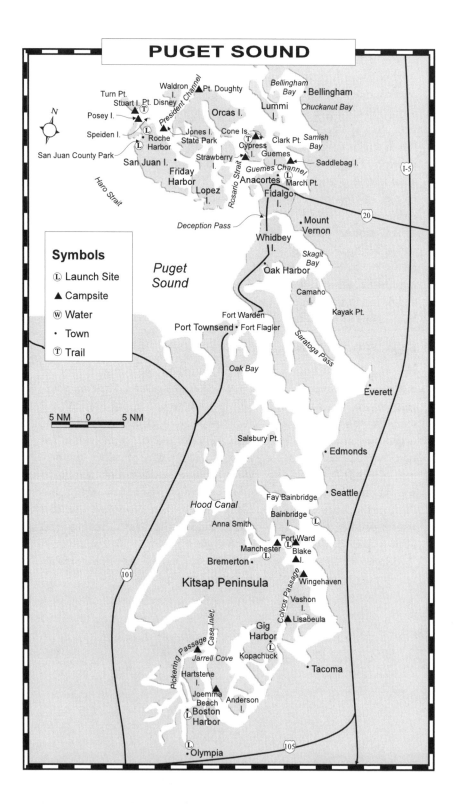

PUGET SOUND

Symbols

- Ⓛ Launch Site
- ▲ Campsite
- Ⓦ Water
- • Town
- Ⓣ Trail

5 NM   0   5 NM

N

Turn Pt.
I.
Stuart I. Pt. Disney
Waldron ▲Pt. Doughty
Posey I.
Speiden I.
Roche
Harbor
San Juan County Park
San Juan I.
Friday
Harbor
Lopez
I.

Orcas I.

President Channel

Jones I.
State Park
Strawberry
I.
Cone Is.
Cypress
I.
Clark Pt.
Guemes
I.

*Bellingham
Bay*
• Bellingham
Lummi
I.
Chuckanut Bay
*Samish
Bay*
Saddlebag I.

Haro Strait

Rosario Strait

Guemes Channel
Anacortes
Fidalgo
I.
March Pt.

Deception Pass

Whidbey
I.

Oak Harbor

• Mount
Vernon

*Skagit
Bay*

Camano
I.

Kayak Pt.

*Puget
Sound*

Fort Warden
Port Townsend • Fort Flagler

Saratoga Pass

Oak Bay

Everett

Salsbury Pt.

• Edmonds

Fay Bainbridge
Bainbridge
I.
• Seattle

Hood Canal

Anna Smith

Fort Ward
Manchester
Blake
I.
Bremerton •

Kitsap Peninsula

Wingehaven

Vashon
I.
▲ Lisabeula

Colvos Passage

Gig
Harbor
Kopachuck

• Tacoma

Case Inlet

Pickering Passage

Jarrell Cove
Hartstene
I.
Joemma
Beach
Boston
Harbor

Anderson
I.

Olympia

I-5
20
101
105

Chapter Two

Puget Sound

Allen Palmer

Native Americans plied the waters of Puget Sound long before the arrival of white explorers. They knew the sound as *Whulge*, which loosely translates as "big salt water." Several tribes inhabited this coast, living on the abundant marine life and using the towering stands of forests to build villages and dugout canoes. Although boats of all kinds now travel these waters, paddling Puget Sound continues to be the best way to explore its beautiful shorelines. The slow, silent pace of a kayak will allow you to absorb the spectacular vistas of Mount Rainier, cabin-dotted islands and wildlife at play.

BACKGROUND

Puget Sound has always been a water highway for the Pacific Northwest. The region's rugged topography and dense, old-growth forests made land travel an arduous if not impossible endeavour for early travellers. Although the region had many visits by Europeans between the 1500s and 1700s, Puget Sound remained relatively unexplored until 1792 when British Capt. George Vancouver sailed the sloop *Discovery* into Juan de Fuca Strait. Two officers from this voyage, Lieut. Peter Puget and Joseph Whidbey, a surveyor, explored much of southern Puget Sound. Originally, only the waters south of Tacoma Narrows were given the name of Puget Sound but over time and with the aid of an unknown chartmaker, the range of Puget Sound was extended to include all of the area south of Admiralty Inlet.

The sound currently has a resident population approaching 2.5 million. Geographically, Puget Sound stretches approximately 242 km (150 mi.)

north to south and 24–32 km (15–20 mi.) east to west with the widest shore-to-shore distance averaging 6–10 km (4–6 mi.). Amazingly, with such a high population in such a small area, there are still many shorelines with stretches of uninterrupted beach and undeveloped coves and bays. This is largely because most of the population is clustered in the six major cities of Olympia, Tacoma, Bremerton, Seattle, Everett and Bellingham. As thousands of people move to the Puget Sound area each year, for its growing employment opportunities and quality of life, public access and water quality issues intensify. The once pristine wilderness is now being loved to death.

In hopes of reversing this trend, the Washington Water Trails Association (WWTA) was formed in 1990. Similar to the B.C. Marine Trail Association, its Canadian counterpart, the WWTA was established by a group of enthusiastic paddlers committed to the vision of a marine trail system designed for kayaks, canoes and other small beachable human- or wind-powered craft. The B.C. Marine Trail and the Washington Water Trail will eventually combine to form a Cascadia Marine Trail that covers the Inside Passage. Currently, the Washington State portion of the marine trail stretches over 242 km (150 mi.), from the state capital in Olympia to the Canadian border, and includes over 35 camping sites throughout Puget Sound and the San Juan Islands. All the trips listed in this chapter utilize Cascadia Marine Trail sites.

GETTING THERE

By land: People planning a trip to the Puget Sound area will find ready access by car, bus or train. Interstate 5 in conjunction with many state and local highways provides vehicle access to the entire Puget Sound basin. The I-5 is the major north-south freeway for the region, and various local roads will take you to the launch sites described below; most of these roads are paved, and others are of good quality gravel and suitable for almost all vehicles. Most Cascadia Marine Trail launch sites are within 160 km (100 mi.) of Seattle. Driving time to these access points will vary depending on road conditions, time of day and destination.

Please note: Be particularly cautious when parking on boat launching ramps or beaches. Ensure that your vehicle is capable of handling soft or slippery conditions, and set the parking brake or chock the tires. Also, don't tie up a boat launch (and annoy other boaters) while loading your kayak. Instead, deposit your boat and gear at the side of the ramp and then move your vehicle out of the way.

Commercial bus service and community transit systems are available throughout the Puget Sound region. Routes and schedules vary, so check with the individual carriers to see how your trip can best be organized.

By water: The Washington State Ferries system provides you with transport across the sound at several points as well as into the San Juan Islands. By using these ferries, you can create shortcuts to points throughout Puget Sound. Ferries provide a welcome break from behind the wheel, terrific views from the water and a valuable fall-back plan if the weather turns rough. You can either drive your car onto the ferry, walk on or, if you have a kayak cart, roll on as you would a bicycle. Check ferry schedules prior to setting out on your trip because conditions may change. The ferry system is very crowded during the summer months, especially in the San Juans over weekends; you should expect delays. Please note: If you walk your kayak onto the ferry, be sure you can legally launch at the other side; contact the WWTA if you are unsure of the launching possibilities.

By air: If coming by air, you will most likely arrive at Seattle-Tacoma International Airport. Rental cars and bus service are available at the airport terminal.

WEATHER AND HAZARDS

Weather in the Puget Sound area varies greatly depending on your location, the current weather pattern and the time of year. With many different microclimates, it may be raining in one spot yet be sunny a few miles away. For most of the summer, the Pacific High brings fair weather westerlies and northwesterlies. These winds enter the Juan de Fuca Strait, often reaching 20–25 knots by early afternoon, and typically spread to the north and south as they approach the mainland. Southwesterlies are sent towards the San Juan Islands, and northwesterlies blow down across Port Townsend and into northern Puget Sound. The south sound typically experiences milder weather conditions during summer months. Still days and flat water prevail, providing the experience of paddling on a glassy, calm sea.

Precipitation is also varied within the sound. Moving northward, you begin to experience more of the effect of the Puget Sound Convergence Zone, which represents an area where marine air collides and frequently produces rain. The San Juan Islands enjoy the benefits of being located in the rain shadow of Vancouver Island, which blocks or diverts many weather systems coming inland from the Pacific Ocean. When it is raining in Seattle, it is often sunny in the San Juans. Nonetheless, water conditions can become quite severe due to a strong blow coming up the Juan de Fuca Strait, causing many of the channels between the islands to become hazardous for small boat travel.

The National Oceanic and Atmospheric Association's Olympia Station broadcasts on wx3 and their Seattle Station on wx1. Be sure to listen to local weather reports and ask advice from other mariners before setting out.

Tides, currents and wind all present challenging water conditions in Puget Sound. The San Juan Islands are especially subject to fast tidal flows, which may create hazardous conditions even in calm weather. Special hazards exist at the north end of Orcas Island in the San Juans and at Deception Pass at the north end of Whidbey Island. Indeed, this region is one of the most hazardous sea kayaking areas in North America.

Water temperatures in Puget Sound range from approximately 9–12°C (48–54°F) year round, and hypothermia resulting from immersion is always a major consideration.

Shipping traffic and a large recreational boating community require the kayaker to always be alert for other watercraft and to yield the right of way when necessary. The speed of tankers and container ships, as well as cross-sound ferries, is quite deceptive. When in doubt, cross behind all such vessels.

SPECIAL CONSIDERATIONS

The Washington State portion of the Cascadia Marine Trail is intertwined with urban and rural areas. Sites on the trail are managed by many different landowning agencies, which have particular conditions under which their site(s) may be used. Please also keep in mind that this part of the coast has a long and rich Native American history. Although none of the sites listed in this chapter are currently recognized as Native American land, they undoubtedly have a history of Native American use. Please treat all the lands you visit with respect but be particularly careful not to disturb any archeological sites. For more information, contact the Governor's Office of Indian Affairs.

You need a Cascadia Marine Trail permit to use most of the water trail sites in this chapter. Permits are for individuals, not for groups or boats. Each person in your group must purchase a permit or expect to pay a nightly fee at each site. The nightly fee may vary on a site by site basis, depending on the landowning manager. Be flexible: you will be encountering a trail system that is subject to ongoing changes. Permits may be purchased at many Washington State Parks and retail stores that sell kayaking equipment; WWTA members can purchase them by mail from the association (Cascadia Marine Trail guidebooks are also available as a WWTA membership benefit). Call the Washington State Parks Information Center at 1-800-233-0321 for the vendor nearest you. To insure goodwill and continuation of the Cascadia Marine Trail, all users should support minimum impact camping standards.

Due to the close proximity of many trail sites to residential areas, fire danger is a very big concern. Most paddlers visit during the summer and early fall months, the driest time in Puget Sound, when fire danger is at its highest. Even where fire containers are provided in a camping area, fires are discouraged. Several sites in the trail were approved based on a "no fire" policy, and these sites will be lost to paddlers if fires are detected. The environmental impacts of fires are another concern in the Puget Sound region. Wood smoke is a serious air and visibility pollutant, and smoky fire is a very unpleasant experience, especially when campers are located in a confined space.

Most campsites have no water so carry your own supply.

Most of the beaches and shoreline in Puget Sound are privately owned. Be aware that you should not beach your watercraft wherever you like, but only at known public access areas. Please obey private property signs. Failure to do so may result in landowners becoming hostile to kayakers' use of the Cascadia Marine Trail.

Finally, please follow the guidelines in Chapters 1, 9, 11 and 13 regarding the minimum distance to be maintained while observing orcas and other marine mammals.

PUGET SOUND TRIPS (1–5)

The Washington State portion of the Cascadia Marine Trail can be travelled in one continuous trip, but most paddlers will pick sections to explore on a daily, weekend or week-long basis. The San Juan Islands are one of the most popular destinations for human- and wind-powered watercraft, which results in crowded conditions at some trail sites during the summer. However, paddling in the relatively isolated southern part of Puget Sound and around Kitsap Peninsula can be just as enjoyable. While it is not possible to describe all of the paddling routes available in the sound, the ones listed in this chapter will give you a good cross-section of the region and its delights. The trips can be paddled in part or in their entirety depending on the experience level of the paddlers, time available and weather and water conditions. Tread lightly—and enjoy!

Trip 1   South Sound

Skill:	Intermediate to advanced
Time:	1–3 days
Hazards:	Traffic and currents
Access:	Boston Harbor/Olympia/Hammersley Inlet
Charts:	18440 Puget Sound 1:150,000
	18445 Puget Sound—Possession
	Sound to Olympia 1:80,000
Tide Tables:	Island Canoe Puget Sound

Southern Puget Sound offers outstanding paddling experiences year round. Long, placid inlets provide habitat for many varieties of birds; harbour seals and river otters are frequently sighted. Acres and acres of sand dollars can be seen in many places as you glide along the beaches, sending red rock crabs scurrying for cover amidst the kelp. Pickering Passage and Case Inlet offer a terrific circular trip for discovering the wonders of the south sound.

Launching

Pickering Passage and Case Inlet form one of the most pristine waterways in southern Puget Sound. You can access this part of the sound via many of the state and county parks in the region. One approach is to launch at Boston Harbor, a small community north of the state capital of Olympia at the head of Budd Inlet. Take an exit on the I-5 for visiting the state capital (105 or 105B) and proceed north on East Bay Drive NE, which runs along the eastern shore of Budd Inlet and into Boston Harbor Road NE. After about 11 km (7 mi.), turn left into Boston Harbor where you will find a marina and protected harbour. Parking is limited, so you may want to consider alternative launching points at Percival Landing in Olympia or the Arcadia boat ramp at the mouth of Hammersley Inlet. These alternative put-ins will obviously affect the distances for this paddle route.

Sites

Jarrell Cove State Park Paddling the waters of Pickering Passage north to Jarrell Cove State Park, you travel a waterway once explored by Lieut. Peter Puget. Plan for a stretching break or lunch at Hope Island State Park. Deer and other wildlife can frequently be sighted as you explore this forested island. Continue north on the west side of Squaxin Island, which is entirely Indian reservation property, and on up to Hartstene Island. As you cruise the shoreline, keep an eye out for bald eagles, kingfishers and the many great blue herons that inhabit the area. If you paddle this route during the fall, watch for salmon doing acrobatic jumps as they prepare to move upriver for spawning. After the 16-km (10-mi.) paddle from Boston Harbor, set up camp at Jarrell Cove and enjoy the showers available in the main camping area. The site is set back from the beach.

Joemma Beach State Park The next day's travel heads around the top end of Hartstene Island across Case Inlet and then south to Joemma Beach State Park. Your route to Joemma Beach can include a stop at McMicken Island State Park, which makes a good lunch break where you can get out of your boat, walk around the island or enjoy the view while you eat. (For the paddler who wants to explore more of Case Inlet, turn your boat north to Stretch Point State Park or Vaughn Bay.)

After paddling about 13 km (8 mi.) south from Jarrell Cove, you can pull your boat onto the smooth stones of Joemma Beach. The water trail site is up the hill, just above and to the left of the group picnic shelter. Even though it is a bit of a hike to make camp, the sunset views from your tent will be worth the effort. For years this park was an undiscovered gem, but with many improvements and the construction of a boat dock, you will likely have to share the pleasures.

As your tour of the south sound winds down, the final leg of the trip takes you through Dana Passage to Boston Harbor. Consult the local tide tables and current guide to determine the best time to paddle this narrow channel. If you are starting out from Joemma Beach on an ebb tide, stay well to the north before rounding the southern end of Hartstene Island, or you may be in for a long, hard paddle to get back to your car. Enjoy the scenic, isolated beaches on the southeast end of Hartstene Island, cruising past into Dana Passage. If you have timed it right, the current will whisk you back to Boston Harbor and your vehicle.

Trip 2 Mid Sound

Skill:	Intermediate to advanced
Time:	1–3 days
Hazards:	Traffic and currents
Access:	Kitsap Peninsula/Bainbridge Island
Charts:	18440 Puget Sound 1:150,000
	18445 Puget Sound—Possession Sound to Olympia 1:80,000
	18449 Puget Sound—Seattle to Bremerton 1:25,000
Tide Tables:	Island Canoe Puget Sound

Located within sight of the towering buildings of Seattle, the mid-sound still offers the paddler a wilderness experience. Blake Island remains a jewel of central Puget Sound, an entire island park where deer and eagles can be seen with regularity—a great spot for your first night out. For paddlers looking for a few more days of adventure, nearby Vashon Island has some great campsites at Wingehaven and Lisabeula.

Launching

To include Blake Island in a tour of Puget Sound, launch from either Manchester State Park on the Kitsap Peninsula or from Fort Ward State Park on the south end of Bainbridge Island. If you are approaching the area from the Seattle side of Puget Sound, ferries can be taken to these launch sites from Edmonds, Seattle or Fauntleroy. Blake Island is about the same distance from Manchester and Fort Ward: around 4.5 km (2.75 mi.). Make sure to cruise by and observe the salmon farms in Rich Passage; you may catch a view of sea lions cruising the same area. Please note: To camp at the following marine trail sites, you must arrive by water (not vehicle).

Sites

Blake Island State Park   The water trail site on Blake Island is on the northwest point of the island and offers excellent views northward and a spectacular night-time view of the Space Needle and Seattle's skyline. If your schedule allows for a one-night stay at Blake, stop and enjoy the deer and other wildlife. Experience the Native American culture at Tillicum Village and treat yourself to the catered salmon buffet. Showers are available in the boat harbour and main camping area. Enjoy a paddle around the island, hike its many trails or enjoy a swim from one of several sandy beaches. The island is a joy to visit at any time, but plan your trip during midweek for a bit more solitude.

Wingehaven and Lisabeula (Vashon Island) With a few more days of paddling available, travel south to Vashon Island and choose either the east or west side. Water trail sites are located at Wingehaven on the eastern shore and at Lisabeula on the western shore—neither will disappoint you. You could even go for a circumnavigation of Vashon and see both sites in one trip.

From Blake Island to Wingehaven it is about 8 km (5 mi.). Be sure to yield to any cross-sound ferry traffic as you paddle around the top of Vashon Island. It is about 16 km (10 mi.) down Colvos Passage to reach the camp at Lisabeula. The tide through Colvos Passage will make your trip either a work-out or an easy cruise, so check the local tide tables and current guide. Current conditions through Colvos almost always run in a northerly direction, on either a flood or ebb tide. No open fires are allowed at either Wingehaven or Lisabeula.

For paddlers charting a course all around Vashon Island, expect at least a 30-km (19-mi.) day between Lisabeula and Wingehaven, and plan for paddling conditions to change at many points along the way, especially as you round Robinson Point on the east end of Maury Island.

Trip 3 Southern San Juan Islands

Skill: Intermediate to advanced
Time: 1–4 days
Hazards: Currents and traffic
Access: March Point
Charts: 18421 Strait of Juan de Fuca to Strait of
                  Georgia 1:80,000
           18423 Bellingham to Everett including
                  San Juan Islands 1:80,000
           18424 Bellingham Bay 1:40,000
           18427 Anacortes to Skagit Bay 1:25,000

18430   Rosario Strait—northern part
1:25,000
Tide Tables: Island Canoe San Juan

The San Juan Islands are known far and wide as a paddling paradise. Unfortunately, access to the waters of the San Juans is at a premium with the ever-increasing push of development and the annual summer rush. Don't despair, however, because islands such as Saddlebag, Cypress and Strawberry offer easy access and solace for the silent paddler.

Launching

Departing from March Point avoids a lot of the harbour traffic that comes and goes from the Anacortes marina. By launching here you will also avoid the strong currents of Guemes Channel. From Highway 20, turn right onto March Point Road after crossing the Swinomish Channel bridge. The road loops around March Point and provides parking around the end of the point. The beach is rocky at high tide so take care when loading boats. Lower tides offer sandy flats but require a lengthy walk back and forth when hauling your gear.

If the tide is low, as you paddle to Saddlebag Island keep your eyes peeled for the raccoons searching for shellfish morsels along the shore of Hat Island. From the launching area at March Point up the shoreline of Hat Island to Saddlebag is about 4 km (2.5 mi.).

Sites

Saddlebag Island The Cascadia Marine Trail site can be found just above the cove on the southern side of Saddlebag. When the wind is out of the south, you may wish to unload in the sheltered cove on the north side and carry your gear to the campsite. Saddlebag is a popular destination for other boaters seeking dungeness crab so expect company just about any time of year.

Cruising up the northeast side of Guemes Island for a stop at the Guemes Island County Park will get you started the next morning. This park is a beautiful stopping point for lunch and offers a good time to check the tide tables and current guide. The county park is another excellent put-in site if Saddlebag Island is not on your itinerary. There is no water at the park. The north end of Guemes Island, at Clark Point, should be watched carefully due to its rip areas. If in doubt, wait for slack tide to paddle around. After your break, plot a course towards the Cone Islands and check out the steep, nearly impassable shoreline as you paddle by.

Cypress Island Your second night's destination is Pelican Beach on the northeast end of Cypress Island. Pelican Beach offers a pebble beach landing, room for up to 10 tents—and no fresh water. Pelican Beach can be unpredictably busy at times; if so, head to the Cypress Head site about 4 km (2.5 mi.) south, which usually isn't as popular. Watch for the current, back eddies and rips off Cypress Head.

Although not all public land, Cypress Island is an incredible place offering extensive hiking and nature activities. Crisscrossed by old logging roads that now serve as trails, you can explore shoreline to mountaintop all in the same day. The diverse geography of the island supports equally diverse species of wildlife. You never know what you may see just around the next bend. Inland lakes and marshes attract varieties of birdlife that you would not expect to see on an island surrounded by salt water. This island is truly deserving of more than one day if your schedule permits.

Strawberry Island If you have a third night available, try circumnavigating Cypress Island by stopping at Strawberry Island on its western side. Once again, make sure to read and understand the currents. Timing is crucial if you want to take advantage of the water movement. Strawberry Island is a paddler's type of island. The steep shores and deep, swift currents prevent anchoring by larger boats, with just enough room for kayaks to land in a cove on the south end. Approach the island from the Strawberry Bay side at any time except slack tide to avoid being swept around the end of the island by the current. Terrific views of Rosario Strait can be found from each of the tent sites. No water will be found on this island so bring what you need. Be sure to place your boats high on the beach because passing tankers create huge breaking waves.

Returning to March Point from Strawberry Island can either be a short or long trip, depending on the time of day. The current velocity in Guemes Channel can be swift; time it right to go with the flow or sit on the side until it changes. Be especially observant of other boaters as you pass through this area. Weekend traffic of all sizes is heavy during the summer season. Keep to the Guemes Island side of the channel to avoid most of the boat wakes and cross over to March Point once you are clear of the channel. Safety first at all times in this area.

Trip 4 Outer San Juan Islands

Skill: Advanced
Time: 3–5 days
Hazards: Variable weather, traffic and currents
Access: Roche Harbor/San Juan County Park
Charts: 18421 Strait of Juan de Fuca to Strait of
Georgia 1:80,000
18423 Bellingham to Everett including
San Juan Islands 1:80,000
18431 Rosario Strait to Cherry Point
1:25,000
18432 Boundary Pass 1:25,000
18433 Haro Strait—Middle Bank to
Stuart Island 1:25,000
18434 San Juan Channel 1:25,000
Tide Tables: Island Canoe San Juan

The northwestern edge of the San Juans offers paddlers an incredible array of wildlife and scenery. Miles of rugged, undeveloped shorelines along Haro Strait provide habitat for a multitude of marine birds and mammals, including orca whales. While this is a great environment for marine life, it is not one to be taken lightly by the paddler. The outer San Juans are for experienced paddlers who are capable of reading tide tables and current guides and are able to respond to the variable weather and water conditions likely to be encountered. Currents in Spieden and President Channels can be treacherous, at times exceeding 4 knots, and should be factored into your trip planning.

Launching

As of 1997, the only realistic put-in sites for paddling this route are Roche Harbor or San Juan County Park on San Juan Island. There is no overnight parking allowed at either Lime Kiln Point or English Camp, neither of which offers adequate access to the water. To get to Roche Harbor or San Juan County Park, take a Washington State ferry from Anacortes to Friday Harbor. Check out the sailing schedule well in advance of your arrival and allow lots of time if you are attempting to do this trip on a summer weekend. Ferry traffic is very heavy on Fridays and Sundays.

At time of writing, you needed your own vehicle to reach these launch sites; however, the wwta is aiming to develop a shuttle service for paddlers, so check with them.

After reaching Friday Harbor, drive about 17 km (10.5 mi.) to Roche Harbor or about 22.5 (14 mi.) to San Juan County Park. Friday Harbor is a little tricky; once you leave the ferry, go west on Spring Street for two blocks, turn right onto Second Street and travel three blocks where you will turn left on Guard. Go one more block and turn right on Tucker at the stop sign. Bear to the left at an upcoming Y in the road. Now you are on Roche Harbor Road. Follow this road for the next 16 km (10 mi.) to Roche Harbor Resort. If you choose to put in at San Juan County Park, turn left after 13.5 km (8.5 mi.) onto West Valley Road and follow the signs.

Deciding on which launch site to use is a matter of economics and distance. Roche Harbor Resort charges $5 a day per vehicle to park and $7 per kayak to launch, including the return use of the boat ramp. San Juan County Park charges $4 a day per vehicle to park and no launching fee. Launching at San Juan park adds around 8 km (5 mi.) to the distance to Stuart Island, so you be the judge.

Sites

Stuart Island State Park   From Roche Harbor, paddle 1.6 km (1 mi.) northwest to Posey Island. The 8.4-km (5.5-mi.) crossing from Posey Island will take you to the first night's campsite on Stuart Island. This region lies in the Vancouver Island rain shadow; you may notice the area is quite dry and even supports cactus, which is how the Cactus Islands, north of Spieden Island, got their name. Spieden even became an African game farm for a short period as entrepreneurs attempted to work with the arid environment. With several of the smaller islands in the area designated as wildlife sanctuaries, there are opportunities to observe a variety of marine birds. Paddlers must remember that landing on these islands is prohibited due to the sensitive nature of local nesting activities. Watch and enjoy from a distance. Unfortunately, landing is also prohibited on Spieden Island because most of the shoreline is privately owned.

As you enter Reid Harbor on the southeast end of Stuart Island, make your way to the head of the bay where the water trail site can be found. There are several campsites in this area so watch for the water trail sign. Many activities abound on Stuart Island. Explore the beaches and tide pools at low tide or try your luck with fishing. If you want some time away

Pelican Beach on Cypress Island. WASHINGTON WATER TRAILS ASSOCIATION

from the water, there are numerous trails and roads on the island that can keep you busy exploring the area's history. For an extended hike, tour out to the Turn Point lighthouse for some spectacular views of Haro Strait.

For the next day's paddle, you will probably want to get an early start to avoid any afternoon wind, but check the current guide to determine that a sun-up departure will have the water going in the right direction through President Channel. The channel takes you north to Orcas Island, past Waldron Island to Point Doughty, about 18.5 km (11.5 mi.). Tour back through the Cactus Islands and then cross over to the stark rocks off Point Disney. Watch for bald eagles soaring overhead as you proceed northerly through President Channel. If you time the current correctly, the paddling will verge on being effortless.

Point Doughty (Orcas Island)   Point Doughty at the northwest corner of Orcas Island is especially suited for kayaks and small, beachable craft, whereas its currents and lack of anchorage provide little protection for larger boats. The campsite does require a bit of an uphill climb but the spectacular views westward to Boundary Pass make it all worthwhile. The point is not road accessible, which usually provides the visitor with a somewhat secluded feeling. There are only a few tent sites so large groups should avoid camping here. Land at the small beach on the south side of the point and be careful of the tide rips on nearby rocks and shoals. There is no fresh water, and the forest is closed to the public because the site is located within a Natural Area Preserve.

Posey Island State Park At this juncture in your trip, you have a few options depending on your schedule. It is about 19 km (12 mi.) to return directly to Roche Harbor; for those who put in at San Juan County Park, it is a long day of about 27 km (17 mi.). If you are destined for San Juan park, consider an overnight stop on Posey Island to make the journey a bit more manageable. Posey Island is off the northwest corner of San Juan Island, about 1.6 km (1 mi.) from Roche Harbor. The entire island is a designated marine trail campsite; however, there are two established campsites that should be used and a limit of 16 people per night. You cannot "hold" campsites for others, and reservations are currently not possible. The site is often crowded and has no source of fresh water.

Jones Island State Park If your trip allows for another day of paddling, plan for a sideline excursion to Jones Island State Park, located .8 km (.5 mi.) off the southwest corner of Orcas Island. You can then return to Roche Harbor or San Juan County Park the following day, with a much shorter distance to cover. Try to catch the President Channel "express" on its southbound trip, but watch for the eddy lines and waves that form as the water pushes out on the ebb tide. Paddling along the western shore of Orcas Island you will see more evidence of people than you did the previous day, but it is still quite scenic. Watch for seals; you may even see some Dalls porpoise around Spring Passage.

Jones Island offers an excellent location for exploring the nooks and crannies of the many smaller islands nearby. The marine trail site on Jones is on the west side of the island. Guard your food and gear bags: the raccoons on the island are very curious and may decide that what is yours is theirs. Watch for the resident black-tailed deer as you explore the trails around the island. For a nice afternoon or evening paddle, tour the Wasp Group for a dip into an area rich in San Juan Island history.

As your paddling adventure comes to a close, you may be tempted to drift off with reflections of the past few days—but stay alert. This area of the San Juan Islands can surprise you at any time. Your last day of paddling should allow plenty of time to return to your vehicle, load up and make one of the afternoon ferries. Even with the ferry schedule in mind, don't miss

Seattle's waterfront. JOEL ROGER

out on the opportunity to carefully enjoy the remaining hours on the water, the wonderful scenery and the magnificent marine life of this special area.

Trip 5 Seattle

Skill:	Beginner to advanced
Time:	Day trip
Hazards:	Traffic
Access:	Waterway #15/Brooklyn Avenue NE
Chart:	18447 Lake Washington 1:25,000

Paddling within sight of downtown Seattle may not be a wilderness experience but it does allow you to travel through waterways with a wealth of maritime history. Several places, such as the Wooden Boat Center at the south end of Lake Union, offer easy access to museums and boating-related activities.

Launching

If you would like to explore the Lake Union/Portage Bay area and are approaching Seattle from the south on the I-5, take exit 169, NE 45th Street, the University of Washington exit. Turn right on 45th and go straight until the intersection with Roosevelt Way. If you are approaching from the north, take the same I-5 exit (169) and turn left onto NE 45th Street and proceed to Roosevelt Way.

Turn right onto Roosevelt Way and travel three blocks. Take another right on NE 42nd Street followed by a left onto 7th Avenue NE. Travel to the stop sign, bearing to the right. Turn left onto 6th Avenue NE. Go underneath an overpass and turn right at the stop sign onto NE Northlake Way. After a couple of blocks you will see the sign for Waterway #15 Public Access and the narrow beach from which you can launch.

An alternative put-in site is just east of Waterway #15. Proceed eastbound on Northlake Way from the Waterway #15 site, turning right on NE Boat Street. Proceed to the intersection with Brooklyn Avenue NE, where there is a small public access ramp.

Sites

This paddle is very popular during the summer and gives you the opportunity to view urban life in a multitude of forms from the water. Observe lakeshore living aboard the many houseboats in Lake Union or paddle down through Ship Canal into Fisherman's Terminal in Ballard to watch the fishing fleet that calls Seattle home. There are a growing number of businesses and restaurants that have floats and docks that boaters can tie up to while visiting their establishment; look for these and plan to stop for lunch or dinner. Paddle quietly in the marsh areas of the Seattle Arboretum to see the diverse bird life that resides here. Continue on via Portage Bay and the Montlake Cut into Lake Washington, or arrange a car shuttle and paddle through the Hiram M. Chittenden (Ballard) Locks out to Shilshole Marina and Golden Gardens. Whichever way you decide to paddle, there will be plenty to see and talk about as you cruise along the historic waterways of Seattle. By the fall of 1998, there will be a brochure showing public boat access to a Seattle Union Bay Trail; for more information, contact the WWTA.

ADDITIONAL ROUTES

Heading north: For those interested in travelling north into the Gulf Islands of British Columbia, your best bet is to cross from the Stuart Island State Park to Isle de Lis Marine Park. Watch for ships and be sure to check in with Canada Customs when you arrive (tel.: 1-888-226-7277).

Heading south: It is hard to go any farther south in Puget Sound than Olympia. One option is to get out of your boat and head for the Olympia Brewery . . . but that's for another type of trip.

THE GULF ISLANDS

STRAIT
OF
GEORGIA

N

VANCOUVER
ISLAND

Newcastle
Ⓦ ▲ I.
Nanaimo • Ⓦ Ⓣ
Ⓛ
Duke Pt.
Gabriola
I.
Dodd
Narrows
Cedar • Ⓛ
Silva Bay
Gabriola Passage
Drumbeg Park
De Courcy
I. ▲
Ⓦ
Pirates Cove
Marine Park
Ⓛ Yellow Pt.
Valdes
I.
Ⓣ
▲ Blackberry Pt.
Thetis
I.
Ⓛ
Ⓦ
Porlier Pass
▲ Dionisio Pt.
Ⓦ Park
Chemainus •
Kuper
I.
Tent
I.
Ⓛ
Ⓦ
Southy Pt.
▲ Wallace I.
Retreat
Cove
Galiano
I.
Crofton • • Vesuvius
Ganges • Ⓦ
Ⓛ
Long
Harbour
Montague Harbour
▲ Ⓛ Ⓦ
Active Pass
Prevost
I. ▲
Saltspring
Island
Mayne
I.
Ⓛ
Ruckle
Ⓛ Park
Fulford ▲
Harbour
Ⓛ
N. Pender
I.
Winter Cove
Marine Park
Ⓛ Ⓦ
Portland I.
Ⓛ Ⓦ
Ⓣ Ⓦ ▲
Swartz
Bay
Beaumont
Marine
Park
▲
Ⓣ Ⓦ
S. Pender
I.
Saturna
I.
Cabbage
▲ I.
Sidney • Ⓛ
Rum
▲ I.
Ⓛ
James
I.
Ⓦ
Sidney
I.
Sidney
Spit
Marine
Park
Saanichton
Bay
D'Arcy
▲ Is.
Sooke
• Victoria
Ⓛ Ten Mile Pt./
Cadboro Pt.
Discovery
I.

Symbols

Ⓛ Launch Site
▲ Campsite
Ⓦ Water
• Town
Ⓣ Trail

5 NM   0   5 NM

Chapter Three

The Gulf Islands
Alan Wilson

Carved from sandstone and marked by twisting, red-bod-
ied arbutus, the Gulf Islands of southern British Columbia offer paddlers
of all ages and abilities endless opportunities for exploration. They are a
kayaker's paradise, with sheltered waters, infrequent summer rain, short
distances between sites and easy access to services. Homes and cabins are
tucked among the trees, provincial marine parks dot the shorelines—the
lifestyle is rural and the pace a bit slow. There is no better place to take a
quick break from urban life.

BACKGROUND

The Strait of Georgia is like a large inland sea, about 220 km (354 mi.)
long, protected from the Pacific Ocean by the great length of Vancouver
Island. Captain Vancouver first referred to the Strait as the "Gulf of Georgia," which is why the islands here are called the Gulf Islands. While each
island has unique characteristics, they all offer a break from urban life—
for a week or a weekend—with a pleasant ferry ride from Vancouver or
Victoria. Saltspring is the largest of the lot with a population of about
10,000. Its town of Ganges is considered the business centre of the south
islands. The next largest in population is Gabriola Island with almost
5,000 people. Galiano, North and South Pender, Mayne and Saturna collectively house over 5,000 residents.

All the islands are in the lee of the Vancouver Island Range and subsequently receive very little rain in the summer. The ensuing mild weather
has attracted thousands of residents over the years, creating development

pressures and, in some opinions, eroding the quiet, rural lifestyle. But there is still an abundance of natural life, particularly in the waters and shores of the islands, with an estimated 3,000 species of plant and animal life. There are hundreds of seaweed and fish species, along with invertebrates such as octopus, starfish, oysters and clams, and large marine mammals such as seals, sea lions, river otters and porpoises. Over a hundred species of bird life including bald eagles, great blue herons, ospreys, gulls, cormorants and a wide array of ducks inhabit the islands year round.

Due to this abundance of wildlife and the sheltered conditions, people have been dipping their paddles into these waters for well over 5,000 years. Many shell middens can be seen throughout the islands, evidence of thousands of years of use, and native communities still exist in a number of traditional areas. Paddlers who are tempted to visit native lands should obtain prior permission from the Lyackson Band (Valdes Island), the Penelakut Band (Tent Island) or the Tsawout Band (Saturna Island).

In geologic terms, the Gulf Islands are fairly uniform, sharing a northwest to southeast orientation. Largely sandstone, with a thin soil layer and frequent outcrops of bedrock, their shores are often eroded in bizarre, picturesque shapes. Despite this rocky nature, and past and present logging, there is still considerable forest cover. To many, there is no sweeter moment than watching the islands' magnificent firs and twisting arbutus, perched on the sea-carved sandstone, glimmering in the setting sun. It is an image that will keep paddlers returning for generations to come.

GETTING THERE

By water: Access to the Gulf Islands is provided by B.C. Ferries from the Tsawwassen terminal, 30 km (19 mi.) south of Vancouver, or from Swartz Bay, 32 km (20 mi.) north of Victoria, on Vancouver Island. There are also smaller Vancouver Island ferry terminals leading to some islands, including Nanaimo for Gabriola Island, Chemainus for Thetis Island and Crofton for Saltspring Island. The southern Gulf Islands have inter-island ferries that call at Saltspring, Pender, Galiano, Saturna and Mayne.

All ferries take vehicles, bikes and passengers. Kayak walk-ons are usually possible. Most terminals have potential launch sites nearby, although you are advised to check with local kayak operators for specific information or rentals. Overloads and waits are very common on holiday weekends and during the summer, so give yourself a bit of extra time. If you are taking a vehicle from Tsawwassen to the Gulf Islands, you must make a

Blackberry Point, Valdes Island. PETER McGEE

reservation; from Swartz Bay to the islands is non-reservable. Call B.C. Ferries for information on routes, rates, schedules and reservations.

In Washington State you can catch ferries from Anacortes and Port Angeles to Sidney and Victoria respectively, or you can drive across the border and head to the Tsawwassen ferry terminal.

By land: It is possible to reach the Gulf Islands by launching directly from Vancouver Island at Swartz Bay, Nanaimo and a number of points in between. Detailed launch information is provided later in the chapter. Occasionally people will paddle from the mainland to the Gulf Islands; however, this crossing is not recommended due to the variable weather conditions and heavy vessel traffic.

By air: Several float plane operations serve the islands, including Harbour Air and Pacific Spirit Air.

WEATHER AND HAZARDS

The Gulf Islands lie in the shelter of Vancouver Island and are well known for their low rainfall and calm conditions. Although the paddling season is generally considered to be May through September, those who live in the Gulf Islands take advantage of the mild climate to paddle year round.

The close proximity of land, short crossings and nearby services make for generally safe paddling. The main exceptions to this rule are the tidal passes where water can run up to 8 knots as it rushes in and out of the Strait of Georgia. These include Gabriola Pass, Porlier Pass, Active Pass,

Sansum Narrows and any of the small passages that open into the strait. For information within the Gulf Islands, use the Fulford Harbour tide table. If you are travelling on the Strait of Georgia side of the islands, use the Point Atkinson table.

In addition to the ever-present fleet of B.C. Ferries, there is considerable small boat traffic in the summer, especially on long weekends. Remember that large objects appear to be moving more slowly than they really are and that large vessels have a very limited ability to manoeuvre. Due to the low visibility of kayaks, it is advisable to paddle defensively. Some paddlers mount a bicycle-type flag from a short mast at the stern of their boat to enhance their visibility.

SPECIAL CONSIDERATIONS

Paddlers are strongly discouraged, and at many sites prohibited, from having fires. The area is simply too dry during the summer and the risk too great. Please *do not* light a fire unless absolutely necessary.

As always, paddlers must take note of Indian Reserves (IR on charts) and contact the respective bands for permission to visit these territories. The Gulf Islands are largely privately owned so try not to alienate landowners when stopping to rest on an attractive beach or point of land. Keep within the high tide zone and do not leave litter or make fires. This is extremely important: paddlers have recently come under the wrath of the local press for abusing some of the smaller islands.

Kayakers are asked to refrain from camping on anything other than established campsites. Although many of the small islets look inviting, they are not able to withstand heavy use and are often noticeably impacted by the end of the summer. For their environmental well-being, please respect this voluntary closure.

Please don't paddle too close to cormorant colonies, especially during nesting season when your approach can scare off adults and expose their young to danger. The same applies to seal haul-outs. Seals seem particularly sensitive to kayakers and can be spooked by your approach. Use your binoculars and try to stay at least 100 m (330 ft.) away. Of course, if you are being followed there isn't much you can do but enjoy.

It is best not to harvest shellfish given the uncertainty over red tide and Paralytic Shellfish Poisoning (see Chapter 1). Also be aware of areas leased

> Gabriola Island. ALAN WILSON

for commercial shellfish growing; these are usually marked by shellfish lease signs. Finally, please respect the wishes of the Marine Life Sanctuary Society and refrain from taking any organism within Gabriola Pass and its surrounding waters, which are a proposed Marine Protected Area.

Trip 6 The Gulf Island Chain

Skill:	Beginner to advanced	
Time:	1–10 days	
Hazards:	Traffic and currents	
Access:	Numerous sites on Vancouver Island and the Gulf Islands	
Charts:	3313	Gulf Islands Various Scales
	3440	Race Rocks to D'Arcy Island 1:40,000
	3441	Haro Strait, Boundary Pass and Satellite Channel 1:40,000
	3442	North Pender to Thetis Island 1:40,000
	3443	Thetis Island to Nanaimo 1:40,000
	3462	Juan de Fuca Strait to Strait of Georgia 1:80,000
	3463	Strait of Georgia, Southern Portion 1:80,000
	3513	Strait of Georgia, Northern Portion 1:80,000
	3527	Baynes Sound 1:40,000
Tide Book:	Vol. 5	

Unlike the rest of this book, there is no single excursion described in this chapter. The following trip is written in a south to north fashion—beginning on Vancouver Island near Swartz Bay and ending in Nanaimo—but multiple launching sites have been listed to allow you to plan an excursion suited to your time frame and abilities. Denman and Hornby Islands are discussed at the end of the chapter. Day trips, weekend excursions and week-long explorations are all possible.

Paddlers who wish to experience the entire chain of Gulf Islands can start their trip near Victoria or Sidney and paddle north to Nanaimo (or the reverse) over a period of 7–10 days. If time is a concern, there are a number of great 2–3-day paddling loops that can be accessed from any of the launch sites listed in this chapter. Especially popular are the routes that launch from Sydney, Swartz Bay and Nanaimo. If you are a little unsure of your paddling skills, you may want to pick a central location, camp at a provincial park or stay at one of the many conveniently located B&BS throughout the islands, and day trip to the surrounding sites.

If you are having trouble planning a trip, call a local operator. Not only do they provide rentals, courses and instruction, some also offer shuttle service to and from ferry terminals. .

Launching

The following three sites are common places to start a Gulf Island exploration.

Swartz Bay You can launch kayaks by the government wharf near the ferry terminal at Swartz Bay on Vancouver Island; this gives you the option of leaving your vehicle behind and walking onto the ferry (with kayak-wheels) at the mainland Tsawwassen terminal. At Swartz Bay, walk your boat through the loading area to the entrance of the employee parking lot. The road access for the government wharf can be seen from the upper left of this lot. Once at the wharf, you can launch from the beach to the left (facing the water). The distance from the ferry to this launch site is about 500 m (547 yd.).

If you are driving to Swartz Bay from Victoria, follow the signs to the passenger pick-up area at the Swartz Bay terminal. Continue beyond the final pick-up turnoff and take the next left to reach the government wharf. You can leave your car in a nearby lot.

Saltspring Island There are several good launches on Saltspring Island. At Long Harbour, after getting off the ferry from Tsawwassen, you can launch from the small park area to the southeast of the terminal or from the beach at Quebec Drive. You can also drive into the main town of Ganges and launch from the boat ramp in Centennial Park. Other launches are Drummond Park and Beddis Beach off Beddis Road (both excellent beach launches) or Ruckle Provincial Park near Fulford Harbour (a short carry down a hill that can be slippery when wet). It is possible to launch at Fulford but the beach is rough. Southey Point, at the north end of Saltspring, has an excellent beach launch, and there is another nearby via a trail off Arbutus Road. There is also a ramp .8 km (.5 mi.) north of the Fernwood dock on the northeast side of the island. At most of these sites, there is limited roadside parking. Please give consideration to the people who live in these areas.

Nanaimo   You can launch at a ramp by the Sealand Public Market near the Departure Bay ferry terminal in Nanaimo for access to Newcastle Island and Gabriola Island, from which the chain of Gulf Islands runs southward. If you are arriving from Horseshoe Bay, turn left at the first set of lights after getting off the ferry and soon after take a right into the market parking lot. If you wish to walk your kayak (with a cart) onto the ferry at Tsawwassen or Horseshoe Bay, you will need to roll approximately 500 m (547 yd.) from the Departure Bay terminal to reach the ramp. North of Nanaimo there are boat ramps at Hammond Bay, in North Nanaimo, at Lantzville and on the First Nations reserve in Nanoose Bay (ask permission).

The new ferry terminal at Duke Point, for travellers arriving from Tsawwassen, provides kayakers with a mediocre launching opportunity, at best. Although B.C. Ferries won't allow launching at the terminal itself, a kilometre or so away is a small park with flat sandstone ledges at the water's edge. The distance is quite far, so you are better off launching at the Sealand Public Market site (above).

If you arrive by vehicle at Duke Point and need parking, you can also go to the nearby community of Cedar and launch at the ramp at the end of Fawcett Road.

Sites

Most of the sites listed below are managed by BC Parks, and the camping fees change over the years. In 1997, the self-registered camping fee for parties of up to four people was between $6–$10.

Discovery Island   East of Victoria Harbour at the junction of Juan de Fuca and Haro Straits sits the 61-ha (151-a.) Discovery Island Marine Park, 3.2 km (2.5 mi.) from Oak Bay Marina. With toilets, trails and room for about 12 campsites, Discovery Island offers spectacular views of the Olympic Peninsula. Approach with caution, however, as there are many rocks and islets and the currents in Haro Strait and Baynes Channel can be extremely strong (consult the tables for Race Passage). Also note that the northern portion of Discovery Island, Chatham Island and some of the smaller islets are Indian Reserve lands and should not be entered without permission. Open fires are not permitted, and there is a self-registered camping fee.

Closest launches: Oak Bay ramp off Beach Drive; Cattle Point ramp off Beach Drive (ample parking); and Ten Mile Point's Smuggler's Cove on McAnally Road (park on roadside, launch from shore). All these launch sites are in or near Victoria.

D'Arcy Island Marine Park Established in 1961, D'Arcy Island Marine Park is a small, undeveloped island lying to the south of Sidney Island. It was a leper colony from 1896 to 1921, and ruins of the facilities are still visible. There are about 12 campsites, a beach landing and a pit toilet though no water. Little D'Arcy Island to the east is private property so please do not intrude. Open fires are not permitted, and there is a self-registered camping fee.

Closest launches: Island View Beach ramp off Island View Road, 5.5 km (3.5 mi.) from D'Arcy; public wharf in Saanichton Bay off James Island Road; and public beach access off Rothsay Road in Sidney.

Sidney Spit Marine Park Sidney Island, 4 km (2.5 mi.) off Sidney, has a famous sand bar, the main attraction to Sidney Spit Marine Park. Although Sidney Spit is a busy anchorage for boaters, the trail around the saltwater lagoon and along the long log-strewn beach to the southeast sees much less use. A large, level, grassy camping area with unlimited room can be found at the old dock partway into the lagoon, too silted up to be used by pleasure craft though paddleable in some tides. You will enjoy drifting along the current scant inches above eel grass, crab and other marine creatures. Toilets and water are available. Camp fees are collected by the park hosts. There is walk-on ferry service available from Sidney.

Closest launches: Sidney or Saanichton launches (see D'Arcy Island launches, above).

Isle de Lis Marine Park Five kilometres (3 mi.) from Sidney is the 4.4-ha (11-a.) Rum Island known as Isle de Lis Marine Park. (Rum Island apparently got its name from rum-running in the prohibition era.) This island borders on Haro Strait, which can indeed be harrowing: it is the main shipping channel from the Pacific into the Strait of Georgia. Rum Island was donated for a public park in 1978 with the owner's stipulation that it be called Isle de Lis for the wild lilies that grow here.

Rum Island is connected to Gooch Island by a steep gravel beach, the only place to land. The next trick is to find a place to perch your tent on the rocky isle. There is a small network of trails, and exploring will reward you with spectacular views to the south, especially of Mount Baker hovering in the distance. Watch for turbulent waters and swift currents off Tom Point. There are toilets and a self-registered camping fee. There is no fresh water.

Closest launch: Sidney (see D'Arcy Island launches, above).

Princess Margaret Marine Park Portland Island lies 4 km (2.5 mi.) to the north of Swartz Bay. The entire island was given to Princess Margaret, sister of Queen Elizabeth, in 1958, but was eventually returned to the people of B.C. and is now the aptly named Princess Margaret Marine Park. Portland is about 200 ha (494 a.) and well forested. Large ferries pass on either side of the island so be careful of ferry traffic and wash. There are a couple of beaches, each with space for several tents. Cross-island and perimeter trails offer pleasant hiking. Toilets and water are available, and there is a self-registered camping fee.

Closest launch: Beach launch near government wharf at the Swartz Bay ferry terminal.

Ruckle Provincial Park (Saltspring Island) Ruckle Provincial Park at Beaver Point on the south end of Saltspring has eight small coves and bays, miles of shoreline, rocky headlands and camping. It is an enormous site, accessible by land and water and hence quite busy during the summer. If you are arriving by boat, watch the ferry wake and unload quickly. One of the nicest beaches is at the south end of the park in the day-use area. A few bays to the north, you can find a suitable landing spot if you are spending the night.

Closest launches: On Saltspring Island, you can launch from the park itself (although the slope can be slippery), Fulford Harbour, Ganges and Long Harbour; on Vancouver Island, launch from the Swartz Bay ferry terminal.

Beaumont Marine Park (South Pender Island) The park is located on the west side of South Pender Island in Bedwell Harbour. Bedwell Harbour has a nearby full-service marine/resort that is busy in summer and acts as a Canada Customs office during those months. The two islands of North and South Pender are joined by a bridge over narrow Pender Canal, site of thousands of years of native habitation and extensive middens. There are good trail links to Mount Norman Regional Park leading to the summit. Water and toilets are available, and a camping fee is collected by the park hosts.

Circumnavigation of South Pender is a nice 14-km (9-mi.) paddle but watch for turbulent waters off the south end, with whirlpools and standing waves when tide and winds oppose. Gowlland Point is a great viewpoint.

Closest launches: The Pender Island ferry terminal at Otter Bay is prohibited for launching so your best bet is to drive to Port Washington on North Pender or to launch from Village Bay on Mayne Island.

Winter Cove Marine Park (Saturna Island) This park on Saturna Island does not allow camping but is worth a visit to watch the waters of the Strait of Georgia rush through narrow Boat Passage at up to 7 knots. Toilets and water are available, and there is a store at the inter-island ferry dock in Lyall Harbour. Fiddlers Cove at the south end of Saturna is on First Nations territory, and anyone wishing to visit should contact the Tsawout Band.

Closest launch: Lyall Harbour ferry terminal wharf.

Cabbage Island Marine Park Beyond Boat Passage and out into the Strait of Georgia are Anniversary Island, Cabbage Island Marine Park and some unnamed islets west of Grainger Point. All but Cabbage Island have rocky landings, and weather conditions on the Strait of Georgia will dictate access. Cabbage Island has toilets, a wonderful sandy beach but no fresh water. There are approximately 6 campsites and a self-registered camping fee.

Closest launch: Cabbage Island is 9.6 km (6 mi.) from Lyall Harbour on Saturna Island.

James Bay (Prevost Island) Prevost Island, lying just off Saltspring Island, is a popular anchorage for boaters due to its long, shallow coves. Until recently it was privately owned, but two properties have been purchased under the joint provincial-federal program, the Pacific Marine Heritage Legacy fund, giving the public legitimate access to the shore. James Bay has a pleasant beach, an abandoned orchard and the potential for hiking trails to Peile Point. There are plans to site a composting toilet at James Bay in the near future, and camping fees will likely follow.

Closest launches: Ganges or Long Harbour on Saltspring Island (launch from small park area southeast of ferry terminal), or Montague Harbour on Galiano Island.

Montague Harbour Marine Park (Galiano Island) Across Trincomali Channel from Prevost and Saltspring Islands is Montague Harbour Marine Park on Galiano Island, one of the best protected and most popular anchorages in the Gulf Islands. The park has established, well-serviced campsites (even a recycling system) and a nearby store. It has a nice beach that is busy in summer due to its road access. Toilets and water are available, and a camping fee is collected by the park hosts. To explore the area, launch from the beach or the public wharf. The Ballingal Islets make a nice paddle some 5 km (3 mi.) north of Montague past a number of small private islands.

Closest launches: From the ferry terminal at Sturdies Bay, drive to Georgeson Bay Road and onto Montague Harbour Road. Launch from the government wharf near the ferry slip in Montague Harbour. You can also drive directly to the marine park to use the boat ramp; parking is available here.

Wallace Island Marine Park Wallace Island Marine Park just north of Montague Harbour is entirely public except for a couple of private homes. It has two coves popular with boaters but there is limited camping available for paddlers. Chivers Point, a scenic site at the north end, consists of rocky fingers projecting north towards the adjacent Secretary Islands. At higher tides the reef and shallows off the southwest side of Wallace offer landings to a sparsely forested area where some level spots can be found. A central trail runs down the length of the island, and there is a dock in Conover Cove. Open fires are not permitted. Water is available from a hand pump but should be boiled before drinking. There is a camping fee collected by the park hosts.

Closest launches: Southey Point on Saltspring Island or Retreat Cove on Galiano Island.

Dionisio Point Provincial Park (Galiano Island) Dionisio Point Provincial Park is at the north end of Galiano Island, on the east side of Porlier

Pass (watch for extreme currents), with nice beaches, rocky headlands and rough road accessibility. There is a hand pump for water and a self-registered camping fee.

Closest launches: There is a government dock, store and phone at North Galiano before the entrance to Porlier Pass. You can also cross over from Saltspring Island.

Tent Island Tent Island at the southern end of Kuper Island is a former provincial park on First Nations territory. The island has reverted to First Nations control, and anyone wishing to visit is asked to contact the Penelakut Band on Kuper Island. For an interesting paddle, enter the narrow, dredged canal that separates Thetis and Kuper Islands. Enter via Clam Bay or Telegraph Harbour, but be careful as the canal is not passable at lowest water. Telegraph Harbour has marinas, toilets, water, a store, phone, pub and restaurant. The Rose Islets, just to the north, are an ecological reserve with abundant bird life. Do not go ashore.

Closest launches: Preedy Harbour on Thetis Island, which can be reached by ferry from Chemainus; and Southey Point on the north end of Saltspring Island.

Blackberry Point (Valdes Island) For years, Blackberry Point on Valdes Island was the most popular campsite for paddlers in the northern islands. However, Blackberry Point is private land owned by forestry giant MacMillan Bloedel, and the company prohibited camping in August 1997 when they found unattended campfires. Since then, the B.C. Marine Trail Association has been working on an agreement with the company that will once again allow overnight camping. For updated information on Blackberry Point, or if you would like to be a "volunteer warden," please contact the BCMTA.

Most other landings on Valdes Island are First Nations territory, under the control of the band living at Shingle Point south of Blackberry. Permission may be sought there or by contracting the Lyackson Band in Chemainus on Vancouver Island.

Closest launches: Drumbeg Park or False Narrows on Gabriola Island, about 10 km (6 mi.) away. It is also possible to launch from the Vancouver Island communities of Cedar (a ramp at the end of Fawcett Road) or Yellowpoint (the beach at Blue Heron Park), both located 20–25 minutes by car south of Nanaimo.

Pirate's Cove Marine Park (De Courcy Island) Pirate's Cove Marine Park on De Courcy Island is a popular anchorage, but the south side of the park on Ruxton Pass is less busy and offers a wide beach with spacious camping areas and good walking trails around the adjacent peninsula. Toilets and fresh water are available, and a self-registered camping fee will likely be introduced in the near future.

Closest launches: Gabriola Island or Cedar on Vancouver Island, both about 3.2 km (2 mi.) from De Courcy.

Gabriola Island As you continue north you will come across Drumbeg Provincial Park at the south end of Gabriola, on the Strait of Georgia side of Gabriola Passage. (Stay alert: this passage has serious currents.) This is a day-use only park. Even so, it is worth a stop as it has a pleasant beach, trails and toilets. When in the passage, follow the voluntary fishing and shellfish harvesting closure introduced by the Marine Life Sanctuary Society. Nearby Brant Reef is a large seal haul-out so please keep your distance. Silva Bay on Gabriola is a popular yacht harbour with marinas, stores, laundry facilities, pub and a restaurant.

For kayakers wanting to camp on Gabriola, your best bet is the privately owned Gabriola Campground at the north end of the island. It has a lovely campsite and beach area and is an easy paddle across from Newcastle Island. Access this site by paddling through False Narrows or Dodd Narrows. Be sure to time the currents and watch for B.C. Ferries and other boat traffic. Don't forget to check out the weathered cliffs on Gabriola and the sea lions on the log booms off the Harmac pulp mill on Vancouver Island near Northumberland Channel.

Closest launch: Sealand Public Market just outside the Departure Bay ferry terminal offers great access to Gabriola and Newcastle Islands. See page 52 for details.

Newcastle Island Marine Park Finally, there is Newcastle Island Marine Park just off Nanaimo. Newcastle Island is such a popular spot, it has its own passenger-only ferry as well as beaches, campsites, toilets and fresh water. The paddle between Newcastle and the launch site at the Sealand Public Market takes only minutes, though be sure to keep your eyes open for ferry, float plane and small boat traffic. Pleasant trails cross the island. Newcastle Island has floats, a concession, a visitor's centre and almost 20 campsites; the camping fee is collected by the park hosts.

ADDITIONAL ROUTES

Heading north: If you wish to paddle north from Newcastle, you will be exposed to the conditions of the Strait of Georgia until you reach Nanoose Bay on Vancouver Island. Nanoose is the site of the controversial Canadian Forces maritime base where the U.S. Navy tests ships and nuclear submarines. Maude Island and Southey Islands, off the tip of Nanoose Peninsula, are potential campsites; Winchelsea Island, the operational headquarters of the naval base, is off limits. North of Nanoose are the sand banks of Rathtrevor Beach and Parksville. Farther north, ferries depart from French Creek for Lasqueti Island and from Buckley Bay for Denman and Hornby Islands.

Denman and Hornby Islands are known as the undiscovered Gulf Islands. With large sections of unpopulated shoreline, the two islands combine with the protected waters of Baynes Sound to provide a tranquil setting that is ideal for the beginner paddler. Unfortunately, there is not much camping in the area, and overnighting is more or less limited to Fillongley Provincial Park and Sandy Island Provincial Park. Fillongley, located on the south end of Denman, is road accessible and has a designated tenting area. North of Fillongley Park, most of the shoreline is owned by logging companies so there is some potential to access these undeveloped lands. Sandy Island is a beautiful park just off Denman's northern tip that is only accessible by water. It has an outhouse but no fresh water, and camping is random. Helliwell and Tribune Bay Provincial Parks on Hornby are stunning but day-use only. Local operators are extremely helpful and will help you plan a trip to the area. It is worthwhile to call them before you arrive because parking and launching can be a little difficult, particularly on Hornby.

Heading south: For those interested in exploring the northern part of Washington State, you can cross from Isle de Lis Marine Park to Stuart Island State Park. Watch for ships and be sure to check in with U.S. Customs when you arrive (tel.: 1-800-562-5943).

For those who want a taste of the exposed West Coast, drive west from Victoria to Sooke. This stretch of coast, with rocky points, sand beaches and rainforests, offers the wild coast within easy reach of the city. On a calm day, you can paddle the outer coast or surf off Jordan River. On a rough day, or if you are new to kayaking, you might choose to paddle in Sooke Basin, a wonderfully protected harbour.

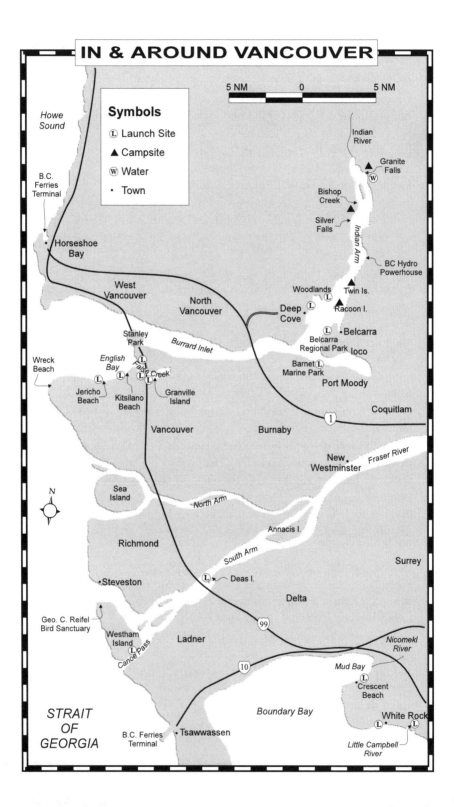

IN & AROUND VANCOUVER

Symbols

- Ⓛ Launch Site
- ▲ Campsite
- ⓦ Water
- • Town

5 NM   0   5 NM

Howe
Sound

B.C.
Ferries
Terminal

Horseshoe
Bay

West
Vancouver

North
Vancouver

Stanley
Park

English Bay

False Creek

Wreck
Beach

Jericho
Beach

Kitsilano
Beach

Granville
Island

Vancouver

Burrard Inlet

Deep
Cove

Woodlands
Ⓛ Twin Is. ▲

Racoon I. ▲

Belcarra
Regional Park

Ⓛ Belcarra

Ioco

Barnet Ⓛ
Marine Park

Port Moody

Indian
River

Granite
Falls ▲ ⓦ

Bishop
Creek ▲

Silver
Falls ▲

Indian Arm

BC Hydro
Powerhouse

Burnaby

Coquitlam

(1)

New
Westminster

Fraser River

Sea
Island

North Arm

Annacis I.

South Arm

Ⓛ Deas I.

Richmond

Surrey

Steveston

Delta

Geo. C. Reifel
Bird Sanctuary

Westham
Island

Canoe Pass

Ladner

(99)

(10)

Nicomekl
River

Mud Bay

Ⓛ
Crescent
Beach

White Rock
Ⓛ   Ⓛ

Little Campbell
River

STRAIT
OF
GEORGIA

Boundary Bay

B.C. Ferries
Terminal

• Tsawwassen

N

Chapter Four

In and Around Vancouver

Peter McGee, Catrin Webb and Howard Zatwarnitski

Living in Vancouver blesses the paddler with many things. The finest boats and paddles in the world are made in our own backyard, and many of the best paddling instructors and outfitters are based here. Most importantly, we and our visitors have the ocean on our doorstep, which means we can experience the joy of paddling 365 days a year. This chapter describes just a few of the trips you can take in and around Vancouver. To find out about additional trips in the Lower Mainland, consider joining the Sea Kayak Association of B.C. or another club listed in Useful Contacts.

BACKGROUND

The influence of the Fraser River on the area in and around Vancouver cannot be overstated. Unlike the rest of the mountainous and rugged B.C. coastline, the Lower Mainland is an area of unusually low and flat land. Most of the region is actually a delta, formed by the Fraser River and its glacial predecessors over a period of about 70 million years. Today the Fraser River basin is one of the largest food reservoirs on the continent, home to millions of salmon, sturgeon, eulachon and trout; it touches, through an elaborate network of tributaries, over 200 000 square km (124,000 sq. mi.) of the province.

Not surprisingly, the magnificence of the Fraser River and the shelter of glacially sculpted Burrard Inlet did not go unnoticed by the First Nations, and several different peoples flourished in the area. Halq'emeylem is the language spoken by the people of the lower Fraser and their histories reach back to the beginning of time, when certain individuals were transformed into the river's first salmon and first sturgeon.

Simon Fraser was the first European to experience the cultures of the Fraser River in 1808. It wasn't until the gold rush of 1858, however, that any substantial immigrant population moved into the area. Even then, the 30,000 miners who came north were a transient folk, and most wintered in Victoria or San Francisco. In an effort to create some stability among the residents, Governor James Douglas introduced a law in 1860 that allowed settlers to claim land not currently "settled" by natives. Unfortunately, this law did not recognize sites that were used seasonally by the First Nations, and thousands of hectares of culturally significant lands were improperly claimed on the assumption they were vacant or abandoned.

Today the Halq'emeylem peoples are striving for a greater self-definition and control over their traditional lands. As you journey in and around Vancouver, you will likely see the Halq'emeylem communities of the X'muzk'i'um (Musqueam), Tsawwassen and Semiahmoo strategically perched at the entrance of the Fraser River. These communities, as well as those of the Squamish Nation on the north shore and the Tsleil Waututh First Nation of Burrard Inlet, serve as a gateway to the city of Vancouver and remind us of a past that contains many lessons for our future.

WEATHER AND HAZARDS

The weather in and around Vancouver varies drastically due to the region's different geographic environments. From the flat Fraser delta to the mountainous Indian Arm, paddlers need to recognize that, though close to a large city, you are ultimately at the mercy of the sea and of highly changeable conditions. Winds, currents and temperature are important considerations wherever you paddle.

Northwesterly winds tend to be dominant during the summer months but these can be strongly influenced by sea breezes, outflow winds from the Fraser Valley and the configuration of mainland inlets. Use care when travelling near the sand and shallows of the Fraser delta, White Rock and Spanish Banks on Vancouver's west side. In addition, be careful travelling near river mouths, particularly when wind and current are opposed.

Finally, be cautious of vessel traffic. In all but the smallest rivers or shallows, you are likely to encounter a number of different boats. Remember, large vessels cannot change course quickly, and you are advised to pick your route on the assumption that other boaters will not be able to see you.

SPECIAL CONSIDERATIONS

As paddlers we often travel in anonymity, but most of the areas in and around Vancouver place us in the company of local residents and other boaters. Please respect private property, be sure to give a wide berth to others while on the water and limit your impacts while on land.

Trip 7 False Creek

Skill:	Beginner to advanced	
Time:	2–4 hours	
Hazards:	Traffic	
Access:	Granville Island/Coast Guard Station	
Charts:	3311	Sunshine Coast—Vancouver Harbour to Desolation Sound 1:40,000
	3493	Vancouver Harbour, Western Portion 1:10,000
	3481	Approaches to Vancouver Harbour 1:25,000
Tide Book:	Vol. 5	

Situated in the heart of Vancouver, False Creek is about as urban as you can get without actually being on land. As the former home of the world fair, Expo 86, and the new home of a massive Concord Pacific development, the area has undergone dramatic changes over the years, but the essential qualities that made it a kayak destination have remained: it is easy to access and extremely well protected. Top this off with fantastic city views and you have the ultimate urban escape for the beginner and advanced paddler alike.

Launching

The most common launch sites for False Creek are the docks on Granville Island. Located under the Granville Street Bridge, Granville Island is home to numerous kayak builders and kayak stores including the Ecomarine Ocean Kayak Centre. Finding a kayak to rent is actually easier than finding a parking space (there is a 3-hour limit on free parking spaces) so if you are planning to rent it might be worthwhile to park off the island and walk to the docks. If you are bringing your own boats, launch on Granville Island or beside the Coast Guard Station located in Vanier Park, at the northwest end of False Creek. To reach Granville Island, head north on Fir Street and take a right on 2nd Avenue; from there, follow the signs. To reach the Coast Guard Station, head east on Cornwall Avenue and take a left two traffic lights before the Burrard Street Bridge.

Once on the water, keep an eye out for other boat traffic and stick to the sides of the inlet. Try to limit your crossings. Paddling the entire length of False Creek should not take more than a couple hours but you might want to leave a little time to visit the restaurants and stores that dot the shore.

Trip 8   English Bay

Skill:	Beginner to advanced
Time:	2–4 hours
Hazards:	Traffic and wind
Access:	Jericho Beach/English Bay/Granville Island
Charts:	3311 Sunshine Coast—Vancouver Harbour to Desolation Sound 1:40,000
	3493 Vancouver Harbour, Western Portion 1:10,000
	3481 Approaches to Vancouver Harbour 1:25,000
Tide Book:	Vol. 5

Paddling in English Bay quickly gives you a sense of Vancouver's beauty. To the north are the often snow-capped mountains, to the east and south are the beaches of Stanley Park, Kitsilano and Jericho, and farther west lie Pacific Spirit Regional Park and the Strait of Georgia. Watching the setting sun reflect off the city's downtown highrises as you drift through this idyllic scene is a great way to finish the day.

Launching

English Bay can be accessed from a variety of launch sites. Jericho Sailing Centre, near the Vancouver Youth Hostel, is the site farthest west. Head west on 4th Avenue until the road forks; go right onto Discovery Road. Follow

Discovery to the water where you will see the Jericho Sailing Centre, an Eco-marine Ocean Kayak rental booth and a pay parking lot. In the West End, near downtown, you can launch and rent from the Old English Bay Bath House at the foot of Denman Street. You can also access English Bay from Granville Island, located under the Granville Street Bridge at the northern end of Fir Street. See False Creek (above) for descriptions.

Early morning and evening are the best times to paddle in the bay as a fair-weather westerly kicks up most afternoons. If conditions are good, consider taking a trip out to the freighters anchored offshore or venture west to Wreck Beach and beyond for a picnic. Although this is an urban area, you are still at the mercy of the sea. It is not uncommon to experience some rather large breaking waves off the shallows of Spanish Banks and the beaches in Stanley Park, and there is quite a strong current in the bay. Plan your trip accordingly and be very cautious when paddling in the major shipping lanes (near the freighters). A final note: Although Burrard Inlet and the inner harbour may look tempting, it is illegal for kayaks, and any boat without power, to go under the Lion's Gate Bridge.

Trip 9   Crescent Beach

Skill:	Intermediate to advanced
Time:	Day trip
Hazards:	Tidal currents
Access:	Boundary Bay
Charts:	3463 Strait of Georgia, Southern Portion 1:80,000
Tide Book:	Vol. 5

If you are looking to add adventure to your local paddling excursions, take the time to visit the communities of Crescent Beach and White Rock. The towns are quaint, and the shoreline between the two is exposed and an exhilarating paddle at any time of year.

Launching

This day tour begins at Blackie Spit, a sandy arm extending into Boundary Bay at Crescent Beach. Take Highways 99 or 99A and follow the signs into Crescent Beach, heading over the railway tracks in the direction of the boat launch signs. There is no launch fee if you launch at the Crescent Beach Sailing Club (Blackie Spit). If you turn before the tracks, you will end up at the yacht club and will be charged.

The park at Blackie Spit is open from dawn to dusk. The gate is locked after dusk so if you expect to be late, move your vehicle in advance or it could end up getting locked inside until morning.

From the spit you can paddle up the Nicomekl River or around Crescent Beach, hugging the shoreline into White Rock. The Nicomekl River is a pleasant day trip that usually has calm, relatively protected water. Remember, if you ride the tide one way, you must leave yourself the energy to paddle back against it.

Paddlers heading from Crescent Beach to White Rock also need to be aware of southerly winds and tides. At low tide the beach extends about 1 km (.6 mi.) from the shore and exposes a number of rocks. The paddle along the shoreline to White Rock is anywhere from 1.5–2 hours if the tide is in. If the tide is out, add at least 1 hour to this trip. There are dolphin markers that outline the deep-water boating channel, where the tidal currents are strongest. If you paddle within the channel markers, watch for boats leading to and from the marina. From January to June you may be lucky to see some of the local gray whales that frequent the bay prior to their journey north.

Trip 10   Fraser Delta

Skill:	Intermediate to advanced	
Time:	Day trip	
Hazards:	Tides	
Access:	Canoe Passage/Deas Island Park	
Charts:	3463	Strait of Georgia, Southern Portion 1:80,000
	3490	Fraser River, Sand Heads to Douglas Island 1:20,000
Tide Book:	Vol. 5	

Westham Island, west of Ladner, is best known for the George C. Reifel Migratory Bird Sanctuary, a congregating place for a variety of marine and predatory birds. Each spring and fall, thousands of our winged friends rest here before their departures north or south, providing paddlers with endless hours of enjoyment. Be sure to bring a bird book and binoculars.

Launching

Launch at the swing bridge located across Canoe Passage. Travel to Ladner via Highway 99, then through Ladner along River Road west. Make a right turn over the bridge on Westham Island Road. Launching can be done on the north side of Canoe Pass by the bridge (parking on the side of the road is limited). This site can be tricky depending on the height of the tide but it allows the best access to the main channels of the area. If you time the tides correctly, you can make both the flood and ebb work for you.

A circumnavigation of Westham Island takes most of the day with the tide in. The best paddling at high tide is on the west side of the island even though it opens up to wind and waves. Be sure you (or your group) is fit for this type of exposure. If the tide is low, you may want to paddle the east side of the island and the many inlets and tributaries of the Fraser delta. If you're seeking an alternate excursion, launch at Deas Island Park and paddle west towards Ladner to explore this historic fishing village.

Paddlers will definitely benefit from a tide table, marine chart and topographical map of the area as the tidal currents here can save time and simplify paddling. The area has many tributaries and islands, and a large-scale chart or map will minimize paddling up channels that lead nowhere.

Trip 11   Little Campbell River

Skill:	Beginner to advanced
Time:	1–3 hours
Hazards:	River currents
Access:	Semiahmoo Park
Charts:	3463 Strait of Georgia, Southern Portion 1:80,000
Tide Book:	Vol. 5

Located on the southwestern edge of B.C., White Rock is a bustling community that faces boldly onto the Strait of Georgia. Its shores are exposed, but escaping the salt, sand and wind is as easy as turning your kayak to nearby Little Campbell River.

Launching

Kayaks can either be launched directly into the river at the Semiahmoo Park parking lot by the baseball diamond (for a 1-hour trip) or from the cartop boat launch located approximately four blocks west of the White Rock pier. Look for the last pay parking lot on the west beach where asphalt crosses the railway tracks; purchase parking tickets from the dispenser: you'll need loonies and/or quarters, and you can park for 4 hours maximum.

Paddle east under the pier past the white rock along the main beach promenade. On the left side you will notice a train bridge, at the mouth of Little Campbell River. The tide must be high or the water in the river system will not be deep enough, even for your kayak. There is a minor current in the channel based on the difference between high and low tides but not anything of concern for paddlers.

The Little Campbell River enters the Semiahmoo Indian Reserve, a beautiful example of the area prior to the encroachment of European civilization. People wanting to fish in this area should check with the Semiahmoo First Nation for necessary permits. Otherwise, feel free to take your time and drift the quiet waterway as the sounds of White Rock fade behind you.

Trip 12 Indian Arm

Skill:	Beginner to advanced
Time:	1–4 days
Hazards:	Traffic and winds
Access:	Deep Cove/Woodlands/Belcarra Park/ Barnet Marine Park
Charts:	3495 Vancouver Harbour / Indian Arm 1:80,000
Tide Book:	Vol. 5

There is no better place within 30 minutes of Vancouver to experience wilderness paddling than Indian Arm. Whether you are day tripping or planning on spending a few nights, Indian Arm has something for everyone.

Indian Arm has recently been protected in cooperation with the Greater Vancouver Regional District's (GVRD) Green Zone Plan and

< Indian Arm. STEVE THRENDYLE

the provincial government's Protected Areas Strategy. In 1995, over 9300 ha (23,000 a.) of wilderness in Indian Arm were designated provincial parkland. According to the government, this is the largest urban green-space initiative in recent Canadian history. BC Parks is currently managing the area and increasing the number of campsites and facilities. The new sites are not yet open as this guide goes to press, but watch for the crowds as soon as they do.

Crowded or not, Indian Arm is still a great location for paddlers of all abilities due to its protected waterway and surprisingly wild setting. Be aware, however, that the winds up and down the arm can cause problems, though your biggest concern may be the wakes from other boaters and water skiers. Make sure to allow extra time for the return portion of your trip, and take your tide table.

Bring fresh water—natural sources are unreliable due to the high volume of recreational activity in Indian Arm. Fires are not allowed.

For a great 2–3 day trip, launch from Deep Cove and travel up the western shore to Bishop Creek. After spending a night at Granite Falls near the Indian River, you can then paddle along the eastern shore and return to your vehicle, stopping at Twin Islands and Racoon Island along the way. Currently there are no fees associated with campsites in Indian Arm and reservations are not required—but this may change in the near future.

Launching

Deep Cove is the most common launch site for Indian Arm. Take Highway 1 north across the Second Narrows Bridge. Both the Dollarton Highway and Mount Seymour Parkway exits will get you to Deep Cove. Follow the Mount Seymour Parkway for 10–15 minutes, then turn left at the lights onto Deep Cove Road. If you are taking the Dollarton Highway, it eventually turns into Deep Cove Road. When Deep Cove Road becomes Gallant Avenue, you've made it.

Follow Gallant Avenue to the water and make a left onto Banbury Road. The first parking lot is just ahead to the left, on Rockcliff Road; another one is just up the hill. Both lots are near the Deep Cove Canoe and Kayak Centre.

Panorama Park also has a day-use parking lot. Follow Deep Cove Road to Gallant Avenue, then take the first left onto Panorama. The parking lot is on your right. Unfortunately, overnight parking is limited to the street and can be difficult to find if you do not arrive first thing in the morning.

If you want to put in farther north than Deep Cove, drive to Woodlands, which has a government dock. To get there, drive along the Mount Seymour Parkway, turn left up towards Mount Seymour Road and then turn right on Indian River Road. Parking can be tricky because there is not much space.

It is also possible to launch at the eastern side of Indian Arm from the regional park at Belcarra. Approaching from Vancouver, take the Barnet Highway east until you reach Ioco Road in Port Moody and follow the signs to Belcarra. You can launch in the park but you will need to carry your boat a little ways. Nonetheless, the park is very kayak-friendly with plenty of day-use parking and a seasonal kayak rental booth. Be warned: The gates to the park are locked every night and vehicles are towed. If it is essential that you launch from this side of the arm but need overnight parking, you can check in the Village of Belcarra (at time of writing there was not much available) or try the Reid Point Marina across Burrard Inlet (off the Barnet Highway) or the Barnet Marine Park.

Sites

Belcarra/Jug Island Off Jug Island on the Belcarra side of the mainland is a nice, small sandy beach. Located on the southeast tip of Indian Arm, the beach is part of Belcarra Regional Park. There are hiking trails and outhouses located up the path from the beach. Belcarra Beach, with its government dock, is farther south and is a great place to explore with kids and adults. There is no camping.

Racoon Island This small island is a good place to stop and explore. Access is limited due to its rocky shoreline but it is close to Deep Cove—30 minutes or so. Camping is permitted; there are no designated spots or water.

Twin Islands These islands get quite busy because they are easily accessible and close to Deep Cove—only 45 minutes one way. The best landing site is in between the two islands, depending on the tide. Be sure to pull your boat up as high as possible. Camping is permitted though there are no designated spots; an outhouse is provided. There is no water.

Silver Falls Silver Falls is a small waterfall located just south of Bishop Creek. This cool, lake-fed waterfall is a great refresher on a hot day. Stopping here can be a bit tricky due to limited pull-in space. There is no camping.

Bishop Creek The rocky shoreline of this alluvial fan provides a flat area frequently used by campers. Bishop Creek/Bergs Landing is located on the west shore, approximately a 3-hour paddle from Deep Cove. Currently the site has room for over 20 tents. There are two pit toilets and a few garbage cans but you are reminded to take out what you bring in.

Indian River The Indian River estuary is located at the top of the arm and is habitat for waterfowl and marine life. Harbour seals are plentiful due to the many species of Pacific salmon that occupy Indian River. The river is accessible by kayak at high tide, and the estuary is a great place for observing wildlife. The Wigwam Inn, privately owned by the Royal Vancouver Yacht Club, is at the northern end of the arm. A short distance behind the Wigwam Inn is a small waterfall known as Spray of Pearls Falls. Those interested in exploring can access the narrow canyon via a primitive trail that follows Wigwam Creek. There is no camping.

Granite Falls This spectacular waterfall, 50-m (165-ft.) high, is located at the northeast end of the arm. The area is currently closed to the public while BC Parks removes natural and man-made hazards; it should be open by the summer of 1998. Although the dock at the site has being designed for power boats, it is still a great spot for paddlers to take a break or pull out and spend a few nights. There are a number of small tent sites, four pit toilets and a spectacular view.

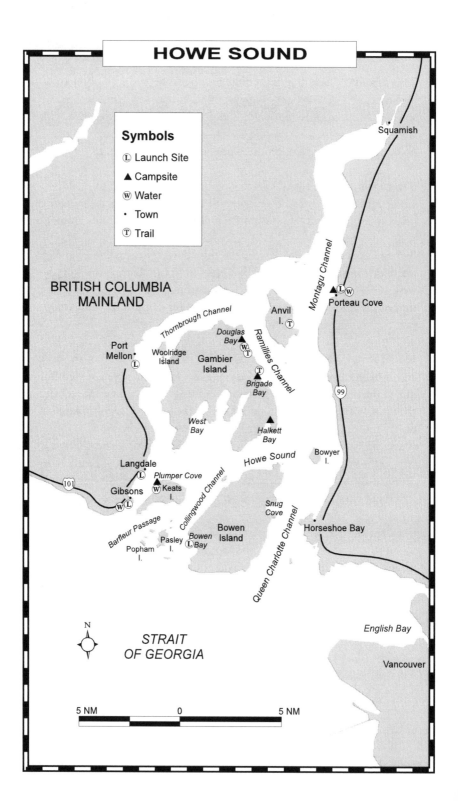

HOWE SOUND

Symbols

- Ⓛ Launch Site
- ▲ Campsite
- Ⓦ Water
- · Town
- Ⓣ Trail

BRITISH COLUMBIA MAINLAND

Squamish

Montagu Channel

Ⓛ Ⓦ Porteau Cove

99

Thornbrough Channel

Anvil I. Ⓣ

Douglas Bay ▲ Ⓦ Ⓣ

Ramillies Channel

Port Mellon Ⓛ

Woolridge Island

Gambier Island

Brigade Bay Ⓣ

West Bay

▲ Halkett Bay

Bowyer I.

Howe Sound

Langdale Ⓛ

Plumper Cove ▲ Ⓦ Keats I.

101

Gibsons Ⓦ Ⓛ

Collingwood Channel

Snug Cove

Horseshoe Bay

Barfleur Passage

Popham I.

Pasley I.

Bowen Ⓛ Bay

Bowen Island

Queen Charlotte Channel

English Bay

N

STRAIT OF GEORGIA

Vancouver

5 NM   0   5 NM

Chapter Five

Howe Sound

Peter McGee

The first strokes I ever took in a kayak were in Howe Sound in the early 1980s. It was my godmother's Klepper, and I distinctly remember exploring every nook and cranny of the reef-strewn bays and coves that surrounded her cabin. Fifteen years later, while finishing a paddling trip that had lasted months and covered much of the coast, I had the opportunity to once again paddle through the sound as my group approached the city of Vancouver. For all I had just seen, Howe Sound still grabbed me as one of the most beautiful spots in British Columbia. Although it may not be wilderness, it still has its own special charms. Nestled among the coastal mountains, speckled with summer homes and flanked by the bright lights of Vancouver, West Vancouver and Gibsons, Howe Sound blends the beauty of the Gulf Islands with the rugged North Coast and places it all invitingly on our doorstep. It is a unique slice of West Coast life well worth exploring.

BACKGROUND

The history of the Howe Sound we see today began 20,000 years ago when a massive ice flow, 1500-m (5,000-ft.) thick, sculpted the fiord. Although the environment was rugged, the Coast Salish peoples inhabited and prospered in the area for thousands of years after the ice receded. The Squamish Nation still resides in the communities of Squamish and North Vancouver; while their political voice is gaining strength, it is the more recent European and Asian influences that have made the most dramatic impacts on the region. The cities and towns that border the sound are testament to this fact as are the many European names attached to the islands, points, passages and mountains. The region was named by Capt. George Vancouver in 1792 after Admiral Howe, a hero of the British navy known as the "sailor's friend" for his fair treatment of his crew. On a more practical note, Passage Island, on the south side of Bowen Island, was named by Captain Vancouver for its use as a navigational aid. The island, when "in one" or in line with the peak on Anvil Island, was used as a mark to pass safely westward of the shoals, known as the Sandheads, off the mouth of the Fraser River.

Yet for all the native and immigrant history in the sound, it is geologic forces that continue to shape its future—and if you plan on visiting, don't wait too long. The sands, silts and clays deposited by the Squamish River and its seven tributaries are advancing the Squamish delta, at the northern end of the Howe Sound, at a rate of about 1 m (3.3 ft.) a year. This may not seem like much but if the present rate continues, the entire sound could be filled in by a fertile valley as early as 27,000 AD. Paddle it while you can.

GETTING THERE

Getting to Howe Sound is not difficult: it is within an easy drive of Vancouver (via Highways 1 and 99) and Gibsons (via Highway 101). Local boat and float plane operators can drop you off wherever you arrange though this added expense really isn't necessary. Prime launch spots can be found on Bowen Island (accessible by B.C. Ferries from Horseshoe Bay), off Highway 99, and near Gibsons and the Langdale ferry terminal on the Sunshine Coast. For the more experienced, you can even launch directly from Vancouver.

WEATHER AND HAZARDS

While weather conditions here are usually quite moderate, paddlers need to be cautious of the winds that funnel down Montagu Channel in front of Porteau Cove. During the summer there is a land/sea breeze (as described in Chapter 1) that gathers strength around Squamish, often reaching speeds of 30 knots. The fact that there is a Squamish Windsurfing Society is testament to the winds' consistency. The period of the strongest onshore wind is between noon and early evening. In winter, particularly dangerous northerly outflow "Squamish" winds occur, as do strong, southerly inflow winds brought about by southeast gales in the Strait of Georgia. Do not let the relatively sheltered environment of northern Howe Sound fool you. In the last decade alone, more than one winter paddler has perished as a result of these winds.

Although tidal rapids are not a concern in Howe Sound, paddlers should be aware of the gap leading into Gibsons from the Strait of Georgia. The funnelling effect of the channel increases the tidal flow, creating dangerously steep waves when the wind is against the tide and the water is shallow. Fog can also be quite common during the fall and spring so be sure to bring a compass.

With any trip in Howe Sound, watch for boat traffic. Paddlers should be particularly cautious about the ferries that travel between Langdale and Horseshoe Bay, Snug Cove (Bowen Island) and Horseshoe Bay, and Nanaimo and Horseshoe Bay (affectionately called the bread slicer routes). There is also considerable small boat traffic.

Finally, you would be well advised to bring your own water on any trip in Howe Sound. There are several fresh water sources (on Gambier Island, for example), but heavy recreational traffic makes this water unreliable. Bring it, treat it or boil it.

HOWE SOUND TRIPS (13–15)

If you are planning a day trip, consider the Pasley Group of islands in the southwestern part of the sound. Although most of the islands are privately owned, they are great to explore from the water and easy to reach from Bowen Island. Unfortunately, there are no camping sites on the outer islands. If you are launching from Gibsons, you will be able to camp at Plumper Cove Marine Park on Keats Island and use it as a staging area to the Pasleys and Keats. If you are looking for further overnight possibilities, your best bet is to take 2–3 days and explore the northern part of the sound around Gambier and Anvil Islands.

If you are concerned about boat traffic and crowds, consider taking a trip in the fall or spring. The wildlife abounds and the snow-capped peaks provide a spectacular backdrop.

Trip 13   The Pasley Group

Skill: Beginner to advanced
Time: Day trip
Hazards: Traffic and winds
Access: Bowen Island/Gibsons Landing
Charts: 3311   Sunshine Coast—Vancouver

	Harbour to Desolation Sound
	1:40,000
3512	Strait of Georgia, Central Portion
	1:80,000
3526	Howe Sound 1:40,000
Tide Book: Vol. 5	

Perched on the edge of the Strait of Georgia, the Pasley Group provides the perfect setting to leisurely dip a paddle and enjoy the company of a few curious seals. Most of the islands are privately owned, and if you want to camp you'll need to paddle to Plumper Cove Marine Park on Keats Island. Don't let this deter you from some of the best day-tripping on the south coast, however, as access from Bowen Island is easy.

Launching

To launch from Bowen Island, take the Bowen ferry from Horseshoe Bay to Snug Cove and drive west across the centre of the island. The road snakes and splits a fair bit—just follow the main route. After about 15 minutes, you will approach the western shore of the island and a fork in the road that leads to Tunstall Bay or Bowen Bay. Keep to the right. At the bottom of the winding, steep hill is the public beach at Bowen Bay. Parking is extremely limited but the bay is relatively protected and launching is easy. It is also possible to launch from Gibsons but this will add a couple of hours to your trip.

Sites

As you leave Bowen Bay and head for Pasley Island, you will encounter Collingwood Channel. Although a short crossing, beware of boat traffic (particularly tugs with barges and booms in tow) and wind funnelling into Howe Sound from the Strait of Georgia. Once across, you will likely be looking at Pasley's East Bay or North Bay (distinguishable by its sand beach, numerous cabins, meadow and sizable wharf). Your decision to go south or north at this point is up to the winds. If a strong westerly is blowing, you are advised to head north towards Mickey Island, wrap around the north end of Pasley and venture off towards Hermit Island. Exploring Popham and Worlcombe would be better left for another day. If conditions are calm, however, circumnavigating Pasley and exploring the smaller islands will give you a great afternoon of paddling.

You are likely to encounter numerous seals and birds among the islands so please respect their space. The seal haul-outs near Hermit and Popham Islands make for great wildlife viewing but the animals are easily disturbed; keep your distance when you see signs of agitation. If you need to stretch your legs, the northeast side of the small island connected to Hermit, locally known as Arbutus Island, is a designated picnic spot but fires and camping are *absolutely prohibited*. Keep in mind that if paddlers are able to show that we are careful and responsible, more private land may be opened for public use. If you are not heading back to Bowen Bay, but instead crossing Barfleur Passage to Keats Island, take a peak into the passage before you cross as the westerlies can bring extremely rough seas.

Trip 14: Keats Island

Skill:	Intermediate to advanced	
Time:	1–3 days	
Hazards:	Traffic and winds	
Access:	Gibsons Landing	
Charts:	3311	Sunshine Coast—Vancouver Harbour to Desolation Sound 1:40,000
	3512	Strait of Georgia, Central Portion 1:80,000
	3526	Howe Sound 1:40,000
Tide Book:	Vol. 5	

If you are approaching Howe Sound from Gibsons on the Sunshine Coast, exploring Keats Island is your best bet for a day trip. Named after Admiral Sir Richard Goodwin Keats, a compatriot of Viscount Nelson, the island has many faces. While much of the north coast is steep and inhospitable, Plumper Cove Marine Park and the community at Eastbourne show its more friendly side.

Launching

If you are not already on the Sunshine Coast, take the ferry from Horseshoe Bay to Langdale (about 45 minutes). As you head off the ferry, turn left and follow the lower road. The best launch near the terminal is from the pier at

Hopkins Landing, a minute or two from the ferry terminal. To launch from the marina in Gibsons, continue along the lower road until you reach Headlands Road and turn left towards the water. Parking is limited during summer. If you are renting boats, Sunshine Kayaking has an office in Lower Gibsons, and you can launch a couple of blocks from their door. Look for the famed Molly's Reach restaurant from the *Beachcombers* television series and follow Molly's Lane for about a block until you see their sign.

Sites

From Gibsons, it is a short hop (about 30 minutes) across Shoal Channel to reach Plumper Cove Marine Park on Keats Island. Although the crossing is relatively sheltered, paddlers still need to be cautious of the boat traffic and ferry wash. As you approach the western shore of the island you will see a number of cabins and the Shelter Islets. Tuck in behind the islets to find the public dock for the park. A park supervisor is there for much of the summer and nightly fees are collected. Call the BC Parks office in Brackendale to see if reservations are required.

Circumnavigating the island provides a good 4–5 hours of paddling and the opportunity to see some great birdlife. Watch the weather as the wave action at the southwestern end (near Home Island—also called Salmon Rock—*hint!*) can be quite severe. Similarly, there is a mile or so of cliffs on the north side that makes landing impossible.

For the truly adventurous, crossing Barfleur Passage puts you in the scenic Pasley group and the land of many seals. Be sure to listen to the weather reports before you go. There is no camping in the islands, and the common summer westerlies can quickly turn Barfleur Passage into a blur of whitecaps, a tough crossing for even the most experienced paddler.

Trip 15   Gambier and Anvil Islands

Skill: Intermediate to advanced
Time: 1-4 days
Hazards: Winds and traffic
Access: Porteau Cove/Port Mellon

Charts: 3311   Sunshine Coast—Vancouver
Harbour to Desolation Sound
1:40,000

    3512   Strait of Georgia, Central Portion
1:80,000

    3526   Howe Sound   1:40,000

Tide Book: Vol. 5

In contrast to the islands and summer homes in the southern part of Howe Sound, surprisingly little development has occurred to the north. Although close to urban civilization and industrialization, with the mill at Port Mellon, Anvil and Gambier Islands provide a fantastic setting for day and weekend trips. Don't let the ease of access fool you, however, as the winds are notoriously strong in this part of Howe Sound (see Weather and Hazards at the beginning of this chapter) and the shores remarkably rugged. With mountains all around and log booms dotting many of the bays, this is truly coastal paddling.

Launching

To access the northern part of Howe Sound, launch from Porteau Cove Provincial Park on the mainland or at Dunham Road near Port Mellon. Porteau Cove can be reached easily from Highway 99 and is located about 30 km (19 mi.) north of Horseshoe Bay. There are a number of facilities at the park, including a dock, boat ramp, toilets and campsites. An extremely popular spot with divers and close to the road, Porteau Cove gets quite crowded on weekends and holidays. Nonetheless, it is a great launch spot.

To reach the launch site near Port Mellon, take the ferry from Horseshoe Bay to Langdale and head north past the ferry terminal for a few minutes; you will pass a small apartment development on your right. Look for Dunham Road soon after and follow it to the water. Be warned: Port Mellon is an active pulp mill and some days the smell is quite bad.

Sites

Heading out from Porteau Cove, your first challenge is crossing the often choppy Montagu Channel. As you approach Anvil Island, named by Captain Vancouver for the "shape of the mountain that composes it," you have a number of options: circumnavigating Anvil to the north, heading south into Ramillies Channel or taking a break on the eastern shore. While there is little accessible public land on Anvil, a cleared area that may have been a scout camp sits midway up its east coast. This is a good place to stretch your legs, though No Trespassing signs have been popping up recently. Heading south towards Gambier Island provides better paddling and camping opportunities.

If you do stop on Anvil Island, you may want to check out the trail that follows the north-south slope. The trail is marked and the view from the top is amazing.

Gambier Island

If you are approaching Gambier from the northwest, the first beach and campsite you will find is Douglas Bay, near the base of Gambier Creek. Farther along the shore is Brigade Bay, and on the southeastern tip of the island is Halkett Bay Marine Park, the only official campsite of the three. From any of these sites you are in a great position to explore the log booms around Gambier and the bird and seal colonies on Christie Islet and the Pam Rocks. For those looking to take a break from paddling, there are several hiking trails on the island that lead to destinations such as Gambier Lake and Mount Artaban.

Circumnavigating the rest of Gambier makes for great paddling as the whole shore is a collection of interesting coves and bays. Unfortunately, most of the land on the southern side is private, and camping is limited to the sites listed above or Plumper Cove on Keats Island. For paddlers starting their northern Howe Sound excursion near Port Mellon, crossing Thornbrough Channel should be relatively easy. For those making the paddle back to Porteau Cove, however, time your crossing carefully and be forever vigilant of changing wind conditions.

ADDITIONAL ROUTES

Heading north: Howe Sound blends into the Sunshine Coast and the trips described in the following chapters.

Heading south: The southern end of Howe Sound lies within sight of the Vancouver skyline and the trips described in Chapter 4.

THE SUNSHINE COAST

Symbols

- Ⓛ Launch Site
- ▲ Campsite
- Ⓦ Water
- • Town

Chatterbox Falls Ⓦ
Princess Louisa Inlet
Queens Reach
▲ •Malibu Camp

Jervis Inlet

Princess Royal Reach

•Powell River

Deserted Bay Ⓦ
(with permission)

Hotham Sound
Harmony Is.
Friel Falls Ⓦ
▲Ⓦ Vancouver Bay (with permission)

Scotch Fir Pt.
Saltery Bay Ⓛ
Goliath Bay
Prince of Wales Reach

BRITISH COLUMBIA MAINLAND

Hardy Is.
Musket I. ▲

Shelter Pt. Ⓛ Park
Texada Island

Nelson I.

Hidden Basin
Cape Cockburn

Agamemnon Channel

Earls Cove Ⓛ
•Egmont Ⓦ
Skookumchuck Narrows

Gillies Bay

Quarry Bay

Narrows Inlet

Sabine Channel

▲ Shingle Beach Ⓛ

Pender Harbour
Ⓛ Madeira Park

▲ Tzoonie Narrows Ⓦ

Malaspina Strait

Ⓦ •False Bay Ⓛ

Lasqueti I.

Jedediah I. ▲

Halfway Pt.
•Kunechin Pt.
Salmon Inlet
Sechelt Inlet

Secret Cove
Smugglers Cove Marine Park Ⓛ
Sechelt Peninsula

▲Thornhill Creek Marine Park

▲

Squitty Bay Ⓦ

Skaiakos Pt.
•Nine Mile Pt.

Stevens Passage

Thormanby Is. ▲
Merry I.
Halfmoon Bay

Ⓛ Ⓦ
Snake Bay
▲Tuwanek

•Parksville

Selma Park Ⓛ
Sargeant Bay
Trail Is.

Porpoise Bay Marine Park
ⓌⓁ
•Sechelt

N

STRAIT OF GEORGIA

Davis Bay
Wilson Creek

Ⓛ

101

•Roberts Creek
Langdale

5 NM   0   5 NM

•Nanaimo

Gibsons
Ⓛ
Keats I.

Chapter Six

The Sunshine Coast

Bodhi Drope, Dorothy Drope and
Howard Zatwarnitski

The stretch of coastline from Gibsons north to Egmont
along the east side of the Strait of Georgia is known as the Sunshine Coast.
It is a region with a mild, dry and semi-Mediterranean climate that has
been attractive to settlement and industry throughout the ages. Despite
these pressures, however, the Sunshine Coast continues to provide a number of superb wilderness experiences for paddlers of all abilities. From the
ideal learning environment of Sechelt Inlet to the exposed 32-km (20-mi.)
coastline between Gibsons and Sechelt, the Sunshine Coast offers some of
the best paddling experiences in southwestern British Columbia.

BACKGROUND

Harry Roberts, the celebrated denizen of the first European family of
Roberts Creek, first coined the name "Sunshine Coast." In fact, he originally called it "The Sunshine Belt" and painted these words in large letters
on his shed in hopes of attracting the tourist trade. Since that beginning in
the 1920s, the name has evolved into the more apt Sunshine Coast, and its
application has crept north to include the Egmont-Jervis Inlet area, with
the advent of ferry service, and now the Powell River district.

Long before Harry Roberts, however, there were the Coast Salish peoples who shared the bounty of the Sunshine Coast since time began. There
were about 80 villages in the area with major settlements of the Hunichin
at the head of Jervis Inlet, the Tsonai in Deserted Bay, the Tuwanek at the
head of Narrows Inlet and in Porpoise Bay, and the Skariakos in Garden
Bay and on the Thormanbys. Large numbers of people would congregate
for the winter in the Pender Harbour area.

The Sechelt people are now in the painful process of reclaiming their traditions. They are deservedly well known as the first natives of Canada to achieve self-government. Enacted by the federal government in 1986, the Sechelt Indian Self Government Act was modelled on municipal governments with additional powers in several areas. A year later the provincial government also ratified this arrangement and, though the model has been criticized by other aboriginal groups, the Sechelts have apparently prospered under it. As with several native bands along the coast, the Sechelts are negotiating with the province to settle their land claims.

The immigrant history of the area is typical of others regions on the south coast, with logging, mining and agriculture the primary incentives for settlement. Evidence of this can be found in the mill town of Powell River and the lime mines of Texada Island.

GETTING THERE

By land and water: Unless you already live on the Sunshine Coast you will need to access the area by vehicle and ferry. B.C. Ferries service runs from Horseshoe Bay (near Vancouver) to Langdale; Comox (on Vancouver Island) to Powell River; and French Creek (on Vancouver Island) to Lasqueti Island. Once on the Sunshine Coast, Highway 101 can take you to most launch sites. You will probably use additional ferry services between Earls Cove and Saltery Bay, and between Powell River and Texada Island. For people coming from Vancouver Island, paddling is an option that is not recommended due to weather and heavy marine traffic.

By air: Check with the local float plane services such as Hanna Air, Coval Air and Vancouver Island Air if you wish to arrange a charter.

WEATHER AND HAZARDS

Winds in this region follow the overall coastal pattern of northwesterly winds in the summer and southeasterly winds in the winter. In summer, west winds indicate warm and sunny conditions, although extremely strong west winds generated by a high pressure system can blow for days. Southeast winds indicate a change in the weather, usually for the worse.

Near Texada Island, winds and tides tend to be stronger due to channelling effects. Welcome Pass, between the Thormanby Islands and the mainland, is also subject to channelling. As always, expect the wind and tidal effect to increase on headlands: the so-called corner effects. Gusty winds and confused, steep seas can occur at the base of high cliffs, such as those found on South Thormanby Island and near Sargeant Bay. In all the inlets be aware of anabatic and katabatic winds as well as winter outflow winds (see Chapter 1).

Tidal rips, overfalls and other nasty stuff occur in the Sechelt Rapids of Skookumchuck Narrows and the Malibu Rapids at the entrance to Princess Louisa Inlet. These rapids should only be attempted by *very experienced* paddlers who have a good handle on tide tables. In other areas the funnelling effect will increase tidal flow, creating steep waves especially when the wind is against the tide and the water is shallow, such as at the "gap" leading into Gibsons.

If you are accessing parts of the Sunshine Coast from Vancouver Island, be cautious of the local wind phenomenon known as a Qualicum. This gap wind, described in Chapter 1, begins on the west coast of Vancouver Island and touches down with amazing force on the east coast near Qualicum Beach. During the morning the weather can be clear with glassy seas on the Strait of Georgia but, very suddenly in the afternoon, southwesterly winds hit the Qualicum Bay area with speeds up to 40 knots. The winds often reach all the way across to the northern tip of Lasqueti Island where they typically diminish and turn southward. One local bit of advice is to watch the cloud movement on summer days; if you see a southwesterly develop, head for cover.

Like much of coastal B.C., the Sunshine Coast is bear country, so be sure to handle your food (and self) appropriately.

Finally, be wary of fresh water sources in all regions of the Sunshine Coast. Even if the area you are visiting seems pristine and uninhabited, its proximity to the Lower Mainland means it is probably heavily used by recreationists of all kinds. Boiling or treating water is a good idea anywhere on the coast, and this is one area where you should make it a mandatory practice.

SUNSHINE COAST TRIPS (16–20)

There are many trips to choose from along the Sunshine Coast depending on whether you prefer sheltered or exposed paddling. If you are looking for an experience suited to beginner paddlers, consider taking a few days to explore the inside coast and Sechelt Inlet. For those with more experience, Hotham Sound awaits, providing fantastic scenery on the edge of magnificent Jervis Inlet.

If inlets and steep-sided hills are a little confining for you, paddling the outer Sunshine Coast will expose you to the beauty of the Strait of Georgia, Jedediah Island and Nelson Island. Most of these trips require a minimum of 3–4 days so, if time is short, you can take a few day trips from the numerous launch sites between Gibsons and Secret Cove. If you are venturing up Jervis Inlet to Princess Louisa Park, leave yourself at least 7–10 days.

People who love the Sunshine Coast ask that you be mindful of the impact of your presence in these waters. Help us to keep a comfortable relationship between the human population and the other creatures that share this space with us. Clean up after yourselves and respect the habitat of the birds and animals.

Trip 16   Sechelt Inlet

Skill:	Beginner to advanced
Time:	1–4 days
Hazards:	Winds and Skookumchuck Narrows
Access:	Sechelt
Charts:	3312 Jervis Inlet and Desolation Sound Various Scales
	3512 Strait of Georgia, Central Portion 1:80,000
Tide Book:	Vol. 5

Se-shalt, meaning "place of shelter from the sea," is the perfect name for the inlet that offers beginner paddlers a taste of coastal kayaking. Over 150 ha (370 a.) located along the shores of Sechelt Inlet, Salmon Inlet and Narrows Inlet are protected in eight marine parks, giving you a chance to experience wilderness without travelling far.

The most common access points are located at the southern end of Sechelt Inlet, near the town of Sechelt. Although it is possible to access the inlet from Egmont in the north, this is not a recommended approach as extreme care must be exercised when crossing Skookumchuck Narrows. To get to Sechelt, take Highway 101 north from the Langdale ferry terminal, about a 30-minute drive.

> Narrows Inlet, off Sechelt Inlet. BODHI DROPE/SUNSHINE KAYAKING

Launching

The most popular launch site is at Porpoise Bay. There is a government wharf with a large parking lot at the end of Wharf Street in Sechelt. If you are heading north through town, turn right on Wharf Street and drive straight down to the water to get to the boat ramp. This launch site gives you the choice of paddling up either side of the inlet depending on winds and what you want to see. The west side is often quieter but has fewer camping opportunities.

If you prefer to launch a little ways from town, there are a number of sites located on the east side of the inlet, including Porpoise Bay Provincial Park. Turn right off Wharf Street onto Porpoise Bay Road and follow it to the park. Here you will find lots of parking, a nice flat beach to launch from and deluxe camping if you choose to stay. Be sure you have made reservations with BC Parks in the summer months as this is a very popular campground.

There are a few other launch sites farther up Porpoise Bay Road but, due to summer congestion and the objection of local residents, they are not listed here. If you are visiting in the late fall or early spring, you may want to check out these sites.

Sites—The West Side

From the launch site at the Porpoise Bay wharf in town, paddle towards Poise Island, keeping to the left to avoid the float planes landing and taking off from the wharf. There is a long mud flat beginning opposite Poise Island and running all the way to Snake Bay. These flats are rich with small fish and other marine life so you can enjoy these creatures and all the birds that feed on them. Expect to see mergansers, cormorants and several other seabirds in their season. There is a pleasant beach in Snake Bay, a good place to head for a short day trip with some swimming. Subdivisions are creeping up this side of the inlet and now overlook the south side of Snake Bay. Past the bay there is only the odd summer cottage.

Around Carlson Point, where Carlson Creek enters the inlet, is the home of one of the coast's most colourful characters. The Solberg sisters were born and raised in the area and made their living as fishers, loggers and hunters. "The Cougar Lady" lives here while her sister lives up Jervis Inlet at Deserted Bay. You will know her home by the animal hide nailed to the shed wall. Piper Point curves out here. This is another of the inlet's marine parks, still undeveloped: no beach, no pit toilets, no camping areas but a nice spot for a break. A few miles north is Skaiakos Point, another park, but also completely undeveloped at time of writing.

Halfway Beach From here, you can continue on to Halfway Beach, another marine park tucked in behind Halfway Islet. This is one of the nicest camping areas in the inlet, with a mountain stream running through the site. Keep in mind that the water is not potable and should be boiled or treated.

At this point, cross the inlet if you plan on heading farther north. If you are returning to Sechelt, double back or cross the inlet and explore Nine Mile Point and Tuwanek Point on your way home.

Sites—The East Side

Tuwanek Point Tuwanek Point is about a 2-hour paddle from the Porpoise Bay park launch site and a great place to stay if you get a late start. The park features a good beach, great swimming, nice campsites and pit toilets. Fires should be laid below the high tide line in the dry season, otherwise use the fire rings on site.

Nine Mile Point Another hour of paddling up the east side brings you to Nine Mile Point, where Salmon Inlet joins Sechelt Inlet. This shoreline is a favourite of eagles, with plenty of snags to sit in and a good supply of food in the water. Watch for the Nine Mile Point Marine Park a short distance before the point. It has the whole nine yards including a fine beach and pit toilets. This is bear country so treat your food cache accordingly.

Winds whistle down the various stretches of water that converge at this point, and a look at the chart will tell you why this is the most dangerous part of this inland sea. In summer, the daily thermal winds move down the inlets and, meeting here, create confused waters and heavy chop. These winds can make for heavy work if you are paddling against them—and a false sense of ease if moving with them. More than one paddler has soared up the inlet on the wings of these winds only to despair at the ordeal of the return journey. Winter outflows are especially severe here.

Kunechin Point Marine Park From Nine Mile Point you are looking at an open water crossing to Kunechin Point, the next marine park on your journey. Be sure to assess conditions carefully before setting out. Experienced paddlers will not find too much difficulty but the inlet often attracts people who are just beginning their paddling careers. If this is you, try to do the crossing in the early morning.

Kunechin Point offers good camping with some hiking opportunities on the hills behind. The HMCS *Chaudière,* a decommissioned naval vessel, was sunk in front of the Kunechin Islets in 1992 and attracts a lot of scuba divers.

Thornhill Creek Marine Park   Salmon Inlet is less well travelled by paddlers for a couple of reasons. First, the shoreline is precipitous for most of its length, providing few good spots to land and camp. Second, there is a power line following the shoreline for miles and lots of logging activity. Having said that, there are some beautiful sights to see along this waterway, and you are more likely to have them to yourself. There is a marine park at Thornhill Creek about halfway up the inlet on the eastern shore where you can camp. Most of the land on either side of the inlet is a tree farm licence. There is a hydro-electric development now in place on Sechelt Creek so the state of this site is unknown at this time. The Clowhom River flows into the end of the inlet from Clowhom Lake.

Instead of heading up Salmon Inlet, you may opt to continue paddling west up Sechelt Inlet towards Narrows Inlet and the Skookumchuck Narrows. Proceeding west up Sechelt Inlet, you will paddle along a series of steep granite cliffs. Again, this is a good opportunity to see intertidal life, especially if the tide is low. Look for both green and purple sea urchins, lots of purple sea stars and tube worms. In the small stands of bull kelp on this stretch, watch for the graceful kelp crab clinging to the fronds with its triangular carapace.

Narrows Inlet   As you round Cawley Point, Storm Bay opens to your right at the very mouth of Narrows Inlet. There is a long mud flat at the top of the bay where Storm Creek runs into it. The north shore is sprinkled with funky little dwellings, relics of the flower children of the sixties—Storm Bay was a haven for hippies heading back to the land. More prosaic dwellings are gradually supplanting them.

Narrows Inlet is generally a kind and gentle place. The mountains rise less steeply here, leaving flats that invite the visitor to wander. Streams come coursing off the mountains, creating myriad waterfalls, especially in the rainy seasons. The stroke of the paddle is often accompanied by the sound of rushing water hidden in the bushes. These lovely spots are definitely worth a stop.

There is a very nice, though not pristine, private campground called the Narrows Inlet Wilderness Camp about halfway to the narrows along the eastern shore. You can enjoy tents on platforms, hot showers, a cooking shack and, best of all, a hot tub on the shoreline—pretty deluxe after a long day of paddling.

Tzoonie Narrows   The inlet narrows drastically, thus its name, at Tzoonie Narrows, creating a little tidal rapid that flows at a maximum of 4 knots—just enough to give you a bit of fun without too much work. Whenever water runs fast it encourages the proliferation of sea life, and Tzoonie Narrows is an excellent example of this.

The marine park runs along both sides of the narrows. The best campsites are on the grassy flat land of the bay beyond Tzoonie Point on the south side of the rapid. This is the only developed part of the park.

The remainder of Narrows Inlet is a peaceful place to explore by kayak. Thermal winds are active from mid-morning to late afternoon on sunny days, but there is not enough fetch in any direction to generate much wave height. It can make for a lot of work though, so relax on a beach to wait out the wind if you prefer.

To continue your trip up Sechelt Inlet, exit Narrows Inlet and paddle northwest along the shore. You'll pass a tiny village called Doriston, consisting of one family and a logging operation on the south shore that harks back to old-time B.C.: no roads, no stores, not much of anything—but interesting to reflect on. Each little bay along here is filled with bull kelp, attesting to the increased tidal flow. As you approach Skookum Island at the top of the inlet, you will notice the water is becoming increasingly active. The Sechelt Rapids begin just beyond this island.

Sechelt Rapids   *Do not paddle* in this area unless you know what you are doing! The full tidal exchange for all the waters you have paddled on to this point rush through Sechelt Rapids, the tightest part of Skookumchuck Narrows, creating awesome and incredibly dangerous conditions. This is a tidal flow that will wax and wane depending on the time and size of the tide. Slack tide in these rapids is really a misnomer as there is no time when water is not flowing one way or the other. Nonetheless, at "slack" the flow is much gentler, the water is flat and very experienced paddlers can safely negotiate the rapids in a kayak. You must have a track record with this sort of paddling, however, because this is not an area for practice or play.

The best route for a kayak is along the northern shore. Once you have calculated the time of slack from the tide table, keep to the right so you can duck behind the many little islets and avoid the fastest moving water. The ebb continues for a while even after the flood tide begins on the south side of the rapids. After rounding the corner at the top of Sechelt Rapids, you will be heading into Egmont and then onto Jervis Inlet, Hotham Sound and the trip that follows.

Trip 17 Hotham Sound/ Jervis Inlet

Skill:	Intermediate to advanced
Time:	3–10 days
Hazards:	Winds and currents
Access:	Egmont / Saltery Bay
Charts:	3312 Jervis Inlet and Desolation Sound Various Scales
	3512 Strait of Georgia, Central Portion 1:80,000
	3415 Jervis Inlet 1:50,000
Tide Book:	Vol. 5

Close to Vancouver, with great fishing and surrealistic beauty, this area is quickly becoming known in paddling circles. Exploring Hotham Sound requires 3–4 days. If you have more than a week, you might want to extend your trip to include the majesty of Jervis Inlet and Princess Louisa Inlet. Be forewarned: Although these inlets are beautiful, they are typically steep sided and provide few camping opportunities—you will have to keep your eyes peeled.

Launching

Hotham Sound and Jervis Inlet are best accessed from Egmont, a small community east of the Earls Cove ferry terminal. If you are coming from the Powell River area, launching at Saltery Bay Provincial Park is also an option.

There are two launching locations in Egmont: the government wharf and the Egmont marina. The advantages of the marina are the store/pub

Jervis Inlet. BODHI DROPE/SUNSHINE KAYAKING

and showers on site. There is a launch fee for kayaks and canoes, which is minimal, and a daily rate for parking. Long weekends are obviously the busiest time, and parking is limited. If you choose to launch from the wharf, ensure your vehicle is locked to avoid theft, especially if you plan to be away for a few days.

Sites

From Egmont looking west, you can see the start of Hotham Sound, a paddle that takes between 1–2 hours depending on wind, current and the speed of your group. The greatest tidal flow will be felt at the wharf or marina, where the current picks up speed when flooding or ebbing from Skookumchuck Narrows to the east. If timed right, you can catch the ebb out and reduce a struggle against the current. You can also hug the shoreline and catch the back eddies to make the paddling easier. The current is strongest towards the centre of the channel.

When paddling across Jervis Inlet, be sensitive to the winds and currents that can stir things up between Hotham Sound and Prince of Wales Reach. The shoreline at the east entrance to Hotham has steep cliff banks; if there is a west wind, paddling close to the Mount Foley side can expose you to rebound waves that may be uncomfortable for people with limited experience. A good option is to paddle close to Captain Island and then watch the wind and weather to ensure the safest crossing to the sound.

Harmony Islands As you head inland, look for Hotham Sound just north of the inlet. You will see Friel Falls plummeting from the top of the mountain fed by Friel Lake. Just past the falls is a cluster of islands, the Harmony Islands, some of which are a marine park. Signs are obvious on those that are private land. These islets offer some small camping areas that are bear-free; groups larger than six people may have trouble finding a spot that can accommodate everyone. Landing at low tide can be quite rough.

On the mainland behind the islands is a small oyster-covered beach with two or three campsites tucked into the forest behind it. A stream runs by the campsite if you need water; Friel Falls is also a source of fresh water. Farther inland on the north side, Goliath Bay has an old log sort where you will find flat ground when in need. At this point, you may want to spend your time exploring Hotham Sound or just return to Egmont. If you are looking for a little more adventure, you can always head west to Nelson Island or east up Jervis Inlet.

Jervis Inlet The deepest of B.C.'s many inlets, Jervis Inlet reaches depths of 720 m (2400 ft.) though it is never more than 1.6 km (1 mi.) wide. As it zigzags 80 km (50 mi.) inland, each reach of the inlet commemorates a member of the British royal family, beginning with Prince of Wales Reach through Princess Royal Reach and Queens Reach. The inlet's banks are high cliffs with occasional pocket beaches, most of which have homes on them. The majority of the land is tenured by forest companies as tree farms.

The winds in Jervis Inlet are notorious: they can pick up quickly and be deflected and funnelled off the steep-sided walls. Aside from Malibu Rapids, the currents here are quite subtle, but it is best to paddle north with the flood and south with the ebb to give yourself a bit of a break. Jervis Inlet is not for beginners.

For those who do head up the inlet, be warned again: Campsites are few and far between. Camping is possible at the mouth of Vancouver Creek on the north side of Vancouver Bay if you first get permission from the Sechelt Indian Band; there is a beautiful hike up the creek featuring a few old-growth cedars. Deserted Bay, farther along, also has some gently sloping land and room for tents. Once again, however, this is Sechelt Indian Band land and permission must be obtained prior to visiting.

Princess Louisa Inlet Princess Louisa Inlet, a canyon 8-km (5-mi.) long and about 1.6 km (1 mi.) across, opens up near the end ofueen's Reach. This lovely inlet, whose towering cliffs are covered with myriad waterfalls, is an internationally known yachting destination beloved by generations of boaters. Its curious ability to inspire the imagination of those who see it is best characterized by Malibu Camp situated at the tidal rapid at the entrance of the inlet. Built by Thomas Hamilton, the inventor of the variable pitch propeller, the camp was conceived as a retreat for the rich and famous, who visited in droves in its heyday in the 1940s. Built of local materials, the camp is an amazing structure and is complemented by the many totem poles that grace the grounds. Malibu Camp is now owned by Young Life International and operated as a summer camp for kids. Be sure to time your entrance and exit to the inlet with slack tide at Malibu Rapids, which can run up to 10 knots at full force.

Much of Princess Louisa Inlet—or *Suivoolot,* meaning sunny and warm—was once owned by James F. "Mac" Macdonald. In 1953, wishing to share and preserve its beauty, Mac turned the property over to the nonprofit Princess Louisa International Society, which subsequently transferred it to the government of B.C. The property is now known as Princess Louisa Marine Park. Although there is little camping in the inlet, the site at Chatterbox Falls can accommodate a large number of people and is partially developed with floats, picnic tables and toilets. A second campsite behind Macdonald Island about midway down the inlet also has room for several tents.

Trip 18 Nelson Island

Skill:	Intermediate to advanced
Time:	3–5 days
Hazards:	Winds and traffic
Access:	Pender Harbour
Charts:	3311 Sunshine Coast—Vancouver

		Harbour to Desolation Sound 1:40,000
	3312	Jervis Inlet and Desolation Sound Various Scales
	3512	Strait of Georgia, Central Portion 1:80,000
	3415	Jervis Inlet 1:50,000
Tide Book:	Vol. 5	

Named after Viscount Horatio Nelson, the hero of the British navy, Nelson Island sits at the mouth of Jervis Inlet guarding the secrets of Prince of Wales Reach and Queens Reach. Famous with the yachting crowd for the scenery and anchorages in Blind Bay and Hidden Basin, the area has a lot to offer paddlers. It is one of the few spots on the coast where you can feel the presence of the towering Coast Mountains while experiencing the expanse of the Strait of Georgia. To explore the west side of Nelson Island, it is best to launch at Pender Harbour.

Launching

The communities of Garden Bay, Madeira Park and Irvines Landing are known collectively as Pender Harbour, a well-known base for salmon sport fishing. Located 37 km (23 mi.) north of Sechelt, Pender Harbour provides all the necessary amenities to get you started on your trip. Launching at Irvines Landing is possible but parking is extremely limited. Similarly, though Garden Bay is a 163-ha (403-a.) park, it has a small parking lot and less than 180 m (600 ft.) of beach front. The day-use waterfront area is only accessible from a small foot path at the southern entrance of the park. In light of this, your best bet is to head out from Madeira Park. The Madeira Park government dock is located next to numerous stores and provides 480 m (1600 ft.) of moorage space and access to the shore. There is plenty of parking but be sure to lock your car. The downside to launching from Madeira Park is the boat traffic you will have to contend with as you cross the harbour and make your way towards Nelson Island.

Sites

Leaving Pender Harbour, you will see the two peaks of Mount Daniel rising behind you. The eastern peak is known as the site where puberty rites were practised by young Sechelt women while young men performed similar rituals on Mount Cecil. Watch for traffic as you cross Agamemnon Channel and continue along the shore of Nelson Island. The shoreline, wrinkled by bays and lagoons, is filled with artifacts of the past that make for interesting paddling. Unfortunately, though movements are afoot to create more parks, most of Nelson Island is private property and is becoming more and more settled.

The first major bay you will encounter is Quarry Bay, the source of much of the granite used in the fine old buildings of Vancouver, the carved lions on the north steps of the Vancouver Art Gallery being a notable example. Be sure to explore this place; the land carries a record of the techniques used to quarry stone. Note that a stream runs out of little Quarry Lake onto the mud flats on the east side of the bay. The hike to the lake along the stream is lovely.

Cape Cockburn   Continuing up the coast, you will find Cape Cockburn, named after Admiral Sir George Cockburn who, in 1814, avenged the burning of York (later Toronto) by sailing up the Chesapeake and marching overland to burn the capitol buildings in Washington, D.C. This headland can see some pretty wild weather. SunRay, the homestead built by Harry Roberts, still graces the shores of Cockburn Bay. The land is now the property of B.C. Hydro and is the object of passionate local lobbying to turn it into another park. Cockburn Bay will dry during the lowest tides of the year.

A rock garden winds along the coast to the entrance to Hidden Basin. A narrow channel that shows on the chart as dry at low tide leads into an enclosed lagoon, a haven for all kinds of wildlife and yet another homestead.

As you move past Kelly Island, Blind Bay opens before you between Nelson Island and Hardy Island. There are lots of little islets and shoals here covered with oysters and other intertidal life. Ballet Bay on the eastern shore of Blind Bay features a walking trail to Hidden Basin, which is a long portage but worth it if you haven't explored the basin yet.

Musket Island   Musket Island, just off Alexander Point on Hardy Island, is a provincial marine park and available for camping. There is a quiet cove with a beautiful, dry arbutus landscape. The site is very small, however, and camping is limited to a few mossy flats. Fires are not recommended, but if necessary, do not burn on or near the moss. There is no fee.

Trip 19 Jedediah Island

Skill:	Intermediate to advanced	
Time:	3–5 days	
Hazards:	Winds and traffic	
Access:	Secret Cove/French Creek/Lasqueti Island/Texada Island	
Charts:	3311	Sunshine Coast—Vancouver Harbour to Desolation Sound 1:40,000
	3312	Jervis Inlet and Desolation Sound Various Scales
	3512	Strait of Georgia, Central Portion 1:80,000
	3513	Strait of Georgia, Northern Portion 1:80,000
Tide Book:	Vol. 5	

Jedediah Island is one of the newest provincial marine parks on the coast and a favourite trip for more experienced paddlers. Nestled between Texada and Lasqueti Islands, Jedediah is a 243-ha (600-a.) jewel with old-growth forests of Douglas-fir and arbutus, a variety of wildlife and a shoreline rich in marine life. In the early 1990s the owners and residents of Jedediah, Mary and Al Palmer, decided it was time to move on and agreed to sell it to the province. The Palmers were committed to the dream of the island being protected as a park, and their price tag of $4.2 million was well below market value. Nonetheless, the province was strapped for cash, and it took contributions from the federal government under the Pacific Marine Heritage Legacy program and from the estate of Dan Culver and numerous individuals, groups and corporations to raise the full purchase price.

Launching

You can reach Jedediah from a number of areas including Vancouver Island, Lasqueti Island, Texada Island and the Sunshine Coast.

If launching from Vancouver Island, you can put in at various boat launches between Nanoose Bay and Parksville; the best spot is French Creek. Here you have the choice of paddling the 13 km (8 mi.) of potentially treacherous water to reach Sangster Island and points beyond or

Jedediah Island. BODHI DROPE / SUNSHINE KAYAKING

of taking the B.C. ferry to False Bay on Lasqueti Island. If you decide to paddle, be very cautious of the vicious and sudden Qualicum wind as well as the usual southeasters. This crossing should not be attempted by beginners.

If you are taking the Lasqueti Island ferry, you will have to deal with its awkward schedule and restrictive capacity. Once on Lasqueti, launching is easily done from the beach by the ferry dock. There is also a store if you need to pick up last-minute supplies. Although it is about 20 km (12.5 mi.) to Home Bay on Jedediah Island, there is some camping on the Finnerty and Fegan Islands just north of False Bay, though the sites are small. From here, Long Bay at the north end of Jedediah is an easy day's paddle, and Home Bay is only a few more kilometres away.

Launching from Texada Island puts you in one of the best positions to access Jedediah. If you are coming from Vancouver Island, take the Comox ferry to Powell River and then the 35-minute ferry to Texada. Once on Texada, you can drive across the island and launch at the Shelter Point Park in Gillies Bay or travel farther south along a gravel road to the free Forest Service Recreation Site at Shingle Beach. You will need local information or a Ministry of Forest Recreation Map (from the Powell River office) if you are heading to Shingle Beach because the road takes quite a few turns.

To launch from Secret Cove on the Sunshine Coast, follow Highway 101 north from Sechelt and past Halfmoon Bay, until you see signs indicating the turnoff. Shortly after exiting the highway, turn onto Secret Cove Road and follow it to the government dock. There isn't a lot of parking, but the atmosphere is a little easier to deal with than the surrounding marinas.

A final option for launching is to hire a charter service or kayak operator to shuttle you and your boats to Jedediah Island. Considering the dangerous crossings involved, this is a good idea for beginners. There are a number of services in French Creek, Nanoose Bay and Gibsons.

The following trip description is written as though you are paddling from Secret Cove. If this is not the case, simply use the camping information to help customize your journey from any of the launch sites.

Sites

The Thormanbys Starting from the mainland, head for the light at Epsom Point at the northwest corner of North Thormanby. The Thormanbys are great islands to explore and provide two marine parks for people wishing to camp (see the following section on trips in the Strait of Georgia for more information). From North Thormanby, paddle directly across to Texada, heading for the point that, at time of writing, was easily identified by an old trailer and a navigation light just off it. As your mother would say, look both ways before you cross. This is a major shipping lane, and no matter what the rules of the waterway may state, most ships have the right of way over the kayaker by virtue of their size. Expect lots of tugs, log booms, the occasional cruise ship and all manner of other vessels.

Texada Island This crossing of about 10 km (6 mi.) is through some of the most treacherous water along the coast. Exposed to the full fetch of the strait to the south, weather here can descend on you rapidly. Tidal currents diverge around the various islands and passes, creating unexpected conditions. The trip is best made in the early morning or late afternoon; evaluate carefully before setting out. Although there are many shallow bays on this shore of Texada Island, they are private and must be treated with respect if you are forced to seek refuge.

As you round the south end of Texada, you will enter Sabine Channel, an area of consistent winds. Note: There is virtually no water on Jedediah. If you need extra water, there is a large stream in a shallow bay just around Texada's south end. There is also an abandoned homestead just up from the beach where you can camp if necessary.

Jedediah Island   Across Sabine Channel you'll find a cluster of islands. The first are huge, bare granite peaks punching out of the water with shoals at their base, followed by Jedediah Island, the largest of the group. Follow the east shore of Jedediah until you find the entrance to Home Bay. This narrow defile is hard to see until you are right on top of it. If the tide is low when you arrive, the lagoon may be dry. You can land on the rock beach before the entrance to the bay or wait till the tide comes in before unloading your boat and setting up camp.

Home Bay offers the paddler a sand beach with a grassy upland for camping. An old horse and a flock of sheep, remnants of an old homestead, share the island with goats reportedly left there by the original explorers of the coast. Although free from bears, the island is home to many a raccoon who will enjoy picking through your camp given half a chance. Take advantage of the walks available through the grassland and over rocky crags. BC Parks is developing the site so call them for the latest camping information.

Home Bay is a favourite camping spot, yet many of the little bays along the west side of the island offer good camping as does Long Bay at the north end. A lot of these bays dry at low tide leaving long mud flats, so time your landings and launchings. Be sure to explore the deluxe paddling in and around the island. Little Bull Passage on the west of Jedediah has a nice tidal flow between high granite cliffs, and the trip to Squitty Bay on the southernmost tip of Lasqueti is a feast for the senses. Although camping is not allowed in Squitty Bay, there is some of the best paddling water around at the head of the bay. There is also camping in and around the Finnerty and Fegan Islands at the north end of Lasqueti.

Shingle Beach (Texada Island)   If you don't want to head directly home, you can explore the southwest shore of Texada Island a little more closely. Shingle Beach is a road-accessible Forest Service Recreation Site (see Launching, above). To find it from the water, look for Texada's Mount Davies and head just to the south. A mile or so away you should be able to recognize the sweeping pebble shoreline of Shingle Beach. There are often cars parked at the north end of the beach—another tip that you are in the right spot. The beach is a beautiful but a little exposed, and landing can be a tricky. There is plenty of room for camping up the road if you can't find anything by the water. If you continue heading north along Texada, you will start to see prominent signs of development and the odd pay-for-use campground.

Whichever route you take, remember that southeast winds will be at their strongest on the open strait and can keep you in camp for a day or two, especially in the spring and fall. You are particularly vulnerable at Squitty Bay and around the tip of Lasqueti. Sabine Channel funnels wind and tide, producing severe chop augmented further when the wind is against the tide. By waiting for slack you will avoid the worst conditions. Remember: These islands are in the middle of shipping lanes from both Powell River and Campbell River, and all that traffic is bigger than you in your kayak. Enjoy one of B.C.'s newest parks but stay alert!

Trip 20   Strait of Georgia

Skill:	Beginner to advanced
Time:	Day trips
Hazards:	Winds and traffic
Access:	Numerous sites on the Sunshine Coast
Charts:	3311 Sunshine Coast—Vancouver Harbour to Desolation Sound 1:40,000
	3512 Strait of Georgia, Central Portion 1:80,000
Tide Book:	Vol. 5

The Georgia Strait trip described below can be used either by long-distance paddlers travelling the coastal marine trail, from the south or the north, or by paddlers out for day trips. The following launch sites are listed in a south to north fashion.

Launching

Launching from Gibsons is quite easy, using either the marina or Hopkins Landing near the Langdale ferry terminal. For more information, see Chapter 5.

To launch from the beach at Davis Bay, follow Highway 101 through Gibsons northwest towards Sechelt. As you are nearing town, just after crossing the Chapman Creek bridge you will see a small lot off the highway at Mission Point. Park in the lot and launch from the beach.

The Selma Park Boat Ramp is another possibility. Look for the boat ramp sign between Davis Bay and Sechelt. Exit the highway and follow

Mason Road to the breakwater. The concrete ramp and small beach offer protected access to the water, and the Trail Islands are only a couple of miles away. There is ample parking.

Sargeant Bay Provincial Park is located a few minutes north of Sechelt. The sandy beach at this day-use area is excellent for launching; you may also want to relax for a few minutes and check out the abundant sea and intertidal life. There is a picnic area and pit toilet, but no overnight parking.

Halfmoon Bay is accessed off Highway 101 about 7 km (4.5 mi.) north of Sechelt. You can launch at the government wharf at the apex of the bay or at Frenchman's Cove at the end of Brooks Road. Limited parking is available.

Secret Cove is located just north of Halfmoon Bay. Turn off the highway where indicated and turn onto Secret Cove Road to reach the government wharf. Limited parking is available.

Sites

The first thing encountered after leaving Gibsons and heading up the Strait of Georgia is "The Stretch." The 32-km (20-mi.) coastline between Gibsons and Sechelt has no offshore islands and rare bits of sand along the rocky shore, which leaves you open to the full fetch of the strait. The estuary of Roberts Creek, the new marina at Davis Bay and the boat ramp at Selma Park offer respite in need. A one-way trip up or down the whole Stretch is a 7–10-hour paddle.

White Islets   Look for the White Islets, a number of granite peaks thrust out of the water with wind-swept austerity, sitting about a mile offshore opposite the Wilson Creek estuary. Although inhospitable in human terms, these rocks offer a welcome haven for a variety of seabirds and mammals. This is a designated bird sanctuary so stay on the water and keep your distance. For a day trip, launch from the beach at Davis Bay.

The next large bay along the coast is Trail Bay, which encompasses the smaller Davis Bay, Selma Park, the Sechelt Indian lands and the town of Sechelt. The Trail Islands are nestled in the northwest corner of the bay. These islands are home to an amazing variety of wildlife, considering their proximity to town. Although the islands are private property, look for the spit on the inland side of the most southerly island if you need to land and enjoy the flocks of oystercatchers that favour this spot. These islands also make a wonderful day trip when you launch from either the Selma Park boat ramp or Sargeant Bay.

Sargeant Bay   Sargeant Bay opens off to the north, a lovely little pocket of protected water with a beach and a park at the apex, though no camping. Take the time to walk through the wetlands at the creek mouth where a wildlife refuge has been developed and maintained by local people and BC Parks. The high bank at the mouth of Sargeant Bay creates a long flat stretching out into the sea, a favourite habitat for herons and other fish-loving birds.

Merry Island   Heading north you will encounter Halfmoon Bay, Merry Island and the Thormanbys. Merry Island has the quintessential lighthouse with its high, white tower topped by the flashing light, red roof and railings—a classic photo opportunity. It guards the entrance to Welcome Passage, the narrow channel between Thormanby Island and the mainland. Be careful: This channel is notorious for nasty weather when the funnelling effect picks up the wind and waves, especially when the wind is against the tide. At time of writing, the lightkeepers were delighted to chat with visitors, but who knows what the story will be when the new order arrives—the Coast Guard has plans to "destaff" lighthouses on the coast. Many varieties of duck patrol the shores of Merry Island due to its great fishing opportunities. Little Franklin hugging the western shore of Merry Island is another sanctuary for nesting seabirds. A number of the older homes on Merry Island are gradually falling down, leaving room for potential campsites. The current Coast Guard shuffle will have to be sorted out, however, before an official site is created here.

The government wharf at the apex of Halfmoon Bay is a good place to stop off to replenish supplies at the great little general store just up the road.

North and South Thormanby   The Thormanby Islands lie just west of Halfmoon Bay and are a study in opposites. South Thormanby is the usual pile of granite with lots of sheer cliffs wrinkled into tiny bays and cobble beaches. North Thormanby, on the other hand, is one enormous sand dune falling into long, shallow flats.

Simson Marine Park covers the entire southeastern side of South Thormanby so camping spots are easy to find. The small bay that sports the marine park sign will lead you to the interior of the island, which was formerly a homestead. Great camping, hiking and birding abound.

North Thormanby arcs out from the western shore of its companion island, creating the wide Buccaneer Bay between them. The apex of the bay is a narrow isthmus that connects the two islands. The public campground is on this little lick of land—lots of sand with great swimming. Mind your feet when walking here as this is the home to a unique cactus-like plant. During big tides, water will flood the spit so you can paddle right through. Resist the impulse to climb the sand cliffs: they are very unstable. The beaches on the open strait offer an opportunity for some gentle kayak surfing.

Smugglers Cove   Buccaneer Bay opens off the western end of Welcome Pass while Smugglers Cove Marine Park lies on the mainland side. The end of a narrow pass marked by the familiar marine park sign reveals a completely enclosed cove sprinkled with tiny islands and shoals.

A favourite with the boating crowd, Smugglers Cove is rich with tales of the booze trade during Prohibition and the often tragic stories of thousands of Chinese workers from CP Railway who came here looking for illegal passage to the United States. Camping is best at the far end where there is a small beach for landing and some facilities. The beach ends up as a long mud flat at low tide so try to arrive and leave at high tide. The cove is also accessible from a 1.3-km (.8-mi.) trail that leads to a parking lot located just off Highway 101, and you can expect company during the summer.

Secret Cove is at the top of the next wide bay on the mainland. Another enclosed patch of water with a couple of marinas, Secret Cove also features a small store with supplies for visiting boaters. Local kayakers often use this cove as the jumping-off place for the trip to Jedediah Island.

ADDITIONAL ROUTES

Heading south: The southern end of the Sunshine Coast blends into Howe Sound and the paddle routes described in Chapter 5.

Heading north: Continuing north along the coast from Muskrat Island Marine Park will take you to Scotch Fir Point, an area of great camping potential though individual sites have not been developed. If you head into Jervis Inlet, you will soon come across Saltery Bay Provincial Park—a nice, though developed, park that sits by the roadside. If you paddle towards Texada Island, check out Pocahontas and Raven Bays. Although they are road accessible, there are plenty of flat areas for camping and reasonably protected landings. Pocahontas Bay is an old log dump and considerably more industrial in feel than Raven Bay. Enjoy!

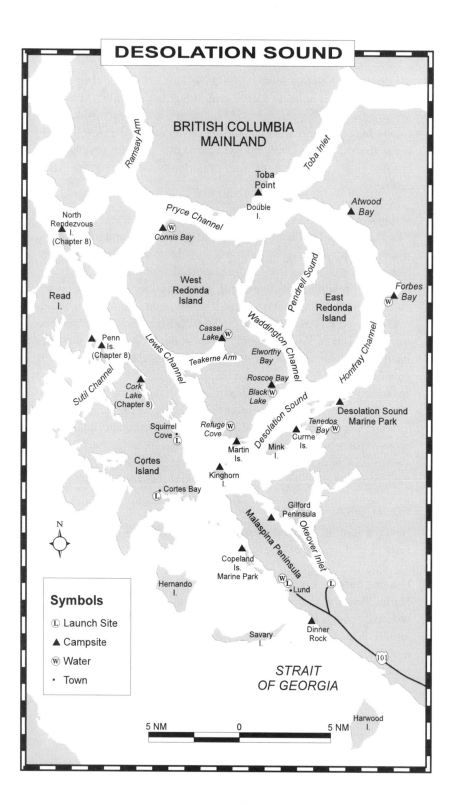

DESOLATION SOUND

BRITISH COLUMBIA
MAINLAND

Ramsay Arm

Toba Inlet

Toba
Point

Pryce Channel

Double
I.

Atwood
Bay

North
Rendezvous
I.
(Chapter 8)

Connis Bay

Pendrell Sound

West
Redonda
Island

East
Redonda
Island

Forbes
Bay

Read
I.

Waddington Channel

Penn
Is.
(Chapter 8)

Lewis Channel

Cassel
Lake

Teakerne Arm

Elworthy
Bay

Homfray Channel

Sutil Channel

Cork
Lake
(Chapter 8)

Roscoe Bay

Black
Lake

Desolation Sound

Desolation Sound
Marine Park

Squirrel
Cove

Refuge
Cove

Tenedos
Bay

Martin
Is.

Mink
I.

Curme
Is.

Cortes
Island

Kinghorn
I.

Cortes Bay

Gilford
Peninsula

Malaspina Peninsula

Okeover Inlet

N

Copeland
Is.
Marine Park

Hernando
I.

Lund

Dinner
Rock

101

Savary
I.

Symbols

- Ⓛ Launch Site
- ▲ Campsite
- Ⓦ Water
- • Town

STRAIT
OF GEORGIA

Harwood
I.

5 NM   0   5 NM

Desolation Sound

Ralph Keller

Located beyond the northern terminus of Highway 101, Desolation Sound greets thousands of boaters every summer with its spectacular scenery and unusually warm waters. Bordered by the Coast Mountains of mainland B.C. to the east and the Discovery Islands to the west, Desolation Sound offers paddlers of all abilities a wilderness unscarred by the development that is so common in southern B.C. It is here that paddlers gain their first taste of the North Coast.

BACKGROUND

When you paddle in Desolation Sound, you are in Sliammon territory and the territories of their friends and relatives, the Klahoose people. As Cheryl Coull writes, the people have always lived here and the winds have always blown. In the very earliest of times, the people of Sliammon tell us, Raven and some other people journeyed north, killed the tiresome Wind-Maker and his wife, and brought their gusty son home with them. Something to remember on your trip.

Capt. George Vancouver referred to Desolation Sound as "a dark and gloomy place." The summer paddler is unlikely to notice that particular effect, though Homfray Channel and Pendrell Sound with their high mountains might well take on a "gloomy" appearance in bad weather. Desolation Sound only receives about 102–152 cm (40–60 in.) of rainfall per year—little of that during the summer.

One of the most interesting facts about Desolation Sound is that it marks the junction of the two tidal streams entering the inside coast of

Vancouver Island—one via Juan de Fuca Strait to the south and one via Johnstone Strait to the north. This junction limits the flushing effects of the tides and dramatically increases the water temperature, creating some of the best swimming on the coast. Pendrell Sound, at the north end of East Redonda Island, the most notable example of this phenomenon, has actually reached temperatures of 26°C (78°F) during the summer, earning it the title of the warmest ocean temperature north of the Gulf of Mexico.

The junction of the two tidal streams also creates inconsistent tides throughout the area. Water wrapping around the north end of Vancouver Island floods in a southerly direction, and water entering from Juan de Fuca Strait floods in a northerly direction (and vice versa for an ebbing tide). It is this change in tidal direction that first tipped Captain Vancouver and his crew to the possibility that the land mass to the west of them— Vancouver Island—was in fact an island.

GETTING THERE

To reach Desolation Sound, your best bet is to launch from Lund or from Okeover Inlet. It is also possible to access the area by launching from Cortes Island, a good option if you are travelling from Vancouver Island or intending to explore the Discovery Islands as well.

By land: From Vancouver, head to Horseshoe Bay and catch the Langdale ferry (45 minutes). The ferries run frequently but expect delays on long weekends. Head north along Highway 101, past Sechelt, to the Earls Cove ferry terminal. Catch the ferry to Saltery Bay (35 minutes) and once again head north along Highway 101 through the town of Powell River, until you reach Lund. Total travel time from Vancouver is about 5 hours.

If you are coming from Vancouver Island, drive to Comox, take the ferry to Powell River and follow Highway 101 north to Lund. The trip from Comox to Lund takes about 2 hours.

If you plan on launching from Cortes Island, drive to Campbell River, take the ferry to Quadra Island (15 minutes), drive across Quadra Island to Heriot Bay (15 minutes) and board the ferry to Cortes Island (40–45 minutes).

By water: Remote water drop-off service, including kayaks, is available from Discovery Launch Water Taxi, Sutil Charters and Coast Mountain Expeditions, which specializes in remote kayak charters (up to 12 paddlers and kayaks per trip).

By air: There are scheduled flights to Campbell River from Vancouver and Seattle with stops in Victoria, Nanaimo and Courtenay. Air B.C. and Canadian Regional Airlines are the two main carriers. There is also float plane service available from Seattle via Kenmore Air. Coval Air, Vancouver Island Air and Rush Air out of Campbell River provide drop-off service to remote outlying areas (a maximum of two hard-shelled boats per trip).

WEATHER AND HAZARDS

Desolation Sound is known for both its fair weather and warm waters. In the summer, air temperatures hover around 22°C (72°F). Winds during June, July and August tend to be reasonably light though be sure to review the note on anabatic and katabatic winds in Chapter 1 if you plan on venturing up any of the inlets. In addition, exercise caution as even a fair-weather westerly can catch you off guard when it is redirected within the convoluted channels of the Discovery Islands. Fog is not typically a problem. There is usually good VHF weather reception on channel 21 International throughout the region.

While the paddling environment in Desolation Sound is fairly benign, other boaters can make certain areas unsafe for kayakers. The danger from larger high-speed powerboats cannot be overstated, so you are best to limit your crossings as much as possible and never assume you are seen. Finally, paddlers should take the necessary precautions against bears when camping on the mainland and the larger islands.

SPECIAL CONSIDERATIONS

As you paddle around Desolation Sound, you will likely notice the striking profile of Mount Addenbrooke on East Redonda Island. This is B.C.'s tallest offshore mountain, aside from those on Vancouver Island, and it has a wonderful array of ecosystems. Because of this, much of East Redonda is an ecological reserve, and paddlers are asked to refrain from camping anywhere on the island.

Due to the dry climate, camp fires and beach fires are not allowed on most of the islands of Desolation Sound without a burning permit. We ask that paddlers use caution at all times with fires of any kind—a major fire would be devastating.

DESOLATION SOUND TRIPS (21–22)

The paddling possibilities of Desolation Sound are limitless. For beginners, there are great 3–4-day trips that begin in Lund or Okeover Inlet and explore the Desolation Sound Marine Park—perfect for a long weekend. If you have a week or so, and a bit more experience, the spectacular vistas, rugged beauty and peace of the Redonda Islands and Toba Inlet await. For those who like to mix things up a little and have the time, see the note at the end of the chapter on combining trips in Desolation Sound and the Discovery Islands. The logistics are a little hard to work out, but the adventure is worth the effort.

Trip 21 Desolation Sound

Skill:	Beginner to intermediate
Time:	3–5 days
Hazards:	Boat traffic
Access:	Lund/Okeover Inlet/Cortes Island
Charts:	3312 Jervis Inlet and Desolation Sound
	Various Scales
	3538 Desolation and Sutil Channel
	1:40,000
Tide Book:	Vols. 5 and 6

This trip passes through Desolation Sound and Homfray Channel. The route leaves from Lund although there is an alternate and more protected launch site in Okeover Inlet on the eastern side of the Malaspina Peninsula.

Paddlers looking for a 3–4-day beginner-to-intermediate exploration of Desolation Sound should limit their paddling to the area south of, and including, Desolation Sound Marine Park. Please keep in mind that exploring farther north and into Toba Inlet requires more time and more skill.

Launching

Launching from Lund provides you with the greatest number of amenities although it also leaves you somewhat exposed to the Strait of Georgia. To reach the best launching site, follow Highway 101 to the centre of Lund. Facing the water, you will have the Lund Hotel to your right and the government wharf in front of you and to your left. Your best bet is to unload all your gear at the wharf and arrange for Dave's Boat Rental to valet park your car. The cost, about $4 a day, saves you the virtually impossible task of finding an overnight parking space. Finally, don't forget to have a few dollars handy to stock up on the cinnamon buns from Nancy's Bakery—perhaps the best start to any kayak trip. Kayak rentals are available in Lund. To reach the provincial park and launching site in Okeover Inlet, turn right at Malaspina Road, 6 km (4 mi.) before Lund, and drive 4 km (2.5 mi.) to the government wharf at Okeover Inlet. Parking here is also hard to find, and there have been a few incidents of vandalism recently. You are advised to park in one of the private pay lots such as the Why Knot Campsite. Check with BC Parks on the status of their overnight camping area; it was closed for much of 1997.

Although Okeover does provide relatively sheltered access to the Desolation Sound Marine Park, the wind has been known to howl quite nastily down the inlet. If you choose to launch in Okeover, please note that Portage Cove at the mouth of the inlet is private land; no matter how tempting, avoid crossing the property. If you need a place to camp near the launch site, look for the small beach on the Malaspina Peninsula that sits directly across from Kakaekae Point on the Gifford Peninsula.

Sites

As you paddle away from Lund, you will be able to see Savary Island to the south and a number of smaller islands to the north. These are the Copeland Islands, a marine park that offers both campsites and anchorages. Although it is a short half hour to an hour's paddle to reach the Copelands, be sure to keep an eye on the winds and boat traffic.

Copeland Islands   The Copeland Islands were named after Joe Copeland, a hand logger who lived here during the early part of the century. It seems this character was a rather unscrupulous officer in the Confederate army during the American Civil War. After the war, he became an outlaw who specialized in holding up stage coaches. He was chased by U.S. officials over the border and into Canada. Fearing apprehension, he lived out the rest of his life in the Copelands.

The islands are beautiful and well known so don't be surprised if you are not alone. Perhaps the best campsite is on the middle island in a west-facing bay. A gently curving beach, lined with arbutus trees, provides access to plenty of tent sites. Watch the setting sun or climb the steep, short hill behind camp to watch the rising moon. There is no fresh water.

Leaving the Copelands and heading north, you will round Sarah Point and enter Desolation Sound. The point is steep-sided and landing can be

difficult; plan this leg of the journey with care—you might be in your boat for a few hours. If the Curme Islands are your next destination, head directly for Mink Island and work your way to its eastern shore. If you are into exploring, a number of sites lie nearby including Kinghorn Island and the Martin Islands (discussed below).

Curme Islands   They may not be big but they sure are pretty. During the high season you can expect to share these gems with other paddlers. Tent and landing sites are a little difficult to find on the rocky shores, but you can find both in the centre of the northern cluster of islets. The Curmes have no fresh water, and the nearest supply of drinking water is a small stream flowing out of Unwin Lake at the top of Tenedos Bay. If you are a large group, avoid camping on the Curmes due to the limited space. All paddlers should be aware of the nearby seal haul-outs and try to maintain a reasonable distance.

It is a short jump from the Curme Islands into Desolation Sound Marine Park. While popular with the big boat crowd, the park offers a number of camping spots for kayakers, including sites in and around Prideaux Haven. Another provincial park, Roscoe Bay, is located close by on the southwestern end of West Redonda Island.

Roscoe Bay and Black Lake (West Redonda Island)   When you first paddle into Roscoe Bay, you'll notice it is wall-to-wall (shore-to-shore) pleasure craft, and you may wonder why it is included in this guide. The truth is, the busyness of the place does not completely diminish its beauty. There are great campsites here and an outhouse compliments of BC Parks. Most noteworthy about the place is Black Lake. There couldn't be a warmer lake anywhere else in B.C., and it is definitely worth the paddle (a few kilometres). Black Lake is a great place to brush up on rescues, rolls or any other kayak-related activity that involves getting wet.

The most obvious place to get water is the small stream running out of the lake past the campsites. Because of the number of people using the lake, however, drinking the stream water is not recommended. The best place to get good drinking water is to paddle about 100 m (330 ft.) to the north side of the bay where a delightful spring splashes over a small cliff. Often, someone will have rigged up a water line to facilitate filling containers.

At this point in the trip, people with time constraints or little paddling

< Toba Inlet. COAST MOUNTAIN EXPEDITIONS

experience should begin working their way back to Lund or Okeover Inlet. Those wanting to carry on should head east and begin the journey up Homfray Channel towards Forbes Bay.

Trip 22 Toba Inlet

Trip 22:	Toba Inlet
Skill:	Intermediate to advanced
Time:	5–14 days
Hazards:	Boat traffic and wind
Access:	Lund/Okeover Inlet/Cortes Island
Charts:	3312 Jervis Inlet and Desolation Sound Various Scales
	3538 Desolation and Sutil Channel 1:40,000
	3541 Approaches to Toba Inlet
Tide Book:	Vols. 5 and 6

Note: The following trip assumes you have already reached Homfray Channel via the Desolation Sound trip described above.

Forbes Bay   There are two good campsites at Forbes Bay. The first is in the middle of a large rocky beach right at the top of the bay, about 300 m (990 ft.) north of Forbes Creek; the second is in an adjacent watershed at the extreme south end of the bay. Pleasure craft tend to anchor at the latter site, which is somewhat more protected than just off the main beach. Both sites are close to the wonderful water of Forbes Creek.

Part of the rocky beach and surrounding watershed belongs to the Klahoose Nation, and you'll notice that the watershed has more or less all its trees intact. You are enjoying much of this extraordinarily beautiful place courtesy of the Klahoose Nation, and their permission should be sought before camping on the northern beach.

Finally, a sobering thought: Forbes Bay is grizzly bear habitat. It is not prime habitat but they are there. This is no place to become complacent about bear protocol. Be careful and do everything right. If you don't remember how to cache your food, read Chapter 1 again.

Atwood Bay   If you are continuing up Homfray Channel, be sure to check out Atwood Bay. On the south side of the bay is a flat, albeit exposed, clearing that used to be a log dump. It is a nice campsite even though the bay can get quite busy with sport fishing boats.

Toba Point   Unnamed on your chart—we gave it this name—it is distinguishable by a navigational light about 300 m (990 ft.) to the west and by Double Island to the east, in the entrance to Toba Inlet. It has a great, steep gravelly beach—easy on your kayak and a short carry to the high tide mark. This site was a real gem until it was clearcut a few years ago. Still, it is a great find in an area where the mountains tend to rise straight out of the ocean. There is good camping on the nearby point just to the west. Once again, this is prime bear country so take appropriate measures.

In the early part of the summer season, you will probably find water in a small stream just above the beach but don't plan on it. Because of the mountainous terrain, however, there are literally dozens of good-sized creeks tumbling down the hills all along your route. During a lunch or bladder break, fill your water containers from one of these. Not only is the water here potable, there is at least one major company that bottles the stuff and sells it internationally at premium prices. So drink up!

Heading farther up Toba Inlet requires quite a commitment from the paddler since campsites become scarce and the weather more temperamental. Nonetheless, experienced paddlers will be rewarded with spectacular vistas and wonderful solitude. For the less adventurous, heading west towards Connis Bay will start you on the path home.

Connis Bay (West Redonda Island)   Connis Bay is several hundred metres west of Connis Point. When you see Connis Point, you'll understand why we prefer to stay at Connis Bay. There are plenty of good campsites among the alders just above high tide. If you're energetic and don't mind doing a little bushwhacking, you can hike up to a small lake about 2 km (1.25 mi.) back into the hills. Be warned: This part of West Redonda Island seems to have a rather healthy black bear population, and you will need to adopt bear protocol during your stay.

Spilling out into the bay is a wonderful creek that is always brimming and bubbling with cold, pure water. If you follow the creek back into the tree line just above the beach—wade up the creek from the beach—you'll

Shorebird. PETER McGEE

discover a wonderful pool fed by a 3-m (10-ft.) waterfall. Invisible from the water and beach, it is shrouded by branches of huge conifers and an awesome array of ferns growing out of the cliff. After a hot, salty day, a minute or two under the falls is a welcome reprieve.

Teakerne Arm and Cassel Lake (West Redonda Island)   As you head south down Lewis Channel, you will come across Teakerne Arm. The journey to the top of this arm on the west side of West Redonda Island is a little out of the way—an 8-km (5-mi.) round trip. Still, the time and energy spent getting here is easily worth it. The setting is as idyllic as anything you will find on the coast: a deep, protected bay whose top is graced by a waterfall—not just any waterfall, a *warm* waterfall that spills out of an equally warm lake. This is also a campsite if a day's visit is not enough.

It is possible to carry kayaks to the top of the falls and paddle the rather large Cassel Lake. Sadly, most of the forest cover along this waterway has long since been removed and what should have been an awesome journey is now quite disappointing. You can always use your imagination as you paddle along the lakeshore. The campsites are near the waterfall.

Leaving Teakerne Arm and continuing south, you soon end up back in Desolation Sound. There are a number of campsites including the Martin Islands, where Lewis Channel and Desolation Sound meet.

Martin Islands   Although the chart shows two islands, for practical purposes there is just one. Evidently the neck that joins the two islands floods during the big winter tides but this never happens in the summer. This relatively flat neck is where most people put their tents. If it is occupied when you arrive, don't be dismayed: there are other good sites nearby. Be advised that you are once again entering the very heart of Desolation Sound—an international pleasure craft destination. A lot of big yachts can be seen cruising by, especially in the pass between the Martin Islands and West Redonda Island. These big boats love to blast through the pass at high speed, throwing off huge amounts of wash. If you're unloading your kayak for the day, be sure to put it well up on shore so it does not get slammed around on the rocky beach whenever a member of the afternoon double-martini crowd zips by.

Unfortunately, there is no fresh water here. The closest source is at Refuge Cove on West Redonda Island, about 1.5 km (1 mi.) away. They not only have water but ice cream, pop and espresso coffee. So if you haven't had a sugar or caffeine fix in a while . . .

If the Martin Islands seem a little crowded or exposed, check out the north end of Kinghorn Island. Although there are no designated campsites, there are a number of rocky beaches to land on and roomy trees to camp among. From here, it is a short jump back to Okeover Inlet or the Copeland Islands and Lund.

Heading north: This leads to the Discovery Islands (Chapter 8).

Heading south: Savary and Hernando Islands, both extremely beautiful, are essentially private. Dinner Rock just south of Lund is a Forest Service Recreation Site but the rest of the coast to Powell River is pretty developed. Farther south, sites appear on Texada and Nelson Islands (Chapter 6).

A Discovery Islands-Desolation Sound combination: The Discovery Islands are situated very close to Desolation Sound, and overlapping the two regions in your planning can produce some great routes. The ultimate trip begins in Lund and finishes at Heriot Bay on Quadra Island (or vice versa). Unfortunately, the pick-up and drop-off logistics are a little hard to work out for this route. If you decide to explore both regions at once, another possibility is to take the ferry to Cortes Island and depart from there. Depending on where you want to go, there are numerous public launch sites, the best ones being Whaletown, Squirrel Cove, Smelt Bay, Cortes Bay and Coulter Bay. Parking is available at all these locations.

THE DISCOVERY ISLANDS

East Thurlow
Island

Johnstone
Strait

Howe Island ▲

Discovery Passage

Small Inlet

Seymour Narrows

(19)

Campbell
River ●

VANCOUVER
ISLAND

Sonora
Island

Okisollo Channel

Hole in the Wall

Waiatt
Bay   Octopus
       Is..   ▲

Maurelle
I.

Elephant
Yeatman ⓦBay
Bay ▲
    ⓦⓉ

Quadra
Island

Surge Narrows

Sheer
Point ▲

Village
Bay ▲

Hoskyn Channel

Heriot
Bay
ⓦⓁ
Heriot Bay ● Rebecca
▲ Spit
ⓁBreton Is.

Stuart
I.

Calm Channel

Church
House ●
ⓦ

North
ⓦ Rendezvous
I.

South
Rendezvous
I.

Read
I.

Penn
▲ Is.
▲

Coulter
▲ Bay

ⓦ
ⓁWhaletown

Ramsay Arm

Frances
▲ⓦ Bay

Connis
▲ⓦ Bay
(Chapter 7)

West
Redonda
Island

Robertson
ⓦ Lake
ⓉⓉ

Von Donup Inlet

Ⓣⓦ▲
Cork
ⓦⓉ Lake
Ⓣ

Squirrel
Cove ●

Cortes
Island

Sutil
Channel

● Quathiaski
Cove

● Mansons
Landing

● Cortes Bay

STRAIT
OF GEORGIA

N

Symbols

Ⓛ Launch Site
▲ Campsite
ⓦ Water
● Town
Ⓣ Trail

5 NM   0   5 NM

Chapter Eight

The Discovery Islands
Ralph Keller

Steps away from urban civilization, the Discovery Islands are gems of tranquillity at the threshold of a majestic wilderness. Guarded by swift ocean currents, the islands offer spectacular vistas, remote beach camps and a solitude that will make each day a journey of discovery.

BACKGROUND

The Discovery Islands or, more technically, the Northern Gulf Archipelago, are in fact the foothills of the highest mountains in the province, some with snowy peaks rising thousands of metres. Nowhere else on the coast will you find a more dramatic backdrop for a kayaking trip. The waterways between these islands are recent glacier tracks that only 15,000 years ago were scoured out to incredible depths—in some instances, to more than 1500 m (5,000 ft.).

Thousands of years ago, the first people moved into this area. Eventually, three distinct groupings formed: the Klahoose, the Homanthko and the Kwakwaka'wakw (Kwakiutl). They still occupy lands within these islands and the mainland coast, and their ancient pictographs still decorate the cliffs of these islands, their traditional homeland.

In the late 1800s, almost a century after European exploration of the area by Capt. George Vancouver and the Spanish navigator Quadra, among others, settlers began to build homesteads using logging and whaling as their means of support. The warm, calm waters of the southern islands were home to about 300 gray whales, and the entire group was hunted out in just three years. The whale population has never recovered, truly one of the world's great tragedies—all for a few barrels of oil. Whaletown and Lund were the two principal whaling stations.

In 1996, a number of dedicated locals successfully lobbied the B.C. government to recognize the rare and outstanding qualities of the region. This led to a significant increase in protected areas, bringing the regional total to about 8000 ha (20,000 a.). On your next trip, consider buying your groceries here, renting a kayak or staying in a B&B as a way of contributing to the local economy and thanking the residents for being the guardians of this magnificent area.

GETTING THERE

By land: Take the ferry from Vancouver to Nanaimo (via either the Horseshoe Bay or Tsawwassen terminals) and drive north along Highway 19 (the Island Highway). You can drive from Nanaimo to Campbell River in 1.5 hours and then take the 15-minute ferry ride to Quadra Island. On Quadra, the best place to put in is the beach by the Heriot Bay government dock or at Rebecca Spit Marine Park. Public parking is available.

By water: Remote water drop-off service, including kayaks, is available from Discovery Launch Water Taxi, Sutil Charters and Coast Mountain Expeditions, which specializes in remote kayak charters (up to 12 paddlers and kayaks per trip).

By air: There are scheduled flights to Campbell River from Vancouver and Seattle with stops in Victoria, Nanaimo and Courtenay. See Chapter 7 for details.

WEATHER AND HAZARDS

Desolation Sound and the Discovery Islands are uniquely situated in that they are affected by currents from the Strait of Georgia to the south and from Johnstone Strait to the north. The result is two very different climates. All of the Okisollo Channel, from Surge Narrows north, lies within the Johnstone Strait Oceanic Ecosection, whereas South Quadra, Read Island and Cortes Island fall into the Georgia Basin Ecosection. When you paddle north through Surge Narrows, you paddle through a bioclimatic door and enter a different world. The Okisollo Channel is clearly a much colder, foggier, rainier place even though it is only a few kilometres away from the sunnier and milder Georgia Basin. Most of the trip suggested in this chapter occurs in that warmer setting, where summer temperatures generally range from 19–26°C (66–78°F).

The Octopus Islands, with Hole in the Wall in the background. PETER McGEE

Two notable natural hazards occur in this region: heavy tidal overfall or tidal rapids, and the anabatic, katabatic and outflow wind conditions of the mainland inlets. There is nothing trivial about tidal rapids or the local wind conditions of the inlets. *Under certain conditions, they are guaranteed to be fatal.* With intelligence and humility, however, they can be negotiated by an experienced paddler. For general information on these phenomena, please refer back to Chapter 1.

There are six distinct sets of tidal rapids in the Discovery Islands, some of which are considered to be the most powerful in the world: Yuculta Rapids, Dent Rapids, Upper and Lower Rapids of the Okisollo, Hole in the Wall, Surge Narrows (Beazley Passage) and Arran Rapids. They run at between 7 and 14 knots. You can use the Surge Narrows current tables to predict the movement of all the rapids in this area. As a general rule, there is a 1-hour window of opportunity to get through any of the region's tidal rapids. Even on the biggest summer tides, the rapids are passable 30 minutes before the current turns and 30 minutes after. You can paddle through any of the rapids within an hour; usually, 30 minutes is ample time. In any event, use extreme caution and plan carefully.

Sometimes you or your group will arrive late at a given pass and, rather than wait 5 or 6 hours for slack current, be tempted to try to get through anyway. Or, sometimes advanced paddlers simply want to play around in the current to see what it is like. Whether you are a beginner paddler or a hot-shot white-water paddler turned sea kayaker, you need to understand two things: The Pacific is not a river and you are not in a white-water boat! I once cautioned an experienced white-water kayaker (a trained guide) about entering a local tidal rapids. He looked at me and exclaimed, "I can't remember the last time I blew a roll!" He was later fished out of the Upper Rapids of the Okisollo by a local who was alert enough to see him and save not only his life but his kayak too. The bottom line is this: No amount of skill—rolling, bracing or paddling—will guarantee you a safe passage through any of the region's rapids. Even in the best conditions, this is no place for beginners.

Trip 23   Discovery Islands

Skill:	Intermediate to advanced	
Time:	4–14 days	
Hazards:	Tidal rapids and winds	
Access:	Quadra Island/Cortes Island	
Charts:	3312	Jervis Inlet and Desolation Sound Various Scales
	3537	Okisollo Channel 1:20,000
	3538	Desolation Sound and Sutil Channel 1:40,000
	3539	Discovery Passage 1:40,000
	3541	Approaches to Toba Inlet 1:40,000
Tide Book:	Vol. 6	

The trip through the Discovery Islands described in this chapter begins at Heriot Bay on Quadra Island and passes through Hoskyn Channel and Hole in the Wall as it circumnavigates Maurelle and Read Islands. It is possible to finish this trip in as little as 4 days, but it is best to leave time to explore.

While there are maintained campsites at locations such as Rebecca Spit on Quadra Island and Smelt Bay on Cortes, kayakers are free to camp most anywhere with a few notable exceptions. Most of the southern half of Quadra is private, as are the western and southern shores of Cortes. Read Island's shoreline is peppered with large, undeveloped industrial lots; by and large, these are unmarked and appear to be public land. To date, most industrial landowners have not seemed to mind having kayakers on their land as long as fundamental concerns are addressed. Take your garbage with you, human feces must be properly dealt with and absolutely no fires!

Fresh water is available at some sites and not at others; you are advised to bring your own supply and, as always, to treat or boil any water from local streams.

Launching

To launch at Heriot Bay, drive across Quadra Island towards the Whale-town-Cortes Island ferry and turn left onto Cramer Road a few hundred metres before the terminal. Drive a few hundred metres more to Antler Road and then down to the Heriot Bay government dock. There is usually adequate and relatively safe parking. The first 3 days are free—$1.50 per day thereafter. Rebecca Spit, another launch site, is located just south of the ferry terminal.

If you are launching from Whaletown, catch the ferry from Quadra Island to Cortes Island. Once on Cortes, you'll see the Whaletown government dock and a store to the right of the ferry terminal. To get there, turn right at each of the two major stop signs. There is safe parking available.

Sites

Hoskyn Channel From Heriot Bay, begin your trip by heading north towards Hoskyn Channel. At the bottom of the channel you will see a number of smaller islands called the Breton Islands. The southernmost island has a fantastic pebble beach on its southwest side that makes a great spot for stretching your legs. At time of writing, the island is believed to be privately owned, though undeveloped, and camping is not permitted without permission. Please, no fires of any kind.

As you paddle north, you have the option of following Quadra Island or Read Island to Surge Narrows. Both routes offer a number of potential campsites including Village Bay and the beaches just north of Sheer Point. For people wanting to mix hiking with paddling, you may want to press on through Surge Narrows to Yeatman Bay. Remember: Surge Narrows is for *very* experienced kayakers only.

Yeatman Bay   While it is not especially picturesque, Yeatman Bay offers lots of campsites. Only .5 km (.3 mi.) north of Surge Narrows (Beazley Pass), it is also a great layover spot for kayakers coming or going through the rapids of the narrows. A time-worn trail starting at the head of the bay will take you on a very short forested walk to a secluded part of Main Lake. If you're just passing through and don't plan to stay overnight, try to leave enough time to hike up to the lake for a swim—it's well worth the time and effort. All the lakes found within the Discovery Islands become unbelievably warm in July and August. At the very top of the bay you'll find a small cold stream that always tastes great—even in the driest summer.

Keep in mind that Yeatman Bay is only marginally protected and is open to the summer westerlies that can blow down Okisollo Channel. Since there is little fetch, the bay rarely ever poses a problem for the kayaker, but any boat left on the beach is prey to a rising tide and battering waves.

Okisollo Channel   Continuing north you will enter upper Okisollo Channel. The water temperature here is noticeably colder—too cold for anything more than a quick swim or splash. You'll notice huge beds of kelp whereas farther south there were few, if any. Here the ocean floor is covered with spiny sea urchins. The Okisollo contains prolific numbers of harbour seals and Dalls porpoises, not to mention huge flocks of gulls, especially Bonaparte's gulls, that congregate by the thousands on the kelp beds of the tidal passages. Expect early morning fog, notably in the latter half of summer. It usually burns off by 10 AM.

Octopus Islands   Also to be found in this part of Okisollo Channel are the enchanting Octopus Islands. Most of the eight Octopus Islands are suitable for hauling out and camping on, with one exception: the large island right in the middle of the group, which is private and well marked. The smaller islands are actually more open and better suited for the kayaker's purpose. Once inside the island group, it should not take you long to locate a pleasant campsite but don't expect any sandy beaches.

It should also come as no surprise to find there is no water on these islands. During an average summer, however, the small streams in Waiatt Bay—in particular, the large one on the south shore as indicated on the chart—do have good water. If you are desperate, there are two other reliable sources, both 4 km (2.5 mi.) away: Yeatman Bay on Quadra Island and Elephant Bay on Maurelle Island.

Just north of the Octopus Islands lie the Upper and Lower Okisollo Rapids. Similar to Surge Narrows, these are not to be taken lightly. Anyone passing through should be experienced and have had a good look at the tide and current tables. There is talk of a portage between Waiatt Bay and Small Inlet, thus negating the need to pass through the rapids if heading north into Johnstone Strait; however, its status was uncertain at time of writing.

To continue your trip in the Discovery Islands, you will most likely want to pass through Hole in the Wall. This is also an area of extreme tidal activity, standing waves and whirlpools, so use caution. If you have the necessary skills, plan carefully—and don't let fear ruin the delightful thrill of being whisked between enormous rock cliffs to the sanctuary of Calm Channel. It is an experience not unlike river travel and gives your aching arms a brief respite. Not far away is a fantastic campsite just off North Rendezvous Island.

North Rendezvous Island While most of North Rendezvous Island is private, there is a 4-ha (10-a.) park at the very northern tip of the island that includes a small islet 50 m (165 ft.) farther north. A small grassy road runs up the interior of the island past several homesteads and cabins. There are a number of good campsites on the islet and a few more near the beach on North Rendezvous.

North Rendezvous has a wonderful spring that is dependable even in the driest summers. Although quite small, the water is clear and cold. You may have a little trouble finding it but don't give up: it is about 150 m (500 ft.) east of the island road in dense salal. You'll also find some small man-made pools 20 m (65 ft.) or so upstream from the beach.

If the site is full, you can try South Rendezvous where there are one or two old homesteads that are suitable for pitching a tent. Frances Bay, just west of Ramsay Arm, also has a couple of campsites and streams. There is plenty of room at both sites; the one at the entrance to Frances Bay is the most attractive. If these are not to your liking, you can try Von Donup Inlet on Cortes Island or the Penn Islands, just south of Read Island.

Von Donup Inlet Von Donup Inlet is extremely well protected and subsequently a favourite anchorage for boaters, which may turn you off at

Packing it in, packing it out. PETER McGEE

first. Pleasure craft or not, the inlet is beautiful and well worth checking out. Once inside Von Donup there are some attractive clearings, perfect kayak haul-outs and campsites. If you don't want to put up with the boaters, try your luck going up into the lagoon and camping where the larger vessels can't go. This is a tidal lagoon, and depending on the tide, you may have trouble getting through its rather small and turbulent entrance. At any rate, it is not considered dangerous.

Cork Lake   Farther up the west side of Van Donup Inlet is a bay that is extremely shallow and impassable by larger vessels. At the base of the Cork Lake Creek is an old Forest Service Recreation Site. While it needs a little work, the site still has room for a few tents. The remnants of the Cork Lake trail are visible for those who want to stretch their legs.

Aside from the creek at Cork Lake, fresh water is limited in Von Donup Inlet during the summer. At Robertson Bay, .5 km (.3 mi.) to the east of the inlet entrance, you will find good drinking water at a small, reliable stream. At the stream mouth there is a trail leading up to Robertson Lake, where you can enjoy a refreshing plunge into this very picturesque and usually warm body of water. Logging activity has left the near end of the

126

lake completely plugged up with logs, and you may have to walk a few hundred metres to find a good place to get in. Fortunately, Robertson Lake is now a protected area.

If you want to explore Desolation Sound, the region described in Chapter 7, you can attempt a portage across Cortes Island to Squirrel Cove. This is a fairly quick way to get across the island, and there are signs marking the trailhead at the southern end of Von Donup Inlet; the distance is about 1 km (.6 mi.) with very little gain in elevation. If you decide to do this, be sure to time your departure on a high tide, especially at the Squirrel Cove side where you can add an extra .5 km (.3 mi.) of carrying on a low tide.

Penn Islands   If you are heading back to Heriot Bay, exit Von Donup Inlet and paddle for the nice campsites among the Penn Islands. One such site is located in a small bay with a gravelly beach on the southeast corner of the most northerly island. The other good site is located .5 km (.3 mi.) from the first campsite almost due south on the extreme eastern point of the next island. The first campsite has the best beach for the kayaker's purpose, but each is beautiful. In late April or May the islands are host to dozens of varieties of wildflowers, some rather rare. Nearby are two seal haul-outs whose inhabitants will likely be your constant companions as you paddle through adjacent islands.

As can be expected of most smaller islands, there is no drinking water on these two sites. The closest reliable supply is the small stream at Robertson Bay. From the Penn Islands to Heriot Bay is about 14.5 km (9 mi.).

ADDITIONAL ROUTES

Heading north: You can pass through the Okisollo Rapids with extreme caution and continue north towards Johnstone Strait. For great camping, be sure to stop at these campsites, about a day's paddle apart: on Sonora Island tucked in behind Howe Island, in the grassy meadow at Camp Point and on the southern shore of Yorke Island.

Heading south: Paddling south through Discovery Passage and Seymour Narrows is not recommended due to the extreme currents and heavy shipping traffic. Your best bet is to cross to Cortes Island and work your way south along the shores of Texada Island or the mainland. Paddling towards Desolation Sound opens up a number of possibilities. See Chapter 7 for more information.

JOHNSTONE STRAIT

Symbols

Ⓛ Launch Site

▲ Campsite

Ⓦ Water

• Town

Sutlej Channel

Kingcome Inlet

Broughton Island

Simoom Sound

Fife Sound

Eden I.

Insect

Ⓦ Echo Bay Park

Bonwick I.

Gilford Island

Sedge Is.

Queen Charlotte Strait

5 NM   0   5 NM

Midsummer I.

Malcolm Island

Knight Inlet Village I.

Blackfish Sound

Swanson I.

Ralph Is.

Mamalilaculla

Compton I.

Mound I.

New Vancouver

Turnour I.

Cormorant I.

Weynton Passage

Ⓛ

Alert Bay

Weynton I.

Hanson I.

Blackney Passage

Harbledown I.

Broughton Strait

Port McNeill

Parson Lagoon

Ⓦ Ⓛ Telegraph Cove

Ⓛ

▲ Ⓦ Blinkhorn Peninsula

Growler Cove

West Cracroft I.

Ⓦ ▲ Pig Ranch

Ⓦ ▲ Kaikash Creek

Johnstone Strait

Robson Bight Ecological Reserve

19

VANCOUVER ISLAND

to Campbell River

Chapter Nine

Johnstone Strait

Fran Hunt-Jinnouchi, Marc Jinnouchi, Peter McGee and Tessa van Scheik

Each summer, pods of resident orcas and lone transients congregate in the waters of Johnstone Strait to feed on salmon, socialize and rub on the pebble beaches of Robson Bight. Similarly, each summer thousands of boaters, kayakers and whale watchers congregate to watch these magnificent mammals in the wild. As paddling experiences go, nothing rivals paddling with the orcas—an awesome event that mixes inspiration, exhilaration and even fear. The area, however, offers a lot more for the true explorer, and a journey into the protected waters north of Johnstone Strait will unleash a world of small bays, protected coves and ancient village sites. It is an area rich in history, wildlife and, above all, beauty.

BACKGROUND

In the early 1900s, Johnstone Strait thrived, full of coastal villages established in response to the booming logging and fishing industries. Apart from Telegraph Cove, however, little is left of these villages today. Sadly this also applies to many of the native sites in the area—the islands are dotted with Kwakwaka'wakw ruins, middens and the odd house but little else. One of the villages still visible is Mamalilaculla, a truly special place located on Village Island. The last major potlatch, held here in 1921 by Emma Bell and Dan Cranmer, was halted by the RCMP under the infamous anti-potlatch laws. The now dilapidated village holds signs of a once-stately village. There are remnants of large fluted house-posts and massive beams, totem poles, some fallen and some still standing. Nearby Telegraph Cove, a thriving tourist destination and the site of a new international resort, presents a very different picture.

Established in 1911, Telegraph Cove served as the terminus of a telegraph line to northern Vancouver Island built by the government. The small town became home to a saltery business, dry-salting salmon for the Japanese market, and then, in 1929, a tiny sawmill. Today an attractive boardwalk links more recent homes and structures with the old village, but the town's popularity is threatening to erode the quaint atmosphere. In the summer Telegraph Cove becomes a bustling sport-fishing community with an RV campground, tourist shops, whale-watching businesses and a new condo development rumoured to have a golf course in its plans. Nonetheless, Telegraph Cove is still a highlight to any visit to Johnstone Strait and continues to be the launching spot for almost every kayaker heading into the area. (There are plans to offer kayak facilities and rentals here; contact the B.C. Marine Trail Association for details.)

Then, of course, there are the whales. During the summer months, pods from up and down the Pacific Coast congregate in the strait to rub on the beaches of Robson Bight and feed on the salmon of the Inside Passage. Two different forms of orcas swim in these waters—residents and transients. They never associate with each other and seem to specialize in different prey—fish for residents and mammals for transients. The social structures of the two also differ, and it has been determined that each resident pod has a unique vocal dialect. Pods with similar dialects form a clan and are most likely to have descended from a common ancestral group. The only other mammals known to have dialects are humans.

There were plans in the early 1980s to turn Robson Bight into a log-booming area, which would have greatly threatened this important whale habitat. Fortunately, lobbying efforts by researchers and conservationists led to the 1982 creation of the Robson Bight (Michael Biggs) Ecological Reserve for whales. Research stations were set up in the islands nearby, producing an enormous amount of information on the four major activities of the whales: foraging, resting, socializing and travelling. The ecological reserve is closed to recreational traffic, and landing in the area is prohibited; however, orcas are easy to view in the surrounding waters throughout June, July, August and September.

GETTING THERE

By land: Coming from the south along Highway 19 (the Island Highway), the turnoff to Telegraph Cove is 345 km (216 mi.) from Nanaimo and is clearly marked. Drive down the paved road until a T-junction. Turn left onto the gravel road and follow the signs to Telegraph Cove, about a 20-minute drive. Those looking for a little more peace and quiet may prefer to launch from the Alder Bay campsite, 2.4 km (1.5 mi.) north of Telegraph Cove. The turnoff is on your left, 10 minutes after leaving the highway, and is well marked.

By water and air: If you want to charter a boat or plane into the region, check out the possibilities in Port McNeill. Although Telegraph Cove has a number of small fishing boats available, you will get a better deal in a less touristy location. For people who would like to avoid Telegraph Cove and Johnstone Strait altogether it is possible to launch from Simoom Sound or Echo Bay. Check with local plane and boat operators in Port McNeill to arrange a charter.

WEATHER AND HAZARDS

The Johnstone Strait Oceanic Ecosection is a much colder, foggier and rainier place than its Georgia Basin counterpart (see Chapter 8) and will give you a feel for the rest of the northern B.C. coast. Nonetheless, summer is usually quite pleasant with warm, sunny days and cool nights. The prevailing winds during summer months are westerly, and it is very important that you take this into account: these winds pick up almost every afternoon, often reaching gale force conditions. The strait also has significant tidal currents that cause hazardous paddling conditions, particularly when an ebb tide mixes with a late afternoon westerly.

Generally Johnstone Strait has a current of 1–2 knots, but some areas have significant currents of 2–3 knots during full flow. An example of this is the northern shore of Johnstone Strait from Hanson Island across to Boat Bay on West Cracroft Island. Blackney and Weynton Passages are even more extreme and are not to be taken lightly: they have very strong currents on big tides and moderate currents on smaller tides. Experienced kayakers can use the ebb and flood to help them, but most paddlers should pass through these areas at slack.

When travelling in Blackfish Sound, you will need the current tables for Weyton Passage, Johnstone Strait and Seymour Narrows. The slack current for Blackney Passage, located between the east side of Hanson Island and West Cracroft Island, is at a different time than Weyton Passage on the west side of Hanson Island. The slack and maximum currents for Weyton Passage are calculated by reading the Weyton Passage current table.

However, figuring out Blackney Passage is more of a challenge. The turn here is 70 minutes before Seymour Narrows. For example, if the turn at Seymour Narrows is at 12 noon during the summer, you would add 60 minutes for daylight savings and then subtract 70 minutes; slack would be at 11:50 AM. However, the turn at Blackney Passage is often 15–45 minutes early (and almost never late). To allow for this local variance, you may wish to attempt your crossing 30 minutes before the official turn.

Calculating the maximum current is done by reading the Johnstone Strait Central current table; there is no variation on maximum flow and time between Johnstone Strait Central and Blackney Passage. If you travel at slack current, you will avoid the dangerous standing waves and whirlpools that form at Blackney Passage and Weyton Passage.

Marine traffic is another hazard as virtually every ship heading north is funnelled through this 3.2-km (2-mi.) wide area. Watch for boat wakes and avoid crossing in the fog. Remember, cruise ships move quickly and have no way of detecting kayaks by radar.

Blackney Passage is an area of high shipping traffic. It is also a blind corner. On several occasions kayaking parties have been split by a large ship while crossing Johnstone Strait from Vancouver Island to West Cracroft point and while crossing Blackfish Sound. Many of the commercial sea kayak guides in the area can be called on to help or give advice on crossings in this region.

Finally, there are numerous black bears on all but the smallest islands, so you should take the appropriate measures to bear-proof your camp.

SPECIAL CONSIDERATIONS

The effects kayakers and other boaters have on orcas has yet to be fully understood. Nonetheless, there are a number of guidelines you should adhere to:

- Never enter the Robson Bight (Michael Biggs) Ecological Reserve.
- Paddle no closer than 100 m (330 ft.) to whales.
- Approach whales from the side, not from the front or rear. Approach and depart slowly. Avoid disturbing a "line" of resting whales. Resting whales are typically grouped tightly together, travel slowly and dive synchronously every 4–5 minutes. Resting episodes usually last 2–3 hours.
- Try to be conscious of the effect of your actions on whales, and do not engage in any activity that will disturb or interfere with them. Under sec-

Bull orca heads south into Robson Bight. PETER McGEE

tion 71(A)(2) of the federal fisheries regulation it is illegal "to disturb or molest orcas." Although orcas can travel over 45 km/hr (28 mph), and easily escape a kayak, your presence can still affect feeding or socializing activities.

· Limit the time spent with any group of whales to no more that 30 minutes.

Telegraph Cove also overlooks the traditional home of many Kwakwaka'-wakw (Kwakiutl) tribes including the Mamaleleqala, the Matlipi and the Tlowitsis. These tribes have a tradition of welcoming respectful visitors but also need to protect their lands and resources in light of the growing numbers of paddlers. Please check with the appropriate band offices prior to your trip to ensure your paddling journey will not upset this balance. A few sites listed in this chapter are midden sites; while currently open for camping, they are susceptible to closures in the future. Please respect any future management changes of these areas. Call the B.C. Marine Trail Association or the appropriate bands for the most recent information.

Trip 24 Johnstone Strait

Skill: Intermediate to advanced

Time: 3–14 days

Hazards: Winds, currents and traffic

Access: Telegraph Cove

Charts: 3515   Knight Inlet   1:80,000

3545   Johnstone Strait, Port Neville to Robson Bight   1:40,000

3546   Broughton Strait   1:40,000

3547   Queen Charlotte Strait, Eastern Portion   1:40,000

Tide Book: Vol. 6

A day trip from Telegraph Cove is possible but not recommended: you won't get a feel for the area, and your chances of seeing orcas will be small. If you have a couple of nights to spend in the area, consider paddling down to Kaikash Creek and exploring the south side of the strait and the waters outside the Robson Bight (Michael Biggs) Ecological Reserve. If you are able to spend several nights in the area, it is worth crossing the strait and exploring Harbledown Island, Village Island and Blackfish Sound; this trip is described below. Regardless of the route you choose, be prepared to sit out bad weather and rough sea conditions. Never paddle in conditions above your ability simply to keep to a schedule.

Launching

Telegraph Cove is by far the most popular launching site for Johnstone Strait. Fees for launching are $5.75 per person, payable at the Telegraph Cove store. Since Telegraph Cove has had problems with kayakers avoiding payment, please be sure to pay or we may all loose our launching privileges. Parking is $5 per day, $7 overnight. Payment is made either at the ticket machine in the parking lot or in the store. You can use a Visa or debit card. The store sells fishing licences, lures and charts of the area. The Bauza Bite Café, located inside the store, has a small grill open for breakfast, lunch and dinners. It is open from 6 AM to 9 PM from July to September.

The boat ramp at Telegraph Cove is a busy place. There are commercial kayak groups, private kayakers and sport-fishing boats all wanting to put in and take out here. Make sure not to occupy the ramp longer than necessary. Kayakers should use the grassy area or gravel above the ramp to load kayaks, then move onto the ramp and launch.

Alder Bay has an easy launch site and a $5 launching fee and parking. Unfortunately, the paddle between Alder Bay and Telegraph Cove is a tedious 1.5 hours of log booms and unspectacular scenery. If you have time, it is also possible to launch from a few different locations in the town of Port McNeill, a full day's paddle north of Telegraph Cove.

Sites

Soon after leaving Telegraph Cove you will encounter the currents of Johnstone Strait at the head of Bauza Cove. In this part of the coast, ebb tides flow north and flood tides flow south as the ocean wraps around the north end of Vancouver Island. Bauza Cove was once a nice picnic spot but is now part of the ongoing development in the area.

Blinkhorn Peninsula   Within an hour you will reach Blinkhorn Peninsula. For reference, there is a light on the eastern side of the small island just off the point. Paddle around the island, or across the spit if the tide is high enough, and land on the east-facing beach. Blinkhorn is not the most attractive site in the area but it is large, has a year-round water source and some older buildings to explore.

Kaikash Creek   Farther south is Kaikash Creek, the most popular site on Johnstone Strait. An enormous site, Kaikash has room for 30 or so tents and is quite often near capacity. Due to pressure from groups such as the B.C. Marine Trail Association, the Ministry of Forests is installing a composting toilet in 1998 to help with the heavy use. Kaikash might also become the terminus of a land-based whale-watching trail that begins in Telegraph Cove, so land and sea travellers may be sharing this site in the years to come. The creek is large, providing year-round water that needs to be treated.

Between Blinkhorn and Kaikash are a number of small pebble beaches that can take a few tents; the upland areas tend to be overgrown. One site a mile or so west of Kaikash proper, known locally as Little Kaikash, is used heavily by commercial groups so don't be surprised to find it quite crowded. There are a few camping opportunities south of Kaikash, again small pebble beaches, but paddlers are reminded to keep a good distance from the ecological reserve.

Pig Ranch and Growler Cove   For people wanting to explore a little more, head across the strait to the west end of West Cracroft Island and a camping area known locally as Pig Ranch. (As discussed in Weather and Hazards, use caution crossing the strait.) This is a great spot to watch for whales and is occasionally used by research teams. Camping is best on the point, nearby or even on the old tent pads. Some of the adjacent small bays have great landings but a lot of salal. If you have time, venturing up Eagle Bluff will give you a spectacular view of the strait. There is a small creek in the northern bay. If camping is limited, try the site in Growler Cove one inlet over. Growler Cove is quite sheltered but much of the area has been logged, allowing winds to funnel over the end of the inlet. For those looking to continue south, camping is possible at nearby Boat Bay though the shore is a little rugged.

Venturing north of the strait lessens your chances of encountering whales but gives you a break from boat traffic. This area has some great inlets, waterways and cultural sites. Heading north from Growler Cove, you can paddle around the western end of Harbledown Island, across Parson Bay and through the numerous islands and islets that guard Knight Inlet.

Village Island   For many, the primary reason for venturing into these waters is to visit the Kwakwaka'wakw village site of Mamalilaculla. Located at the western end of Village Island, the remnants of this significant village are definitely worth exploring. Permission is absolutely required before visiting Mamalilaculla and can be obtained from the Mamaleleqala Que'Qwa'Sot'Enox Band in Campbell River for a $7.50 fee/donation per person ($5 per person for groups of six or more). If the cultural riches of Village Island don't interest all members of your group, there are lots of berries and a huge, fat black bear to keep them occupied.

Mound Island   Since camping is not allowed anywhere on Village Island, you will probably want to hole up in a place nearby. The islets just off Ralph Island have room for a few tents, though your best bet is the midden site at the western end of Mound Island. This is one of the most beautiful sites in the area and is heavily used in the summer. It is well protected from the wind and has a large grassy area that can accommodate upwards of 10 tents. Although not an officially designated Indian Reserve, evidence of past use is obvious and it is best to get permission to use this site from the band office (see above). Since this site is a midden, be extremely careful

Mamalilaculla on Village Island. PETER McGEE

and practise zero impact camping. If this does not occur, a closure of the site may result. There is no water onsite. If you need an overflow area, check the small island immediately off the midden site or Dead Point on Harbledown Island a few hundred metres due west.

Harbledown and Compton Islands Dead Point was once used by the Kwakwaka'wkw as a winter village and is also worth exploring. In 1914 there were at least 10 houses standing; in later years the village moved to the west side of the point. Today it consists of a pier and a couple of houses and is known as New Vancouver. Camping can be found in the little bay just south of New Vancouver. Before you set up camp, ask permission from the villagers and, if possible, make a small donation to the community. If you're lucky, they will also supply you with fresh spring water (the stream provides an irregular water supply).

Nearby Compton Island is an Indian Reserve that can be used for camping if permission is granted and a fee is paid. Again, write to the band office in Campbell River prior to visiting the area. The fee for camping is $7.50 per person per night ($5 per person per night for groups of six or more). Compton Island is often used by large commercial groups.

If you're looking for something a little different, a paddle into Parson Lagoon won't disappoint. This is not the typical kayaker's site—it has an extremely rugged landing and a long haul at low tide—but the surrounding forest and lagoon provide an incredibly serene setting. Your best bet is to approach from the north, in Parson Bay, and head for the pass between Parson and Harbledown Islands. Camping can be found on the Harbledown side but be warned: there are no developed campsites or water, and the landing is not for everyone.

Hanson Island   For paddlers with little time left, you can head back to Telegraph Cove the way you came or work your way west to Hanson Island. The northern side of Hanson is full of little coves, streams and pretty good campsites for small groups. Keep your eyes peeled for the orca research stations as well as beaches lined with cottonwoods, a sure sign of an old homestead. Double Bay, though it may look tempting on the chart, is home to a fish farm and various amenities for the yachting crowd. However, tucked in behind Weynton Island at the western tip of Hanson is a small site if needed. The currents here can run up to 5.5 knots, causing some steep waves when opposing the wind—best avoided by inexperienced paddlers. Commercial groups use this site so expect company.

Broughton Archipelago   If you are not ready to head home, consider taking a trip into the Broughton Archipelago and its maze of intricate islands and waterways. Camping can be difficult for large groups but don't let that deter you: this is some of the nicest paddling B.C. has to offer. Highlights include the Sedge Islands to the west of Bonwick Island and the massive camping area on the southern tip of Insect Island. Owl Island and the Echo Bay Provincial Park on Gilford Island provide additional campsites, though the park may be too developed for some. There is a large grass field to camp on in Echo Bay as well as a dock, water supply and store at the adjacent Echo Bay Resort.

ADDITIONAL ROUTES

Heading north: From the Broughton Archipelago, you will enter the exposed waters of Queen Charlotte Strait. Once again, camping spots for more than one or two tents are sparse. For larger groups, check out Robinson Island near Blunden Harbour, Shelter Bay just off Richards Channel and Burnett Bay south of Cape Caution.

If you are heading towards Port Hardy from Telegraph Cove, there are a number of great campsites in the islands just off Fort Rupert. For those venturing north of Port Hardy, some of the most beautiful spots on the coast can be found on the islands of Nigei and Balaklava. Contact the B.C. Marine Trail Association for more information.

Heading south: Down Johnstone Strait provides some surprisingly good camping. Just south of the ecological reserve (make sure you are well south of the sign marking the ER) is a pebble beach at the mouth of a creek with some camping above the high tide line. On the north side of the strait are great sites at the Broken Islands and, farther along, Yorke Island. From here you begin to venture into the territory discussed in Chapter 8, the Discovery Islands.

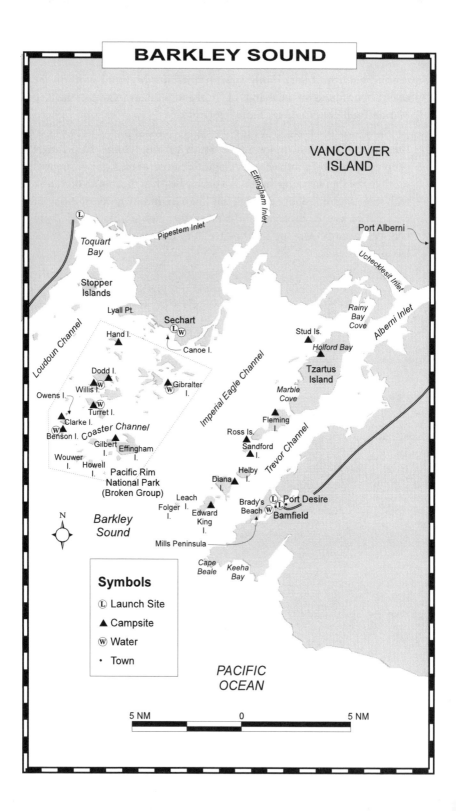

BARKLEY SOUND

VANCOUVER
ISLAND

Port Alberni

Effingham Inlet

Uchucklesit Inlet

Pipestem Inlet

Toquart Bay

Stopper Islands

Loudoun Channel

Lyall Pt.

Sechart

Hand I.

Canoe I.

Dodd I.

Willis I.

Owens I.

Turret I.

Clarke I.

Benson I.

Coaster Channel

Gilbert I.

Effingham I.

Wouwer I.

Howell I.

Pacific Rim
National Park
(Broken Group)

Leach I.

Folger I.

Edward King I.

Mills Peninsula

Barkley Sound

N

Imperial Eagle Channel

Gibralter I.

Rainy Bay Cove

Alberni Inlet

Stud Is.

Holford Bay

Tzartus Island

Marble Cove

Fleming I.

Ross Is.

Sandford I.

Helby I.

Diana I.

Brady's Beach

Port Desire

Bamfield

Trevor Channel

Cape Beale

Keeha Bay

Symbols

- Ⓛ Launch Site
- ▲ Campsite
- Ⓦ Water
- • Town

PACIFIC OCEAN

5 NM   0   5 NM

Chapter Ten

Barkley Sound

Liz Hicks, Edwin Hubert and
Bill McIntyre

The pounding surf and relentless swells of Vancouver Island's west coast breed fear in the minds of many kayakers. Yet within Barkley Sound lie two clusters of islands that tame the ruggedness of the open ocean: the Broken Group and the Deer Group. These are places where advanced paddlers can test their skills among outer islands, sea arches and caves, and where beginners and families can discover the joys of ocean kayaking while drifting through a maze of protected coves and passages. Barkley Sound encompasses all that is special about the West Coast and lets everyone enjoy its treasures.

BACKGROUND

Barkley Sound is the traditional home of the Nuu-chah-nulth people. For thousands of years, the Nuu-chah-nulth led a semi-nomadic existence, living part of the year in the protected islands and bays of the sound and part of the year on the outer islands and exposed shores, closer to the Pacific. *Nuu-chah-nulth* can be loosely translated as "all along the mountains." The name refers not only to the natives of Barkley Sound but to all the bands living alongside the mountains on Vancouver Island's west coast, from Cape Cook to the Jordan River.

Although explored and named in 1787 by Capt. Charles William Barkley of the British trading ship *Imperial Eagle,* European settlement in the Barkley Sound area did not occur until the 1850s. As the European population and exploration of the land and marine resources expanded, disease and government intervention forced native peoples to abandon their traditional way of life and relocate in permanent villages near stores and mills. Indian Reserves and the tragedies of missions and residential schools followed. Today, the Nuu-chah-nulth reserves of the Broken Group are limited to Effingham, Nettle and Keith Islands, but the more than one hundred culturally significant sites scattered throughout the islands remind us of a more prosperous time when close to 10,000 native people lived here. As always, please treat all archeological sites with proper respect and avoid trespassing on Indian Reserves.

In 1970, close to 50 000 ha (123,500 a.) of land and ocean on the west coast of Vancouver Island were put into the Pacific Rim National Park Reserve, including the Broken Group Islands, Long Beach and the West Coast Trail. The Broken Group Islands Unit consists of about one hundred islands and islets between Loudoun Channel to the west and Imperial Eagle Channel to the east, encompassing an area of 10 607 ha (26,200 a.) of which only 1350 ha (3335 a.) are land.

Pacific Rim is currently classified as a national park reserve due to the comprehensive claim of the Nuu-chah-nulth Tribal Council. The federal government accepted the claim for negotiation in June 1983, and the establishment of a full-fledged national park is subject to the outcome of these negotiations. In the interim, the National Parks Act, and all the rules and regulations associated with it, apply to the Broken Group.

To the east of the Broken Group are the Deer Group Islands, the smaller chain of islands dividing Imperial Eagle Channel from Trevor Channel. Although not within the Pacific Rim National Park Reserve, these remote islands offer an incredible diversity of paddling options and, best of all, are easily accessed from the quaint coastal community of Bamfield.

Romantically known as "the Venice of Vancouver Island," Bamfield is a village of approximately 400 people. Bamfield Inlet splits the village into east and west sides, with no road access to the west side. The village is known for its famous boardwalk along the harbour, small art galleries and shops where you can sit and watch the boats go by. The Bamfield Marine Station on the east side was previously the site of the historic Bamfield Cable Station and is known worldwide for its contribution to marine biology and education. The Bamfield Coast Guard and Rescue Training Station also contributes to the unique flavour of the village.

Truly the jewel of the west coast of Vancouver Island, this little fishing village is still magical, wild and relatively untouched—the perfect jumping-off point for paddlers headed for the Deer Group Islands.

GETTING THERE

The Broken Group

By land and water: For most paddlers, the easiest way to get to the Broken Group is by freighter from Port Alberni on Vancouver Island. Both the MV *Lady Rose* and MV *Frances Barkley* travel to Sechart, a site outside the Broken Group Islands about 1 km (.6 mi.) north of Gibraltar Island. A former whaling station, Sechart is now used as a land base by Alberni Marine Transport Ltd.; phone them for schedules and reservations. Reservations are strongly advised during July and August.

To reach Port Alberni from the mainland, catch the ferry to Nanaimo from either Horseshoe Bay or Tsawwassen. From Nanaimo, head north along Highway 19 (the Island Highway) towards Qualicum Beach. Exit at the Qualicum Beach/Port Alberni turnoff and follow the signs for Highway 4 to Port Alberni.

If you are approaching from Seattle, you can also catch the ferry from Seattle to Victoria, then drive north 2 hours to Nanaimo. From Nanaimo, follow the directions above.

Island Coach out of Nanaimo offers bus service to Port Alberni.

For experienced paddlers, the islands can be reached by launching from Toquart Bay and crossing Loudoun Channel to Hand Island, a distance of 8 km (5 mi.). A logging road connects Toquart Bay to Highway 4. From Port Alberni follow Highway 4 west for 88 km (55 mi.). Look for the gravel turnoff to your left—you will have just come down a steep hill, and Kennedy Lake will be on your right. (The turnoff is about 12 km (7.5 mi.) before the junction of Highway 4 and the Tofino-Ucluelet highway.) Follow the logging road to the Forest Service Recreation Site and boat launch at Toquart Bay. It is a large site that fills up with RVs and power boaters during the summer months. Be sure to lock your vehicle. If weather and time permit, take to the water and make the passage to the Broken Group—the camping on the islands is far superior.

The Deer Group

By land: In earlier years, Bamfield could only be accessed by water via the Port Alberni Inlet or by the dangerous, exposed "Graveyard of the Pacific" route from Victoria. The famous "West Coast Life-Saving Trail" starts 5 km (3 mi.) south of Bamfield at Pachena Bay. Even today, accessing

The sea arches of Marble Cove on Tzartus Island, the Deer Group. PETER McGEE

the town from logging roads and waterways is definitely part of the challenge of these expeditions.

By vehicle, you can reach Bamfield by either the Lake Cowichan route or the Port Alberni route. It is a 3-hour drive from Nanaimo to Bamfield via Port Alberni, with 80 km (50 mi.) of gravel logging road. It is a 4-hour drive from Victoria to Bamfield via Cowichan Lake, with 90 km (56 mi.) of logging road after Youbou or Honeymoon Bay; you can use either side of the lake. The logging roads are fairly good, but they are very active, rough and often dusty. Two spare tires are recommended; before leaving, check that your car jack works and your wheel nuts can be loosened. If you can

144

make the journey in the evening or on a Sunday, after the logging crews are off, chances are you will have a more relaxing drive. Forestry maps are helpful though there are directional signs on the roads. Always drive with your headlights on.

There are two bus services available to Bamfield: Western Bus Lines, which travels between Port Alberni and Bamfield, and the West Coast Trail Express, which travels between Victoria and Bamfield. These bus services run during the summer only, and you need to make a reservation.

By water: Alberni Marine Transport offers day trips aboard the famous MV *Lady Rose* into Bamfield on a summer schedule. The vessel, one of the favourite means of transportation for tourists, transports kayaks and freight into Bamfield, Ucluelet and the Broken Group Islands. They also rent kayaks and equipment. The Bamfield Express Water Taxi will make special passenger trips from Port Alberni to Bamfield or the Deer Group on request.

By air: There is a small, privately owned airstrip in Bamfield. There is no scheduled air service, but charters can be arranged from any major town, by land or float planes.

WEATHER AND HAZARDS

From July to September, prevailing high pressure systems in Barkley Sound create warmer air temperatures with westerly winds, building typically in the late morning and subsiding overnight. Be prepared, however, as storm conditions can occur unexpectedly. Low pressure systems, dominated by strong southeast winds and heavy rain, can produce dangerous seas and extreme exposure conditions along the southeast shores of the islands. Storms can occur at any time of year but are more common from October through June.

Fog is also a serious concern. Always travel with a compass as fog banks can move in with alarming speed, even in the absence of wind. Paddlers are advised to avoid surge channels, sea caves and submerged rocks.

Sea lions are present in both the Broken Group and the Deer Group, especially off Wouwer, Howell and Folger Islands. While these animals are not usually aggressive, they are territorial and it is best to keep your distance. If the smell and pounding surf that surround their haul-outs haven't already alerted you to their presence, 900 kg (2000 lb.) of growling blubber probably will.

Near Bamfield, the Cape Beale Headlands are very hazardous. Strong tidal currents from Barkley Sound create very large and steep waves to the point of breaking. Combined with excessive rebounding waves from boomers, exposed rocks and a strong rip tide, these currents make this one of the most hazardous spots on the west coast of Vancouver Island. Westerly winds on an ebb tide can also cause steep waves in Trevor Channel. In the summer, winds usually build to moderate during the late morning and often die down in the evening, making the crossing of Trevor Channel best in the early morning or evening.

Paddling across Imperial Eagle Channel to the Broken Group from Bamfield via the Deer Group Islands is not recommended for any skill level. Similarly, crossing Loudoun Channel from Ucluelet is dangerous and not recommended for anyone but the most experienced paddler.

Parks Canada would like to remind paddlers in the Broken Group that they are expected to be self-sufficient and responsible for their personal safety. Should you require emergency response, such as search and rescue, and are found to be negligent, you could be held financially responsible.

SPECIAL CONSIDERATIONS

Park wardens patrol the Broken Group Islands and are based at the floating warden station located at Nettle Island, due north of the Gibraltar Island campsite. To preserve the delicate wilderness character of the Broken Group Islands, Parks Canada has various rules and guidelines.

- The maximum stay in the Broken Group is 14 days; maximum stay at any one campsite is 4 days. Maximum group size allowed in the Broken Group is 10 persons. This applies to private, commercial and non-profit groups alike.
- All island users and visitors must camp in the designated campsites located on Hand, Turret, Gibraltar, Willis, Dodd, Clarke, Benson and Gilbert Islands. Camping fees are $5/person a night from May 1 to September 30. Fees are collected at the campsites and a Use Permit issued. Fees are payable in cash or by credit card.
- Campfires are allowed only on beaches and only below the high tide line; driftwood may be used but collecting wood from forested areas is not permitted.
- You must pack out all items you bring to the islands, including garbage.
- Limit your travel in and around sea caves due to the nesting of cormorants and other seabirds.

To further protect the fragile ecosystems of the Broken Group, Parks Canada is considering a quota and reservation system. For more information, contact the Park Superintendent at Pacific Rim National Park Reserve.

Trip 25 The Broken Group

Skill:	Beginner to advanced
Time:	3–7 days
Hazards:	Outer coast, fog and winds
Access:	Sechart (MV *Lady Rose* or *Frances Barkley*)/Toquart Bay
Charts:	3670 Broken Group 1:20,000
	3671 Barkley Sound 1:40,000
Tide Book:	Vol. 6

There are eight official campsites in the Broken Group, but the islands are so close together it is unlikely you will use them all on any one trip. Setting up a base camp and exploring for a few days is a popular option. Experienced paddlers will undoubtedly want to visit the outer islands, and staying at Gilbert, Clarke, Benson and Turret Islands will give you easy access to the open ocean. For beginner paddlers or those with children, the campsites on Hand, Willis, Dodd and Gibraltar Islands make great base camps for exploring some of the more sheltered waterways. Although Parks Canada has marked a number of water sources on the marine chart for the area, most of them are unreliable in the summer. Bring your own supply and treat any water you find. For more information on the Broken Group, see the *Official Guide to Pacific Rim National Park Reserve*. Much of the following information is used with permission of Parks Canada and was extracted from this guide.

Launching

Most paddlers will approach the Broken Group via the MV *Lady Rose* or MV *Frances Barkley* from Port Alberni. You will be dropped off at Sechart Lodge, located just behind Canoe Island, a mile or so from the northern park boundary. Kayak rentals and lodging are available at Sechart, though food and additional supplies weren't being sold at time of writing.

If you launch from Toquart Bay, you will need to cross Loudoun

Channel, a body of water that is open to the Pacific and subject to strong winds and ocean swells. Once again, this access is not recommended for inexperienced paddlers or those travelling with children. As you cross, it is worthwhile to use the Stopper Islands and the light on Lyall Point to help find you bearings. Your first stop in the park will likely be Hand Island.

Sites

Hand Island   The site at the north end of Hand Island is the largest of the designated campsites, accommodating up to 20 tents, and a favourite among paddlers for its shell and sand beaches and unobstructed views. Be sure to keep an eye out for native fish traps. These traps consist of a circular wall of stones, placed in the shallow bays, that acts as a corral at high tide, trapping fish when the tide recedes. Another item you might notice on Hand is the outhouse. These solar composting units, at many national park campsites throughout B.C., are particularly important to the Broken Group. Not only are they clean and efficient, which they should be at $20,000 a piece, they are raised above ground so as not to disturb the archeological record contained within the soil and middens.

Dodd and Willis Islands   Leaving Hand Island and heading south puts you in the natural harbour created by Dodd, Willis and Turtle Islands, one of the most sheltered spots in the Broken Group. Crossing Peacock Channel to reach the harbour should be done with care as strong westerlies can kick up in the afternoon. Once in the harbour, however, there is little to worry about, and examining the abundant sea life and intricate maze of islets nearby makes for a great afternoon. Bald eagles are common on Dodd Island so don't be surprised if there are more than a few pairs of eyes on you as you drift by. Campsites are located on Dodd and Willis. There is a good water source on Willis.

Turret Island   Thiepval Channel, named after a fisheries patrol boat that went aground here in 1930, is quite small, but its western end is exposed and paddlers should exercise caution when crossing. The most direct route from the campsite on Willis to the campsite on Turret is to work your way through the tiny islets off the western end of Trickett Island, as tides permit. It is here the paddler begins to feel some of the energy of the open ocean—both an intimidating and exhilarating experience. Heading back towards the southern side of Turret, you will soon see the campsite tucked in behind a small unnamed islet. Land on the south-facing beach and head into the giant sitka spruce forest to pick your site for the night.

Owens, Clarke and Benson Islands   From here on, the seas can get quite nasty, and continuing south should only be attempted by paddlers with experience. Owens, Clarke and Benson Islands sit just across from Turret Island and, though their eastern sides are normally sheltered, the western shores of all three are fully exposed to the pounding Pacific. Clarke has a stunning sand beach and campsite at its northern end; camping on Benson takes place in a large meadow, remnants of an orchard Capt. John Benson planted in 1893 when he built a hotel on the island. The hotel shut its doors in 1922. Benson is also the site of a blowhole near the water catchment station at the island's south end. It takes a bit of hiking to reach but is worth the effort.

Gilbert Island   The campsite at Gilbert Island lies across Coaster Channel, an area subject to Pacific swells and strong winds that should only be accessed by more experienced paddlers. Once across the channel, exploring the extremely rugged shores and watching the sea lions off Wouwer and Howell Islands will give you a taste of the wild Pacific in all its glory. Fittingly, the Nuu-chah-nulth name for nearby Dicebox Island is "a place you don't want to leave." Keep in mind that, some days, you actually *can't* leave due to fog, so be sure to allow yourself a little time for waiting it out. Due to the sensitive nature of Dicebox, please restrict your movements to the pocket beach.

Look for the beach at the southeastern end of Gilbert to find the campsite. The forest can seem quite dark yet is worth wandering through; many of the trees have been "culturally modified"—stripped of their bark by native peoples to make clothing, blankets, baskets, rope and even diapers. These culturally modified trees are distinguished by a bare patch on the side of an otherwise normal living cedar.

Gibraltar Island   Effingham Island, the largest of the islands, sits right next to Gilbert and is home to one of the Nuu-chah-nulth reserves. Meares Bluff, over 100-m (330-ft.) high with a large sea arch spanning the foreshore, is truly spectacular—the island's most prominent feature. Heading north from Effingham will take you to Wiebe and Dempster Islands and, finally, Gibraltar, the last campsite in the Broken Island circuit.

The eastern shores of all these islands are constantly pounded by the storm-driven waters of Imperial Eagle Channel, and previous paddling experience is a must. If you are looking for a less intense experience, the quiet lagoon between Jacques and Jarvis Islands is an excellent place for exploring marine life and a number of ancient fishtraps. Please do not land on the beaches on the south side of Nettle Island, as they are part of the Tsheshaht First Nations reserve. Gibraltar is a short jump to the launch site at Sechart Lodge, and a good 3–4-hour paddle to the launch site at Toquart Bay.

Trip 26 Bamfield and the Deer Group

Skill:	Intermediate to advanced
Time:	2–5 days
Hazards:	Outer coast, fog and winds
Access:	Bamfield
Charts:	3646 Plans Barkley Sound, Bamfield Inlet 1:12,000
	3671 Barkley Sound 1:40,000
Tide Book:	Vol. 6

The trips in the Bamfield area are numerous and range from a few hours in the inner harbour to a few days in the Deer Group. Although campsites in the Deer Group are generally quite small and will only accommodate a few tents, the views over Barkley Sound and the Pacific make them some of the best on the coast. The trip described below begins in Bamfield and covers most of the islands in the Deer Group. For paddlers looking for a shorter excursion, a couple of day trips around Bamfield are described at the end of the chapter. If you plan on visiting any Indian Reserves in the area, make sure you have received prior permission and a visitor's pass from the Huu-ay-aht (Ohiats) First Nation.

Launching

There are a few options for launching boats in and around Bamfield. The best spot is the boat ramp in Port Desire. To get there, turn right at the four-way stop when you first get into Bamfield and follow Grappler Road to the government wharf at Port Desire. Parking is on the side of the road. There is also a government wharf in east Bamfield but it doesn't have the convenience of a boat launch.

There is a summer information centre, store and campground when you arrive by road on the east side of the inlet. If you arrive by boat on the west side of Bamfield Inlet, information is available at the Coast Guard Station or the Bamfield General Store.

Sites

Day trips to the Deer Group are easy if wind and weather are steady, but it is best to leave yourself a few days. The crossing from Bamfield to the islands should be undertaken in the morning, with winds and tides taken into account. Crossing Trevor Channel to Helby Island usually takes about 30 minutes. Although Helby Island is private, you can land and stretch your legs at Self Point if necessary.

Diana Island   Much of Diana Island is an Indian Reserve, but camping is possible at the sand beach on the northern point. For people hoping to explore the island by foot, or wanting to land at the beaches near Kirby Point on the island's south end, you must have a pass from the Huu-ay-aht First Nation. Although you can usually find sheltered waters in Dodger Channel, Kirby Point and Voss Point are exposed and should only be attempted under the right conditions. From here, intermediate paddlers should start to head east (see Sandford Island, below). Those with more experience may want to include Folger and Leach Islands to the west in their trip.

Folger, Leach and Edward King Islands   It is among these islands that sea and land meet in full fury, carving and twisting the shore into beautifully bizarre shapes and providing an ideal environment for birds, seals and sea lions. Always use caution when approaching sea lions and keep a reasonable distance from their haul-outs and rookeries. This is the wild West Coast so be prepared for anything, especially fog.

The closest camping spot in the western end of the Deer Group is on the northeast corner of Edward King Island. The island was named for Capt. Edward Hammond King, who was accidentally killed here in 1861, unloading his rifle from a boat while on a deer hunting expedition. It is quite rugged, though beautiful, with few sheltered landings.

Sandford Island Heading back to Diana and Helby Islands will put you into calmer waters again, and you can continue your journey east by crossing over to Sandford Island from Helby. This crossing can also be rough, with Satellite Passage open to the ocean swell. Please do not land at Wizard Island; there are often breeding seabirds on this island and any disturbance can have a large impact on their success. For people looking to camp, head to the eastern shore of Sandford where there are a number of good campsites tucked above a small sandy beach. The nearby Ross Islets also have a few small sites; don't be surprised if you have company.

From the Ross Islets, paddle around the western corner of Fleming Island and into the large bay on the north side. Use caution: the southwest point of Fleming can be quite rough under certain conditions. There is a beach on the northwest side of the island that is suitable for camping, though it is quite a small area when the tide is high.

Tzartus Island The last of the major islands in the Deer Group to explore is Tzartus. Named from a native word for "place of the seasonal or intermittent waterfall" or "place where the water flows inside the beach," Tzartus has much to offer the paddler, including the absolutely stunning sea arches of Marble Cove and the intricate Chain Group of Islands off its northern shores. In and around Robbers Passage and Marble Cove are a number of floating cabins and the Canadian King Lodge, which leaves little in the way of campsites. This shouldn't deter you from extending your trip to include Tzartus, however, as the largest of the Stud Islets and Holford Bay each have room for a few tents.

From this point you can either retrace your strokes back to Bamfield or head directly across Trevor Channel to Vancouver Island and work your way west along the shores.

ADDITIONAL ROUTES

In and around Bamfield: For those less inclined to venture to the Deer Group but still looking for some paddling adventures, consider the following suggestions.

Mills Peninsula offers terrific day trips both in and right outside Bamfield Harbour. The inside waters of Bamfield and Grappler Inlets are calm in most weather and offer lots of little inlets and side coves; the estuaries at the heads of the inlets are a treasure of wildlife. Beyond the harbour, the peninsula has magnificent white sand beaches and rugged rock formations with numerous caves. The coast can be rough, with a constant swell—experienced paddlers only!—but it is spectacular. This paddle is best started in the morning because the wind from the open Pacific picks up towards the afternoon, and it is always exhilarating riding the swells home accompanied by a brisk westerly. Brady's Beach is the most famous beach along this southward route, with easy landing.

As you continue south, you will come to the Blow Hole, an impressive phenomenon at the right tide, spraying cascades of ocean up to 15 m (50 ft.) into the air, creating rainbows. Past the Blow Hole you will find incredible beaches, including First Beach, Second Beach and Keeshan. These three are on Indian Reserve 9, and visits to First and Second Beaches require a pass. Keeshan is off limits completely: it is one of the region's most sensitive historic village sites. The lookout here, with its commanding view of the entrance to Barkley Sound, is known as Execution Rock and is rich in native lore and history. The cliffs and caves are breathtaking and the waters very turbulent as ocean swells smash and reverberate off the rugged coast.

The last large beach before Cape Beale is Tapoltos. This is a most inviting crescent-shaped beach about 1 km- (.6 mi.-) long with a spectacular double sea arch at the southwest end. Landings are more often than not treacherous as the surf can be wicked. The Tapoltos Bay Hilton is a rough little shack at the south end of the beach. With its beachcomber treasures, rainbow graffiti and stunning view, this is a place to enjoy lunch and relax. From Tapoltos Beach, trails lead to Keeha Beach and the Cape Beale lighthouse.

To paddle beyond this point and around Cape Beale requires extreme caution and experience. There is a slip of an entrance into a magical cove just before reaching Cape Beale. The cove is used to bring in supplies by boat to the lighthouse, and there is a trail from the beach up to the lighthouse. You can paddle through the cove or portage your kayak across the mud at low tide and do the "shortcut"; this will bring you to the other side of Cape Beale, avoiding the reef and famous breakers. However, you will still find it tricky negotiating through the rocks and surf before reaching open ocean—experience is a must. From here you can paddle around into Keeha Bay, a spectacular 2-km (1.25-mi.) beach with wonderful caves at the west end. Floats in the middle of the beach mark the Keeha trail back to Bamfield.

Heading north or south from Barkley Sound: Neither direction is recommended. Both shorelines are exposed to the full fury of the Pacific and should only be attempted by paddlers very familiar with the open ocean.

CLAYOQUOT SOUND

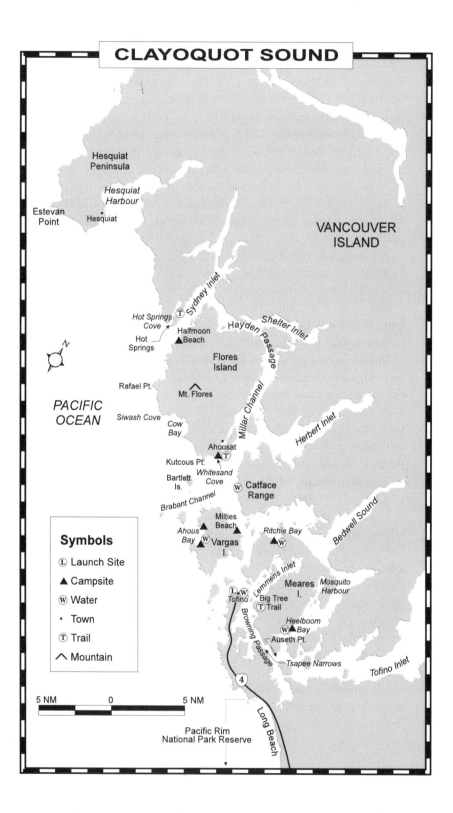

Hesquiat
Peninsula

*Hesquiat
Harbour*

Estevan
Point

· Hesquiat

VANCOUVER
ISLAND

Sydney Inlet

Ⓣ

*Hot Springs
Cove*

Hot
Springs

Halfmoon
▲Beach

Hayden Passage

Shelter Inlet

Flores
Island

Rafael Pt.

PACIFIC
OCEAN

⌃
Mt. Flores

Siwash Cove

Millar Channel

Herbert Inlet

*Cow
Bay*

· Ahousat
▲Ⓣ

Kutcous Pt.

Bartlett
Is.

*Whitesand
Cove*

ⓦ Catface
Range

Brabant Channel

Bedwell Sound

Milties
Beach
▲

*Ahous
Bay*
▲
ⓦ Vargas
I.

Ritchie Bay

▲ⓦ

Symbols

Ⓛ Launch Site

▲ Campsite

ⓦ Water

· Town

Ⓣ Trail

⌃ Mountain

Lemmens Inlet

Meares
I.

*Mosquito
Harbour*

Ⓛ.ⓦ
Tofino

Big Tree
Ⓣ Trail

Heelboom
ⓦ▲*Bay*

Auseth Pt.

Browning Passage

Tsapee Narrows

Tofino Inlet

4

5 NM   0   5 NM

Pacific Rim
National Park Reserve

Long Beach

N

Chapter Eleven

Clayoquot Sound

Bonny Glambeck and Dan Lewis

Home to ancient rainforests and white sand beaches, Clayoquot Sound is a gem on the rugged West Coast. Once known only for its stunning scenery, hot springs and whales, the area was flung into the international spotlight during the infamous summer of 1993. Over 12,000 people attended the Clayoquot Sound Peace Camp that summer to protest the provincial government's decision to open up 62 per cent of the sound to clearcut logging. It was the largest civil disobedience action in Canadian history and led to the arrest of 932 people. Although the future of the area is still uncertain, the summer of 1993 highlighted a very clear and important message supported by people around the world: The temperate rainforests of Clayoquot Sound must be cared for differently in the future.

BACKGROUND

Located halfway up the west coast of Vancouver Island, Clayoquot Sound encompasses 262 000 ha (647,140 a.) between Tofino and the Hesquiat Peninsula. Its 10 major river systems support the largest lowland temperate rainforest remaining on Earth.

Clayoquot Sound is also the traditional home and unceded territory of three Nuu-chah-nulth First Nations: the Hesquiaht, Ahousaht and Tla-o-qui-aht peoples. Clayoquot (pronounced Klak-wit) is an anglicization of the native term *tla-o-qui-aht* (pronounced tla-oo-quee-at), meaning different or changing. The provincial and federal governments have recognized the ancestral claim of the Nuu-chah-nulth Tribal Council and are now in the process of negotiating a treaty. In 1997, the local native population was approximately 800, largely concentrated in the village sites of

Opitsaht on Meares Island, Hot Springs Cove north of Flores Island and Ahousat on Flores. The majority of the 1,100 non-native residents in Clayoquot Sound live in Tofino.

First incorporated as a village municipality in 1932, the town of Tofino has served as the gateway to Clayoquot Sound since the lifeboat station was established in 1913. Named after Vincente Tofino, a Spanish rear-admiral and prominent astronomer, Tofino has undergone some dramatic changes over the last decade, transforming itself from a quiet coastal community to a booming tourist destination. This change comes as no surprise, however, as Tofino sits just north of Long Beach and the Pacific Rim National Park Reserve, an area that receives over 450,000 visitors annually, about 80 per cent of those between May and October.

GETTING THERE

By land: Tofino is approximately 250 km (155 mi.) from Nanaimo at the end of Highway 4 (the Pacific Rim Highway). Coming from the mainland, catch the ferry to Nanaimo from either Horseshoe Bay or Tsawwassen. Once in Nanaimo, head north along Highway 19 (the Island Highway) towards Qualicum Beach. Exit at the Qualicum Beach/Port Alberni turnoff and take Highway 4 to Port Alberni. Follow the signs to Tofino as you head west, through the town of Port Alberni and beyond. When you run out of road, you've reached Tofino. Total driving time from Nanaimo is roughly 3 hours though there are some sights along the way (such as the MacMillan Provincial Park/Cathedral Grove) and a few curves in the road that may slow you down a bit. Island Coach out of Nanaimo offers bus service to Tofino.

If you are approaching from Seattle, you can also catch the ferry directly from Seattle to Victoria, then drive north for 2 hours to Nanaimo along Highway 19. From Nanaimo, follow the directions above. If you are approaching from Port Hardy, head south on Highway 19 until you reach the turnoff at Qualicum Beach for Port Alberni, and follow the directions above.

By air: North Vancouver Air, based at the ESSO Avitat Terminal in Richmond, flies daily to Tofino, landing at the Tofino Golf Course. Flight time is approximately 1 hour.

WEATHER AND HAZARDS

Winds typically blow northwest or west in the summer in this region, particularly on sunny days. Westerly winds of 20–30 knots are common on

Ahous Bay on Vargas Island. PETER McGEE

most fair-weather afternoons, quickly blowing fog away but also kicking up a chop. Do not be caught midway on an exposed crossing by this predictable phenomenon. Another potential hazard is the presence of fog during July and August. While this fog generally lifts by the early afternoon, do not count on it clearing—and avoid crossings while it persists. On shore, fog makes for cool, damp camping conditions so be prepared with the appropriate clothing. Clayoquot Sound receives 250 cm (98.5 in.) of precipitation annually, though the summer months tend to be relatively dry with temperatures ranging from 10–25°C (50–77°F).

Because of the dangers of the exposed coast, beginner paddlers should only plan trips on the protected waters behind Meares Island. If you do not have experience landing in surf, pull over at Long Beach in Pacific Rim National Park, and get out and play in the surf. Best of all, take a kayak surfing course from a reputable instructor.

Regardless of the trip you decide upon, you will likely face currents of 2–3 knots around the harbour at Tofino. These currents can be particularly dangerous if running counter to the prevailing winds and/or mixed with the heavy boat and plane traffic in the area. Tofino Harbour is a beehive of activity, especially during the summer. Water taxis, float planes, whale watchers and fishing charters all add to the excitement. As at other locations throughout the province, locals affectionately refer to kayakers as "speed bumps," so stay together in a tight pod and make your presence known.

No matter how visible you are, however, there are still two areas that require extra caution. The first is the harbourfront traffic flow running along the shore of Tofino. Cross this area in a tight group perpendicular to traffic. The other area is the traffic route between Tofino and Opitsaht Village on Meares Island, marked by red and green buoys. This is the main route for all traffic coming and going in Clayoquot Sound. If you are heading for Vargas or Flores Islands, avoid this fairway by paddling out towards Stubbs (Clayoquot) Island. If the tide is too low to do this, paddle down the right side of the lane in single file, keeping clear of traffic.

SPECIAL CONSIDERATIONS

Gray whales migrate past Clayoquot Sound every spring, and several stay each year as summer residents. Encountering whales while paddling is a thrilling experience. The kayak, however, is not the ideal craft for whale watching. Although grays appear to be gentle and slow-moving creatures, they are powerful wild animals that deserve space and respect. If you encounter whales of any kind, please keep these guidelines in mind.

- Always approach slowly from the side, no closer than 100 m (330 ft.). (The same distance applies to sea lion haul-outs.)
- Make noise by tapping on your kayak frequently so that the whales know where you are at all times.
- Do not restrict or interrupt a whale's normal movement.
- Do not disturb a motionless or sleeping whale on the water surface.
- Do not split up groups, especially mothers and calves.
- Do not box whales in with other boats or in shallow water.
- Keep in mind: The best encounters with whales are the ones where they choose to visit you.

Finally, please remember that all of the beaches you land on, camp on and explore have been home to the Nuu-chah-nulth since time immemorial. Some of them are designated Indian Reserves. Do not land at an IR without permission from the appropriate band office.

CLAYOQUOT SOUND TRIPS (27–29)

There are several popular trips in Clayoquot Sound. If you have only a day, the Big Tree Trail on Meares Island is a must see. Three to 4 days will provide enough time to circumnavigate either Meares Island or, for more advanced paddlers, Vargas Island. Finally, for those of you lucky enough to have at least 7 days on the water, the increasingly popular trip to the natural hot springs north of Flores Island awaits. Each trip departs from, and returns to, Tofino.

Trip 27 Big Tree Trail (Meares Island)

Skill:	Intermediate
Time:	Day trip
Hazards:	Traffic and currents
Access:	Tofino
Charts:	3673 Clayoquot Sound, Tofino Inlet to Millar Channel 1:40,000
	3685 Tofino 1:20,000
Tide Book:	Vol. 6

This spectacular hike through a grove of giant cedars is an essential ingredient for any visit to Clayoquot Sound. A short paddle, the trip is suitable for all but complete novices. If you have never kayaked before, consider taking a guided trip—it makes dealing with the harbour traffic, complex currents, float planes and potential winds a lot easier. If you are heading out into the sound for a longer trip, plan on working Meares Island into your schedule; it is one of the best hiking opportunities into Clayoquot Sound's ancient forests.

Launching

As you approach the town of Tofino, you will likely be driving along Campbell Street. Go all the way to 1st Street, turn right, go to the bottom of the hill and turn left. You will see the kayak launch sign. This site is conveniently near the Common Loaf Bakery, in case you need to make a last minute dash for treats, and the Tofino Sea Kayaking Company, a good local resource centre for kayakers. It is recommended that you book any sort of accommodation well in advance.

Starfish on Flores Island. PETER McGEE

The municipality of Tofino is working on a strategy to deal with the shortage of parking space in the summer. Parking in the downtown core is limited to 1 hour. Your best bet is to park on Main Street between 2nd and 4th Streets. If you have questions about parking, call or visit the village office.

Big Tree Trail If you leave Tofino on a rising tide, the currents will push you over to Meares, making for a relaxed paddle. The trailhead can be a little hard to find: it is located in the passage between Morpheus and Meares Islands, about halfway down the Meares side. In summer there will likely be other boats coming and going, which makes the trail easier to find. Be sure to park your boats up high and tie them to a tree; tides and currents have been known to strand the occasional visitor. Overnight camping is not permitted.

The trail was originally built in 1984 by the Friends of Clayoquot Sound. Local photographer Adrian Dorst thought that more people would be motivated to help save Meares Island if they saw for themselves the awesome forests at stake. In 1992, a boardwalk was developed in a joint effort between the Tla-o-qui-aht First Nation and the Western Canada Wilderness Committee. The boardwalk was built to protect the forest, especially the tree roots, from the damage caused by thousands of visitors each year. Please stay on the boardwalk and do not pick or remove anything.

The boardwalk winds its way through a varied forest of cedar, hemlock and spruce. The trail ends at the famous Hanging Garden Tree, a huge cedar with hundreds of smaller plants, shrubs and trees growing on it. All of this lush rainforest would have been clearcut in the 1980s were it not for the valiant efforts on the part of concerned locals, native and non-native alike. The fate of Meares Island is still in limbo. Although the Nuu-chah-nulth won a court injunction that halts all development on the island, the future of Meares depends on how the native land question is settled. In the meantime, the Nuu-chah-nulth declared Meares Island a tribal park in 1984, set aside for continued traditional use and for the recreational enjoyment of all who wish to visit the island and leave it as they find it.

Trip 28 Meares Island

Skill:	Intermediate
Time:	3 days
Hazards:	Traffic and currents
Access:	Tofino
Charts:	3673 Clayoquot Sound, Tofino Inlet to Millar Channel 1:40,000
	3685 Tofino 1:20,000
Tide Book:	Vol. 6

Circumnavigating Meares Island is an excellent 3-day trip, especially if you are a less experienced kayaker and want to ease yourself into West Coast paddling.

See the trip above for launching details. It is best to leave Tofino on a rising tide, no more than 4 hours after low tide; this way you will have the current pushing you down Browning Passage. There is a small tidal rapids at Tsapee Narrows—another good reason to be going with the tide. If you are not with the tides, creep along the shore of Meares Island in the back eddies. Tsapee Narrows is a popular sport-fishing location and can be busy with local traffic, so stay close to shore.

Rounding Auseth Point, head north. You will note on the charts that the rapids at Dawley Pass flow north on the ebb, not on the flood as you might logically expect. If you have timed things right, you can picnic at Auseth Point at high tide and then allow the current to push you through Dawley Pass. Again, watch for traffic in these narrow passages and stay close to shore.

Sites

Heelboom Bay/Cis'a'quis   As you head north, Heelboom Bay is the first big bay on your left. Known locally as Cis'a'quis, this was the site of the 1984 confrontation between MacMillan Bloedel and local natives and environmentalists. A sign declaring the area a Meares Tribal Park can be seen on your left; a cabin built for the blockade is located on the west side of the bay. There is good camping across the little bridge behind the cabin. Water can be gathered from creeks on either side of the cabin though following the creek up the left side of the cabin will reward you with the purest water. In adverse weather the cabin can be used. Sign into the logbook, even if you camp outside.

Mosquito Harbour is a day's paddle away from Cis'a'quis and a great place to visit. The harbour has a trail that leads to the largest cedar on Meares: 19 m (64 ft.) in circumference.

Milties Beach and Ritchie Bay   From Heelboom Bay or Mosquito Harbour, you can head back to Tofino the way you came, catching the tides in reverse, or continue to circumnavigate Meares. A careful look at the charts will show the steep, cliffy coast along the north side of Meares Island that makes camping impossible. One option is to go all the way to Milties Beach on Vargas Island (see the route to Hot Springs below). Another is to camp at Ritchie Bay at the base of a couple of old clearcuts; there is a creek running down the middle of the beach. Both these beaches may be underwater at spring tides (full and new moons), but otherwise there should be enough room to fit a small to medium-sized group.

Trip 29 Hot Springs Cove

Skill:	Intermediate (inside route) to advanced (outside route)	
Time:	5–10 days	
Hazards:	Traffic, currents and open coast	
Access:	Tofino	
Charts:	3673	Clayoquot Sound, Tofino Inlet to Millar Channel 1:40,000
	3674	Clayoquot Sound, Millar Channel

to Estevan Point   1:40,000
3685   Tofino   1:20,000
Tide Book: Vol. 6

Few trips along B.C. waters combine as many pleasures as the trip from Tofino to Hot Springs Cove. Not only is the scenery beautiful and the wildlife abundant, but at the end of it all you can soak away your troubles in one of the most picturesque hot springs on the coast. To reach the hot springs, you can either take an exposed route along the outside of Flores and Vargas Islands or travel the protected inside passage. As mentioned earlier, intermediate paddlers who do not have surf experience should choose the protected route.

Launching

As you leave Tofino for Vargas Island, be cautious of the harbourfront traffic flow and the designated traffic lane between Tofino and Opitsaht Village on Meares Island (as mentioned earlier). You can avoid much of this traffic by paddling out towards Stubbs (Clayoquot) Island but only if the tide is high. If not, paddle down the right side of the lane in single file. Once on Vargas, follow the northern shore to Milties Beach. Leave yourself at least 3 hours to reach Milties from Tofino and be particularly careful about other boat traffic in the event of fog.

Sites

Milties Beach (Vargas Island)   This is a good destination for the first day of a trip into the sound: a sandy beach with a western exposure, far enough removed to feel you are "out there" yet not too far for the frenzy of last-minute runs to the bakery and packing to catch the tide. This site is often busy in the summer so bring along your common courtesy and patience. There can be a bit of a surf landing here. Be prepared for a dunking, and make sure loose bits of gear will not be scattered along the beach should you tip.

At the north end of Milties Beach is an abandoned homestead with excellent camping on a large, flat and shaded spot. Otherwise there is .4 km (.25 mi.) of sandy beach for you to choose from; just check the tide tables carefully to ensure a dry night's sleep. There is no water source. Just north of Milties, across Brabant Channel, lies an alternative spot at Whitesand Cove.

Whitesand Cove (Flores Island) As the name suggests, this area is a heaven on earth. Gibsons Marine Park covers most of the beachfront, which is where you should plan to camp. Similar to Milties Beach and other spots throughout the sound, you may find that you are not the first to discover this prime campsite. If you do appear to be alone, keep your camp compact and avoid spreading out in case more paddlers show up later in the day or evening. There is no water source here.

Nearby is the Ahousat Wild Side Trail. The result of a 1996 collaboration between the Ahousat First Nation and the Western Canada Wilderness Committee, this trail runs along the outer coast of Flores Island, from Ahousat to Mount Flores, and offers paddlers a great chance to stretch their legs. You can start the trail at Ahousat or pick it up on any of the nearby beaches.

If you are day-tripping in the Whitesand's area, a couple of cautions. First, Bartlett Island is an Indian Reserve in its entirety: do not plan on landing here, even for a picnic. You can picnic at nearby Whaler Island, an ideal location to play *Gilligan's Island* for a few hours. Second, the unprotected coastline west of Kutcous Point is not a good place for less experienced paddlers. The beaches require surf landings and the entire area is exposed to the typical afternoon westerly winds, as well as to the infrequent summer storms with southeast winds.

Flores Island There is not a lot of camping along the inside of Flores Island, though several small sites are scattered along Millar Channel and Shelter Inlet. If you can, plan to go up Millar Channel on a flood, arriving at the south end of Hayden Passage at high tide. The current races through Hayden Passage—try to go with it. Take the ebb through the pass then carry on around Flores to Halfmoon Beach.

Halfmoon Beach and the Hot Springs Although there is no water, Halfmoon Beach is an excellent base camp for a day at the hot springs. The surf is usually quite small by the time it works its way up Sydney Inlet and into the bay. Give yourself a full day to visit Hot Springs Cove. Paddle around Sharpe Point and up into the cove. Park your boats at the government wharf (it is difficult to land at the peninsula near the springs) and hike the easy, well-marked boardwalk to the springs. Once there, you get to shed your gear and enjoy one of the finest natural pleasures known to paddlers around the world. Rounding Sharp Point in big swell or strong winds is not recommended.

Flores Island (Outer Coast) Paddling down the outside of Flores Island can be a thrilling trip, but only attempt this trip if the conditions are good to excellent and you are experienced and prepared. If you are not, the trip can be harrowing, as more than one paddler has found out. Conditions to avoid include seas greater than 2 m (6.5 ft.), winds above 15 knots, fog and nighttime. What makes this paddle especially challenging is that there are no safe landings between Rafael Point and Siwash Cove—you are 100 percent committed out here and will feel it. If you are not an experienced open-coast paddler, it is better to learn in a relatively safe setting such as the outside of Vargas Island.

Ahous Bay Ahous Bay, on the exposed outside of Vargas Island, is another kayaker's dream come true. A 1.6-km- (1-mi.-) long sand beach looks out over Blunden Island and the open ocean beyond. This is a surf beach, and on a large swell you can actually get out and practise your surfing skills—if you brought a helmet.

Camping can be found at both ends of the bay, making the landings a little easier as the surf is smaller at the edges than at the middle of the beach. There are also a few small creeks at the southern and northern ends of the bay. The southern point is an Indian Reserve and off limits.

If you decide to paddle around the southern end of Vargas Island on your way back to Tofino, be sure to take care passing through the La Croix Group. Not only are the islands exposed to surf, but reefs, fog and sportfishing boats can make them particularly dangerous.

ADDITIONAL ROUTES

Heading north and south: There is currently a tourism moratorium in Hesquiat territory, so we cannot recommend a route north towards Hesquiat Peninsula. Similarly, we don't recommend a route heading south: the coastline is rugged and completely exposed to the full fury of the Pacific for 20 nautical miles.

Chapter Twelve

Nootka Sound

Jamie Boulding

For all its natural beauty, it is the history of Nootka Sound that makes this area unique. Nootka Sound is where Capt. James Cook first set foot in British Columbia and where the sea otter fur trade began. Most importantly, Nootka is the ancestral home of the Mowachaht/ Muchalaht people. As the Mowachaht/Muchalaht have said, it is not just a place: Nootka is a feeling, and if you listen closely as you paddle the shores and walk the beaches, you might just hear the elders talking.

BACKGROUND

Long before Europeans arrived in Nootka Sound, the area was populated by dozens of Mowachaht communities. On March 29, 1778, Capt. James Cook, commander of the ships *Resolution* and the *Discovery,* moored off the Mowachaht village of Yuquot/Friendly Cove. Believing the area to be officially Spanish, based on the voyage of Juan Perez in 1774, Cook did not bother to claim it for the British Empire. Instead, while repairing his ships he explored the area and traded European goods for sea otter furs. Many of these furs were later sold for outrageous prices in China, and the trans-Pacific trade between Nootka and China began.

In light of this sudden interest in the area, the Spanish felt their rather dubious claim was being threatened and, in a show of force, seized American and British ships. The seizure caused an uproar in London, and Britain mobilized its forces for war. Spain, not wishing to embroil itself in yet another conflict, relinquished her claim to the region in the Nootka Convention of 1790. Shortly after gaining title to the northwest coast of the continent, however, the British withdrew from the area, concentrating their forces on the defence of the homeland. For the next 80 years following the abandonment of the Spanish fort at Yuquot/Friendly Cove, no Europeans occupied any land on the west coast of Vancouver Island.

When Europeans once again started to settle the area, the sea otters were long gone and livelihoods were created from fish, forests and mines. Logging still makes its mark on Nootka Sound, with many slopes visibly scarred. Recognizing the importance of the region, the provincial government has finally started to look more closely at the protection and management of Nootka Sound and Nuchatlitz Inlet. There are four new parks in the district—Catala Island, Nuchatlitz, Santa-Boca, Bligh Island—though there is still very little information on the plans for their management. The Mowachaht/Muchalaht Band has development plans for Yuquot/Friendly Cove including a museum, rental cabins (these are in place) and improvements to the west coast hiking trail on Nootka Island. Although the Mowachaht/Muchalaht are encouraging tourism at Yuquot/Friendly Cove, it is best to obtain permission and information from the Ahaninaquus Tourist Centre, near Gold River, if you plan on stopping there.

GETTING THERE

By land: Most visitors to Nootka Sound and Nuchatlitz Inlet will pass through the town of Gold River, approximately 1.5 hours west of Campbell River along Highway 28. Campbell River lies about 153 km (95 mi.) north of Nanaimo along Highway 19 (the Island Highway).

If you are heading to Nootka Sound, you can launch from Ahaninaquus, approximately 14 km (8.5 mi.) west of Gold River on Pulp Mill Road. Closer launch sites to the sound can be found at Cougar Creek and Tuta Marina, which can be reached via the logging road that connects Gold River to Tahsis. The total driving time from Gold River to either site is about 1.5 hours, but you will avoid the long paddle down Muchalat Inlet that is necessary if you launch at Ahaninaquus.

If you are heading directly to Nuchatlitz Inlet, drive 125 km (76 mi.) north along Highway 19 from Campbell River to Woss and then head west 60 km (37 mi.) to Zeballos. It is possible to launch from Zeballos, but your best bet is to take the logging road leading to Fair Harbour and stop short at the bridge that crosses Little Espinosa Inlet. From here you can avoid the winds and extra paddling associated with Zeballos Inlet.

> Bligh Island. GRANT THOMPSON/TOFINO EXPEDITIONS

By water and air: For paddlers who want to customize a trip into Nootka Sound or want a quick drop-off, head to Ahaninaquus (see above). From here the region can be accessed by the MV *Uchuck III*, Maxi's Water Taxi, Air Nootka or a private boat. *Uchuck* owner Fred Mather reports that their weekly summer passage to Nootka is often fully subscribed, with paddlers contributing a significant portion to the list; reservations are essential. Should you choose to use the *Uchuck,* bear in mind that your travel plans will be dependent on her return schedule.

WEATHER AND HAZARDS

The weather in Nootka Sound is typical of the southern section of the west coast of Vancouver Island and a little less severe than its northern counterpart. The paddler must be continually aware of boat and ship traffic, large swells, changing wind patterns, surf landings, breaking waves and boomers. Various inlets funnel and redirect the winds, particularly in Muchalat and Tlupana Inlets, and afternoon winds typically become quite strong during the summer. On the outer coast expect serious weather. Ocean swell and fog can combine at any time of year to make a deadly combination. Many stretches of the exposed coastline have limited take-outs so plan your routes carefully.

Animals are not generally a problem here, but cougars can be a danger to small children left unattended. Half of the over 60 recorded cougar attacks in North America have taken place on Vancouver Island. There have been a few problems with bears getting into people's boats and food, most recently on Strange Island, so remember to cache your food unless you are on a small island. It only takes one careless kayaker to create a problem bear.

NOOTKA SOUND TRIPS (30–31)

The paddling possibilities in and around Nootka Sound are seemingly endless. The route from Cougar Creek or Tuta Marina along the west side of Bligh Island and through the Spanish Pilot Group is ideal for intermediate paddlers who want a feel for the West Coast. Those with more experience can lengthen their trip with excursions to Yuquot/Friendly Cove, Burdwood Bay and beyond. North of Nootka Sound lie the Esperanza and Nuchatlitz Inlets. From the launch site at Little Espinosa Inlet, paddlers can easily spend a few days exploring the new parks at Catala Island and Mary Basin (in Nuchatlitz Park). For the truly adventurous, a circumnavigation of Nootka Island is possible, but both experience and time are essential.

Trip 30 Nootka Sound

Skill:	Intermediate to advanced
Time:	3–7 days
Hazards:	Open coast
Access:	Gold River/Cougar Creek/Tuta Marina/
	MV *Uchuck III*
Charts:	3662 Nootka Sound to Esperanza Inlet
	1:75,000
	3664 Nootka Sound 1:40,000
Tide Book:	Vol. 6

Exploring the Spanish Pilot Group is a great 2–4-day tour that will give you a good taste of Nootka Sound and most likely whet your appetite for further adventures. For the more experienced, taking a few more days to explore Yuquot/Friendly Cove and Burdwood Bay is time well spent. Campsites on the inner islands are much more limited than on the outer coast, but you can still find spots if you are a small group equipped with bivouac sacs.

From your put-in location to the Spanish Pilot Group, the ocean is generally calm with perhaps a slight swell; your main consideration when landing in this area is the nature of the seabed. Once you reach the southern parts of the islands, and points beyond, the water becomes considerably more challenging.

Launching

The most convenient put-ins for a short trip in Nootka Sound are either the Cougar Creek Forest Service Recreation Site or Tutu Marina. To drive to these sites, take the gravel road from Gold River towards Tahsis. (The road from Gold River to either of the put-ins is gravel, and vehicles with high clearance are recommended.) After you come down the steep pass from the obvious high point, look for a left turn marked Nesook Log Dump and take that road. Watch for logging trucks along the road and at the dump itself: this is an active logging area and drivers should be wary at all times. When you reach the paved dry-sort area at the Nesook Dump, stay left and continue along Tlupana Inlet road. This is perhaps the most confusing part of the drive, and many newcomers to the area have turned around here thinking they were lost. Cougar Creek, approximately 6 km (3.7 mi.) past the dump, is well marked and will be obvious especially in summer when up to one hundred RVs, filled with overzealous sport fishers, arrive on their annual migration. Tuta Marina is another 6 km (3.7 mi.) past Cougar Creek on the same road. This private marina was opened in 1995 and has big plans to offer full services. Although there is a small parking fee at Tuta Marina, the site allows you to put in on Hanna Channel where you can avoid the head winds that blow up Tlupana Inlet most afternoons.

Sites

Spanish Pilot Group   The most common route from these put-ins is to paddle around San Carlos Point at the northern tip of Bligh Island and then down the west side of the island. The most desirable destination for the first night out is at a location commonly called the Isthmus, located on the southwest tip of Bligh Island directly north of Clotchman Island. This is a very special campsite with two beaches that offer great morning and evening light. The downside of the Isthmus is that it is too popular, hence crowded and occasionally dirty. The most popular back-up site is in the small bay on the east side of Vernaci Island. This site is a little buggy but has good flat places to camp and some beautiful culturally modified trees.

Water is hard to find in the Spanish Pilot Group unless it has been very rainy before your trip. Your best plan is to carry lots of water and/or make water collection trips to Bligh Island streams, which are marked on the chart.

On the second day of this short tour, if weather reports for the seas and winds are moderate or less, head to the Yuquot/Friendly Cove area. If the weather is not agreeable, fishing and exploring in the Spanish Pilot Group are excellent. If you travel to Yuquot/Friendly Cove, the Cook Channel crossing should not be taken lightly. In low visibility conditions, your major consideration will be the large ocean-going ships that, though infrequent, are still a significant hazard. You should also consider other boat traffic in Cook Channel and around the Saavedra Islands. Remember that kayaks, unless outfitted with radar reflectors, are not detectable on the equipment used to pilot many ships. Wind patterns should also be assessed before setting off as full-sized ocean swells are not uncommon in Cook Channel. If there is any chance of challenging conditions, try crossing Cook Channel from the north end of Narvaez Island, heading directly for the north end of the Saavedra Islands—or don't cross at all. This route will minimize your time in the channel and allow you a scenic paddle through McKay Passage south towards Friendly Cove. There is a nice campsite in the southwest corner of Santa Gertrudis Cove.

Yuquot/Friendly Cove   Yuquot/Friendly Cove is part of the Mowachaht Indian Band Reserve. If you plan to stay at Yuquot/Friendly Cove or on any part of the reserve property in this area, call or write the Mowachaht/ Muchalaht Band Office in Gold River for permission and reservations. The band charges a $5 per person landing fee, so be sure to bring cash. If you arrive without prior arrangements with the band, talk to Ray and Terry Williams, band members who permanently reside at Yuquot/Friendly Cove.

You can easily spend a whole day exploring and visiting Yuquot/ Friendly Cove. The highlights include the pebble beach on the west coast, the church (with permission), a swim in the lake (the water is surprisingly warm) or a walk along the exposed beach on the west side of the cove. A visit to the lighthouse is also recommended. The view is excellent, and the keepers are always friendly and keen to inform citizens of their views regarding Ottawa's plans to destaff the stations. It is also possible to camp or even stay in a small rental hut at Yuquot/Friendly Cove. Again, call the band to make the appropriate arrangements and for a list of current fees.

Resolution Cove   After visiting Yuquot/Friendly Cove, the safest route out is to retrace your strokes back to Narvaez Island. Once back in the Spanish Pilot Group, you can return to your vehicle via San Carlos Point, the easiest way back, or circumnavigate Bligh Island. If you plan to paddle around the island, be wary of the headlands on the tip of Clerke Peninsula: they can cause nasty rebound waves with even moderate swells. History buffs may want to stop in Resolution Cove to look at the plaques that commemorate Captain Cook's first landing on the West Coast of North America. Although Cook made contact with the Mowachaht at Yuquot, Resolution Cove is the site where British explorers first actually set foot in what is now British Columbia. The native name for Resolution Cove is *Kathni-aktl,* meaning "a place of driftwood."

It is possible to cross from Yuquot/Friendly Cove directly to the southern tip of Clerke Peninsula but paddlers must exercise caution during such a long and exposed crossing. This option is not recommended if there are any concerns about weather, wind or visibility.

Burdwood Bay   For paddlers who are comfortable in open water, try a trip to the beautiful beach in Burdwood Bay. The bay will likely require you to execute a surf landing, and the size of the surf will vary depending upon the wind speed and direction of the waves. The best campsite on Burdwood beach is on the far left side of the bay when coming in. A dependable water source is inland about 50 m (164 ft.); follow the trail that leaves from the corner of the beach—you will likely have to cross over a section of piled driftwood to find the trailhead.

If you arrive in Burdwood Bay and the surf landing looks like more than you bargained for, paddle instead to the little bay due west on Burdwood Point. This is the easiest beach to land on near the bay.

Escalante   Advanced paddlers can also consider making a trip down to Escalante Island from Burdwood Bay. This trip involves paddling 5 km (3 mi.) of exposed coast. The best route south along the coast is to stay inside the two groups of islets while weaving through the boomers. The chart accurately shows the rocks that are likely to boomer, but you should not attempt this route unless you are comfortable and experienced with these types of challenges. In the Escalante area, the easiest landing and standard campsite is called Jim's Refuge. To get there travel around Escalante Point and land on the beach between the rock shelves directly inland from the centre of Escalante Island. Other possible landing and campsites in the area are on the inside of Escalante Island, Escalante River (the landing into the mouth of the river should only be attempted in very small swell) and the south end of the beach beside Escalante River before you round Escalante Point. Also noteworthy in the Escalante area are the prospector's cabin at Escalante River and the trail overland to avoid the headlands at Escalante Point.

Trip 31   Nuchatlitz Inlet and Nootka Island

Skill: Intermediate to advanced
Time: 3–14 days
Hazards: Open coast
Access: Little Espinosa Inlet/Zeballos

174

Charts:	3662	Nootka Sound to Esperanza Inlet
		1:75,000
	3663	Esperanza Inlet 1:40,000
	3664	Nootka Sound 1:40,000
Tide Book:	Vol. 6	

Paddling the bays, basins and islands around Nuchatlitz Inlet is a great 4–5-day trip. Those with the skill and mental preparation needed for the open coast can try the waters of Nootka Island's west side. The beaches at Skuna Bay, Calvin Creek and Beano Creek are some of the nicest on the coast, rewarding paddlers who are able to negotiate surf landings and quickly punishing those who are not. Travelling the inside of Nootka Island is a little less exciting. Nonetheless, a circumnavigation of Nootka Island will give you the best feel for the area and may bring a certain closure to your trip.

Launching

If you are planning road access, the best places to start a tour of the Nuchatlitz area are at Little Espinosa Inlet or the town of Zeballos. From the put-in at Little Espinosa, you have a shorter and more protected paddle into the sound, avoiding the winds that are so common in Zeballos Inlet. For this reason it is the favoured launch site even though Zeballos is a little more secure.

To reach the launch site at Little Espinosa, follow the road that leads from Zeballos to Fair Harbour. A few kilometres out of town the road crosses a small bridge over the inlet. There is no sign, but it is a fairly obvious launching area. Park on the side of the road. Be sure to lock your car and remove all valuables as this area is quite isolated.

Sites

Garden Point   After launching from Little Espinosa Inlet, a good objective for the first day is the Forest Service Recreation Site at Garden Point. Paddling out of Espinosa Inlet, stick to the east of Centre Island and head for the sand and pebble beach at the base of Brodick Creek. There are a number of tent sites in the old growth and the setting is relatively wild. Hopefully, the Ministry of Forests won't be putting in too many picnic tables in the near future.

Catala and Rosa Islands   From Garden Point, you can head to either Catala or Rosa Islands. Catala is a provincial marine park that offers some nice camping and plenty of beach to explore. Rosa Island is contained within the larger and newly designated provincial park, Nuchatlitz. You may want to use the camp on the centre of Rosa for a base when exploring the park. Although there are some pleasant little islands to camp on in Nuchatlitz, there are also numerous private holdings, Indian Reserves and burial sites that should be avoided unless you have permission. BC Parks should be releasing a new map soon to give the paddler an idea of where to go.

Continuing past Nuchatlitz involves paddling in some exposed areas. The three options in order of increasing difficulty are to head up Nuchatlitz Inlet to Mary Basin, cross Nuchatlitz Inlet to Louie Bay or paddle around Ferrer Point and continue along the outside of Nootka Island.

The trip into Mary Basin and the Inner Basin is a good option for a couple of days of exploring. This section of coast has an impressive sea cave to visit in calm conditions, but watch out for the boomers between Belmont Point and Benson Point. It is possible to avoid some of the exposed paddling en route to Port Langford by taking either of the two narrow portages from Nuchatlitz Park.

Louie Bay   The crossing over to Louie Bay from Nuchatlitz is 5-km- (3-mi.-) long and receives huge seas at times. Louie Bay has some good campsites on the sand beaches just south of Florence Point. There is a derelict radar station that was formerly used as a Christian camp by the Esperanza mission near Tongue Point. Do not try to paddle to the outside coast through the passage from Louie Bay; it is only covered in extremely high tides and you will likely end up stuck in a mud flat. If you venture into the small inlet directly south of Louie Bay, try to catch the tide midway between high and low or you will be dragging your boat over some very slippery rocks. At the far end of this inlet is a trail that leads to a very beautiful beach camp on the west side of Nootka Island. This trail is actually the north end of a trail that runs down the outside coast of Nootka. Hiking parties often fly into this small inlet and hike down to Yuquot/Friendly Cove.

Nootka Island (West Side)   Only expert paddlers should attempt the trip down the exposed coast of Nootka Island. It is best paddled from north to south to take advantage of the fair-weather westerlies. The route takes you around Ferrer Point, with the first possible landing at what is sometimes called Third Beach (the beach described above as the spot to hike to from Louie Bay). Landing at Third Beach is only possible if the swell is not very big; the swell direction will dictate which side of the rocks in front of the beach you should come in on. If the landing looks bad, you must be prepared to paddle down the coast to Skuna Bay or Calvin Creek. Both of these landings can be attempted in large swell without much danger as long as you are comfortable in surf. The beach at Calvin Creek is one of the most spectacular on the B.C. coast. Calvin Creek has a 10-m (33-ft.) waterfall called Crawfish Falls that creates a little swimming hole right on the beach.

The next landing on this coast is inside the reef at Bajo Point. This is the easiest landing on the outside of Nootka Island and the only place where a skilled operator who knows the area can land a powerboat. There is also a landing at Beano Creek, another spot you would not want to land on if the swell is too big. The final stretch from Beano Creek around Maquinna Point to Yuquot/Friendly Cove is the most dangerous part of the trip. Even in moderate swell, you should expect unstable rebound waves if you get too close to Maquinna Point.

Nootka Island (East Side)   The paddle along the inside of Nootka Island, while not exciting, should be your route unless you have the weather window and expertise to attempt the outside. Recommended camps include Santa Gertrudis Cove, the Spanish Pilot Group, Santiago Creek (between Toswin Narrows and Tahsis), then through Tahsis Narrows and west to Haven Cove and on to Garden Point

ADDITIONAL ROUTES

Heading north: This advanced paddle route puts you on the dramatic and exposed coastline between Tatchu Point and Kyuquot Sound. The odd pebble beach breaks up an otherwise rocky shore, and much of the area has being subjected to substantial logging. At the northern edge of this stretch of coastline lies Rugged Point Marine Park (see Chapter 13).

Heading south: Heading south should only be attempted by advanced paddlers. Rounding Estevan Point in strong winds and heavy seas or swell is hazardous as waves steepen on the strong tidal currents close to the point. Once around the point, you are on the way to Clayoquot Sound (see Chapter 11).

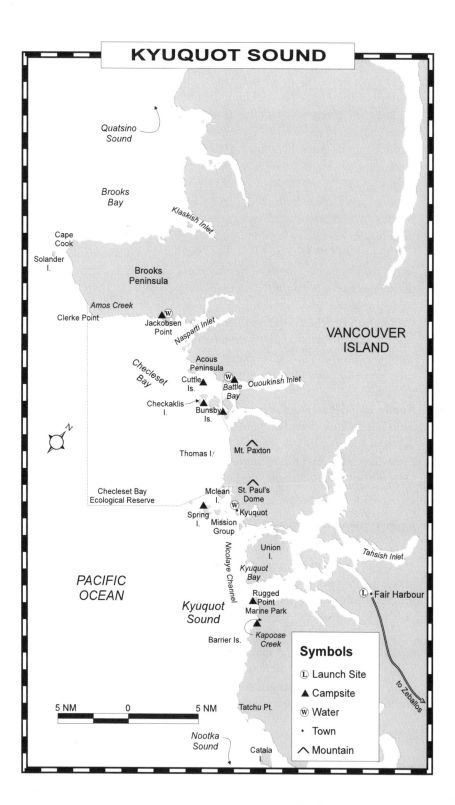

KYUQUOT SOUND

Quatsino Sound

Brooks Bay

Klaskish Inlet

Cape Cook

Solander I.

Brooks Peninsula

Amos Creek

Clerke Point

Jackobsen Point ▲Ⓦ

Nasparti Inlet

VANCOUVER ISLAND

Checleset Bay

Acous Peninsula

Cuttle Is. ▲

Ⓦ▲ *Battle Bay*

Ououkinsh Inlet

Checkaklis I. ▲

Bunsby Is.▲

Thomas I.

Mt. Paxton ⌃

Checleset Bay Ecological Reserve

Mclean I.

St. Paul's Dome ⌃

Spring I. ▲

Ⓦ • Kyuquot

Mission Group

Nicolaye Channel

Union I.

Kyuquot Bay

Tahsish Inlet

PACIFIC OCEAN

Kyuquot Sound

Rugged ▲Point Marine Park ▲

Ⓛ • Fair Harbour

Kapoose Creek

Barrier Is.

to Zeballos

Symbols

Ⓛ Launch Site

▲ Campsite

Ⓦ Water

• Town

⌃ Mountain

5 NM   0   5 NM

Tatchu Pt.

Nootka Sound

Catala I.

Chapter Thirteen

Kyuquot Sound

Rupert Wong

When a local sea kayak guide was asked once why she loved returning to Kyuquot every season, she closed her eyes, inhaled the salty air, smiled and said it was the bone-coloured nights when moonlight bathes the moss-covered trees, the sound of smacking as sea otters dine while nothing else is stirring, the fascinating stories and people of Kyuquot, and the way the place changes people in a matter of days.

BACKGROUND

Fewer than 5,000 people live in the northwest quadrant of Vancouver Island, with approximately 300 in the Kyuquot area. The coastline is rugged and folded with fjords, and the surrounding waters are strewn with reefs. The village of Kyuquot is one of the only communities on Vancouver Island's 400-km- (250-mi.-) long outer coast that remains isolated and without road access. For recreationists, the key attraction of the Kyuquot wilderness area is the Checleset Bay Ecological Reserve for sea otters and the recently designated Brooks/Nasparti Protected Area northwest of the community of Kyuquot. Unfortunately, these protected areas are situated in a region that has been heavily logged over the last 15 years, and visitors are often shocked by the dramatic contrast between pristine coastlines and ravaged slopes.

Some clearcuts, such as those on the slopes of Mount Paxton, are so atrocious that *National Geographic*'s 1992 article on temperate rainforests highlighted them as among the world's most ugly faces. It was such articles and the passionate lobbying of locals like Sam Kayra and Cindy Lee that alerted a stunned public to the devastation and ultimately helped save what remained. Although much of the logging has stopped, the steep slopes are struggling to recover while erosion and blow-down continue to remind us of the simple physical laws that the province and logging companies chose to ignore.

Considering this recent history, it comes as no surprise that many locals remain wary of outsiders. It also sheds some light on this message from the Checleset and Kyuquot First Nations, written by elder Lucy Paivio: "So I ask of the visitors that come to enjoy the beauty of our land and sea, please do not upset or damage them during your visit. Someone may be coming today to see what you took yesterday. Our people have all learned a hard lesson from history. Let us all learn a lesson from this and approach with clear minds, your reasons for coming to our Checleset Kyuquot Territory. And ensure they are such that the beauty remains to share for a long time to come."

The paddling routes suggested in this chapter should be approached with a generous degree of care, and all travellers should be mindful of the many natural forces that have humbled locals for centuries. Today, Kyuquot is in flux with impending First Nations treaty negotiations, forestry issues and a growing tourism industry. The fate of Kyuquot is in everyone's hands.

GETTING THERE

By land: The most economical means of reaching Kyuquot is to drive the 220 km (136 mi.) of Highway 19 (the Island Highway) and logging roads from Campbell River to Fair Harbour. Once a forestry-based community, Fair Harbour now acts as a parking lot for people who live and work beyond. During the summer, there is some space for tents though paddlers generally launch immediately after finding parking. It is often worthwhile to spend the evening in Campbell River or Courtney so you can get a morning start for Fair Harbour.

Drive 125 km (76 mi.) north along Highway 19 from Campbell River to Woss. (Woss and Zeballos are the only places to stop for fuel en route to Fair Harbour.) From Woss to Zeballos is about 60 km (37 mi.) and usually takes about 1 hour. Take the Zeballos turnoff, approximately 22 km (14 mi.) north of Woss, just past the Steele River bridge along Highway 19. This is the start of the gravel logging road to Fair Harbour. Use your headlights and be aware of logging trucks. From Zeballos, follow the main logging road along the 35-km (22-mi.) stretch (roughly 30 minutes) to Fair Harbour. Forks in the road are usually well marked, but if you encounter one that is not sign posted, follow the route most travelled until you reach the gravel parking lot of Fair Harbour.

If you want to avoid the paddle from the parking lot, a water taxi service can be arranged whereby all your gear, including kayaks, is moved from Fair Harbour to almost any drop point of your choice.

By water: You could also drive to Gold River and board the 24-m (80-ft.) freighter MV *Uchuck III*. The *Uchuck* serves northwest coastal communities between Gold River and Kyuquot, and reservations are essential. The romance of the 7-hour *Uchuck* sail into Kyuquot is well worth the effort. Should you choose to use the *Uchuck*, bear in mind that your travel plans will be dependent on her return schedule.

By air: Finally, you can always fly. Air Nootka presently holds the contract to deliver mail to Kyuquot on scheduled flights departing from Gold River. For $130 one way, you can join the mail run after carefully lashing your kayak onto the pontoon. This is an excellent way to gain a lofty perspective on forestry, the coastline and the lay of the land. Ask about air and water packages that combine charter service using Air Nootka and the *Uchuck III*.

WEATHER AND HAZARDS

The remote and rugged nature of Kyuquot can be a hazard in itself, and paddlers are reminded that this is not an area for beginners. Even during the popular summer months, you are reasonably likely to encounter storms or fog. Storms generally approach from the southeast or northwest. During the summer there are the added local effects of katabatic and anabatic winds amplified by inlets and warmer weather. Storms are usually accurately forecast by Environment Canada and broadcast on the area weather channel (wx 01). Southeast storms pose the most serious threat to paddlers as wind and wave energy easily and quickly develops to unsafe levels. Northwest storms seem to be deflected to some degree by the hulking mass of the Brooks Peninsula, which protects Checleset Bay in its lee. The challenge in Kyuquot Sound is weighing the risks of negotiating a certain exposed body of water in light of the forecast. It is always best to err on the side of caution and build in ample contingency measures to your travel plan.

For inexperienced and unprepared paddlers, fog can present an insurmountable challenge. Familiarity and confidence with navigation can make fog less of a problem, but there is always the concern of ensuring your own visibility to oncoming motor vessels. See Chapter 1 for more information on fog and wind.

Finally, some of the emergency resources typically available in more populated communities cannot be found in Kyuquot. There is no regional hospital within striking distance and the Coast Guard's nearest port is Tofino. Nonetheless, the Coast Guard can often be reached on channel 16 with a transmitting VHF radio, and there is a Red Cross outpost hospital attended by a registered nurse located outside the southeast entrance of Kyuquot. Since 1996, an RCMP officer has been posted in Kyuquot.

SPECIAL CONSIDERATIONS

Checleset and Kyuquot First Nations: As with any other First Nations traditional territory, you should seek permission to visit the area as part of your trip-planning process. The Checleset Kyuquot traditional territory includes Checleset Bay to Kyuquot Sound, south of Rugged Point, and points inland including channels inlets and watersheds. The key concern, particularly with elders in the community, is the degradation of heritage sites. Trespassing on mortuary sites, including burial caves and sacred islands, is strictly forbidden. Most of these sites are virtually unknown except to family members and the odd visitor who has accidentally stumbled upon them while exploring. As for uninhabited village sites, hereditary chiefs and their families usually do not mind sharing their beauty, but travellers should secure permission first, limit their visits to day use only and minimize their impacts by not destroying vegetation, removing materials, building fires or constructing structures.

If you have not prearranged your visit with the Che:k'tles7et'h' (Checleset) and Ka:'yu:'k't'h' (Kyuquot) Nation, a visit to the band office to register is advised. At time of writing, recreational use permits and registration were not mandatory, but this is being considered by both BC Parks and the First Nations. A 1995 pamphlet titled "Checleset Bay/Kyuquot Sound— The traditional areas of the Checleset and Kyuquot First Nations" is a guide towards a voluntary registration program. The pamphlet also provides information on heritage sites, environmental etiquette and sea otter viewing guidelines, among other things.

Waste management: Garbage disposal is another serious issue in the community of Kyuquot. At present, there is no garbage disposal or

Spring Island in the Mission Group. PETER McGEE

recycling program, and garbage generated by the community is dumped directly into the ocean for lack of better alternatives. Domestic sewage from Walters Island is piped straight into the cove. Untreated sewage from Houpsitas is discharged into Nicolaye Channel. Although there is a dumpster on the government wharf intended for tourist use and serviced by the *Uchuck III*, it is often brimming with waste. Local residents remove refuse from the area at considerable effort and expense. In short, do not plan on leaving your garbage in Kyuquot.

The Checleset Bay Ecological Reserve: Unique to the B.C. coastline is the 34 650-ha (85,585-a.) Checleset Bay Ecological Reserve established in 1981 for sea otters and their habitat. The reserve is located immediately south of the Brooks Peninsula and encompasses such prime paddling destinations as the Bunsby and Cuttle Islands.

It was once thought that the B.C. coast had been completely stripped of sea otters (not to be confused with river otters) during the greed-driven fur trade of the late 1700s. The last sea otter was reportedly shot near the village of Kyuquot. Through recolonization efforts largely initiated by Ian MacAskie, then director of the Western Canada Whale Research Foundation, sea otter populations have begun to make a dramatic recovery. The Checleset Bay area was selected as the recolonization site for its remoteness, sheltered waters and extensive shallow beds for feeding.

Sea otters rank at the top of the food chain, their only threat being humans, eagles and orcas. When a marine ecosystem such as the one in Checleset Bay is in equilibrium, the sea otter plays a key role in controlling the numbers of kelp-grazing shellfish. An average adult sea otter weighs about 30 kg (66 lb.) and will eat a quarter of its body weight per day, a diet that consists of sea urchins, abalone, clams, crabs, snails and other invertebrates collected on dives to the bottom.

The presence of the sea otter is so significant that whole ecosystems are altered by their positive influence on kelp growth in nearshore waters. Like a terrestrial forest, kelp provides both food and shelter for its inhabitants. Kelp forests also act as natural breakwaters, absorbing the force of waves and currents. When these forests disappear, nearshore productivity diminishes as beaches become exposed, while fish and other animals dependent on kelp become less abundant.

According to marine biologist Jane Watson, there are now over 6,000 sea otters on the west coast of Vancouver Island, from Quatsino to Hesquiat— an almost 600 per cent increase since they were reintroduced in the late 1960s and early 1970s. The otters may be encountered singly, in small groups or in large colonies called rafts. They are very cautious animals and difficult to observe in the wild. If their space is intruded upon, they will disappear by either diving, swimming underwater or porpoising along the surface.

Since sea otters are usually above water, grooming or eating, a kayaker's presence can be stressful to them. If you observe a sea otter in an upright position with head and shoulders above the water, they are most likely assessing their surroundings and possibly you. Many other marine mammals do this "spy hopping," especially orcas.

Kayakers should approach sea otter habitats carefully, observing the animals from a distance that will not startle them. This distance will vary, so use common sense. Female sea otters caring for pups, though entertaining to watch, are also the most vulnerable due to their protective nature. Stay clear of crying sea otter pups. A mother will temporarily leave her dependent pup while foraging for food, and your presence may prevent them from reuniting.

In addition to Checleset Bay, there are four other ecological reserves in the area that paddlers should avoid when camping: Solander Island, Klaskish River, Tahsish River and Clanninick Creek.

Trip 32 Kyuquot and the Bunsby Islands

Skill:	Intermediate to advanced
Time:	5–14 days
Hazards:	Open coast and winds.
Access:	Fair Harbour / MV *Uchuck III*
Charts:	3623 Kyuquot Sound to Cape Cook 1:80,000
	3682 Kyuquot Sound 1:36,700
	3683 Checleset Bay 1:36,500
Tide Book:	Vol. 6

The most common trip leaves from Fair Harbour and heads north towards the Bunsby Islands and the south side of the Brooks Peninsula. Due to the exposed coast and the varying weather conditions, it is wise to leave at least one week for this trip. If you are short on time, consider establishing a camp in the Mission Group or at the Rugged Point Marine Park and taking day trips to explore Kyuquot Sound.

Launching

Launching at Fair Harbour is easy: there is good water access and plenty of room for parking. Be prepared, however, as there are no facilities—only the large gravel parking lot used by logging companies and residents of Kyuquot. Lock all vehicle doors and do not leave valuables inside. Theft is uncommon but you never know.

Sites

The paddle to Kyuquot Sound from Fair Harbour is approximately 4–6 hours depending on inflow or outflow wind strength and tidal exchange. (The unofficial record of 2.5 hours is held by Bill Noble who started from

Spring Island.) Although there are no choice camping spots en route to Kyuquot, small groups can certainly improvise without too much difficulty. The best site at the southern edge of the sound, and the first camp on this route, is at Rugged Point.

Rugged Point Marine Park Precariously balanced between extensive mountainside clearcuts and the open ocean, this park represents how the exposed coastline between Rugged Point and Tatchu Point appeared before logging. Relentless surf over a shallow shoreline helps to maintain this stretch of fine sand beach, interrupted only by the occasional rock outcrop. The area is used frequently by boaters, with the highest concentration of use at the northwest end where a protected anchorage exists. Paddlers capable of surf landings and launchings can venture southeast of Rugged Point towards Kapoose Creek, where more secluded camping can be found. Creeks that run through the park are not reliable for drinking without some method of treatment. It should also be noted that black bear, cougar and wolf are not uncommon, and care should be taken not to intrude upon their space if you suspect they are in the vicinity.

The Rugged Point geology is characterized by tilted seabeds dating back to the Jurassic Period, and marine fossils can be found in most rock outcrops. For the enjoyment of others who come after you, and in the spirit of conservation, BC Parks advises visitors not to remove or destroy specimens.

This subtidal habitat offshore of Rugged Point park is ideal gray whale feeding grounds, used each spring and winter during their annual migration. Occasionally, non-reproductive whales take up residence here.

Union Island and Nicolaye Channel The paddling routes between Rugged Point and the Mission Group depend on the weather. On calm days, it is feasible and fun to travel offshore between the largest of the Barrier Islands. A more conservative approach is along Union Island and through Nicolaye Channel. Kyuquot Bay on Union Island offers protection and a place to beach if necessary. Both routes are about 13.5 km (8.5 mi.) and leave you vulnerable to wind and waves. If you must push the journey to Kyuquot or the Mission Group, taking the 21-km (13-mi.) inside passage around Union Island can be accomplished in all but extreme weather.

Mission Group and Spring Island Located approximately 13.5 km (8.5 mi.) northwest of Rugged Point is Spring Island, the largest of the Mission

Group. Spring Island historically provided many resources for the Checle-set and Kyuquot community that resided on the neighbouring islands of Aktis and Kamils.

More recently Spring Island served as a military radar station until the mid 1970s. Old road bed, building remnants and other debris are evidence of this previous occupation. The old service road is now a Forest Service Recreation Site that provides easy access between Spring Island's exposed coast and the more protected bay on the northeast side. Both protected and exposed aspects of the island offer good camping, with the most breathtaking vistas facing the open ocean. The finest sand, and certainly the least damaging to the hull of your kayak, can be found on the central and eastern portions of the more protected, shallow bay. On the exposed side of Spring Island, winter storms leave steep gravel beaches that offer suitable camping over flat terraces, which wet only on the most extreme summer tides.

Spring Island is 3.2 km (2 mi.) from Houpsitas Village and the community of Kyuquot, which has such modern conveniences as restaurants, a general store, post office, telephones and fax machines. Spring Island was not named for its water, so paddlers must either bring water from Kyuquot or collect it from Clanninick Creek located 3.5 km (2.25 mi.) north of Spring Island.

Day tripping around the tightly knit Mission Group of islands is richly rewarding, with shallows teeming with life and sea otters displaying their curious antics. Due to the proximity of Kyuquot, however, this region has more powerboat traffic than you will find elsewhere in the area. Avoid paddling on powerboat corridors wherever possible. Certain islands in the Mission Group such as Aktis, Ahmacinnit, Sobry and Kamils are off limits to visitors without prior permission from the hereditary chiefs. Other islands located between Favourite Entrance and Minx Rocks offer suitable beaches for resting or camping for small groups.

To Checleset Bay   Perhaps the most daunting leg of a paddler's journey to Checleset Bay is the 13-km (8-mi.) stretch between the Mission Group and Bunsby Islands. The first portion of your paddle should be made close to outer McLean Island. Except in extreme weather, this water is protected by offshore islands, extensive kelp beds and shallow reefs. While paddling you can observe the exposed water and make an informed judgement regarding the more open portion of the journey to the Bunsby Islands.

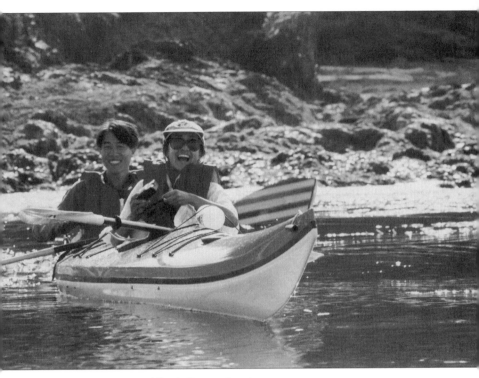

Paddling in Kyuquot Sound. WEST COAST EXPEDITIONS

The 5-km (3-mi.) shoreline along the base of the Mount Paxton clear-cut is characterized by inhospitable bedrock, steep cliffs and beaches—an exposed body of water with few opportunities to seek refuge. Rebounding waves can cause localized confused water that should be avoided by travelling offshore where wave patterns are more predictable. Thomas Island is approximately halfway to the Bunsbys and offers some leeward protection from wind, but the island is often too rough to land on safely. On calm water days, watch for large feeding groups of gulls, murres and cormorants or the harbour porpoises that frequently play in the area.

Bunsby Islands Ranked high in kayaking circles as a must-do destination, the Bunsby Islands are nothing short of a paddler's paradise. However, growing popularity and the Checleset people's recent interest in returning to occupy traditional village sites may soon change the character of this cherished place.

The two primary campsites in the Bunsby Islands can comfortably accommodate medium-sized groups of six to eight people. One is located in a sandy cove near the southeast entrance to Gay Passage. The other is located on an outer Bunsby Island with a chart elevation designation of 195 ft. Both sites offer camping on or above the beach, but it is critical for the conservation of these sites that any necessary fires are below the high tide line and that campers follow basic minimum impact principles.

Checkaclis remains as one of the most well-visited islands in the Bunsby archipelago. Historically, it was a Checleset village site. Its proximity to excellent clam beaches and channels for trapping fish provided ample resources to sustain people through the winter. Due to the heritage features of this ancient village site (i.e., little to no evidence of structures, modified terrain from generations of inhabitation), this site makes for excellent camping. Unfortunately, overuse in the past five years has permanently damaged many of its sensitive features, and public education and regulation are urgently needed to help preserve it. A 1994 decision by the Checleset hereditary chief of Checkaclis was to allow day-use visitors but forbid overnight camping, fires and harvesting. Please respect this decision.

Acous Peninsula, Battle Bay and Cuttle Islands   The Cuttle Islands are located less than 8 km (5 mi.) northwest of the Bunsby Islands. Crossing the entrance of Ououkinsh Inlet is generally manageable except against headwinds or extreme weather. Two of the larger Cuttle Islands offer suitable camping for small groups.

Acous was the largest of the traditional Checleset village sites. Also known as Byer's Cone, its proximity to Battle Creek made it an ideal village location. It is a popular heritage site with more new paths created every year by foot traffic; there is even evidence of excavation by people searching for artifacts to take home. For this regrettable reason, it is fortunate that this is not a suitable campsite for sea kayakers due to the presence of black bears and mosquitoes. To help preserve the quality of this heritage site, access has been restricted to day use only, and voluntary permits should be picked up at the Checleset Kyuquot Band office.

Beaches at the northeast end of Battle Bay are good for beachcombing and also suitable for camping. Reliable water can be collected from Battle Creek above the estuary. Look for wolf and elk prints along the streambanks. Be cautious of black bears.

Brooks Peninsula and Nasparti Inlet   The Brooks Peninsula and Nasparti and Battle watersheds make up the Brooks Protected Area, proclaimed in 1995. For many paddlers it is the unfragmented view of this 51 631-ha (127,525-a.) protected area that makes the paddle from the Bunsby Islands worthwhile.

The Brooks Peninsula appears as a mountainous obstruction protruding from Vancouver Island's otherwise uniform coastline. Cape Cook, at the peninsula's outermost extremity, is regarded by many as the worst section of water on the West Coast. Winds either accelerate around Cape Cook, or push over the top generating cloud en route. This wild domain separates the traditional territories of the Nuu-chah-nulth and Kwakwaka'wak'w Nations. For botanists and ecologists, the Brooks is endlessly fascinating. Evidence collected from botanical and geological samples suggest that parts of the Brooks may have escaped the ice that deeply blanketed Vancouver Island during the Fraser Glaciation, ending about 10,000 years ago. As a glacial refugium, the Brooks likely supported hardy plant communities unchanged throughout the millennia.

Roosevelt elk are the largest ungulates found on Vancouver Island. They prefer browsing in primary forest and inhabit larger watersheds such as the Tahsish River, Battle Creek and the Nasparti River. The Brooks Peninsula Provincial Park will further ensure the protection of Roosevelt elk habitat.

Few beaches on the Brooks Peninsula guarantee launching after you manage to land. Peddler's Cove, inside of Jackobsen Point, is the only refuge from extreme weather on the south side of the Brooks. A BC Parks interpretive sign at the head of a small trail greets you with insightful information about the area before showing the way to an outer beach. Several camping sites can be found along the stretch of beach west of Jackobsen Point. You can choose between accessing a beach from the outside or taking the more conservative approach of hiking your gear over the trail from the protected side of Peddler's Cove. Water sources on the rarely visited Brooks Peninsula are usually reliable.

ADDITIONAL ROUTES

Heading north: Venturing north of the Brooks Peninsula from Checleset Bay is nothing short of exhilarating. This area is for advanced paddlers only. If you can land at Amos Creek, a strenuous day's meander up the drainage will take you to fascinating alpine zones and breathtaking vistas. Off Cape Cook lies monolithic Solander Island, often circled by birds such as tufted puffins and rhinoceros auklets. Solander is off limits to humans as an ecological reserve for marine birds; it also bears the brunt of the weather that accelerates around the cape. North of the Brooks Peninsula, on its wild and rain-swept coast, the watersheds of Klaskish and East Creek are being threatened with large-scale clearcut logging by two forest companies. At time of writing, these watersheds are being drafted in the Vancouver Island Resource Target Plan, which unfortunately seems to have few provisions to protect drainages and wildlife habitat.

Heading south: Immediately south of Rugged Point is an expanse of sand beach interrupted by rocky outcrops. Rugged Point Marine Park includes this remote beach up to Kapoose Creek. Prior to the establishment of the Rugged Point park, a forestry reserve protected the line of trees that provide a scenic backdrop for the popular destination. Behind this veil of trees, however, you will find large clearcuts and tree farms. South of Kapoose Creek, clearcut logging has reached the water's edge. The dramatic coastline towards Tatchu Point is primarily rocky with pockets of gravel beach constantly being worked by the swell and surf of the Pacific; this is for advanced paddlers only. A few hours of paddling down this exposed coast will put you in Esperanza Inlet and the waters described in Chapter 12.

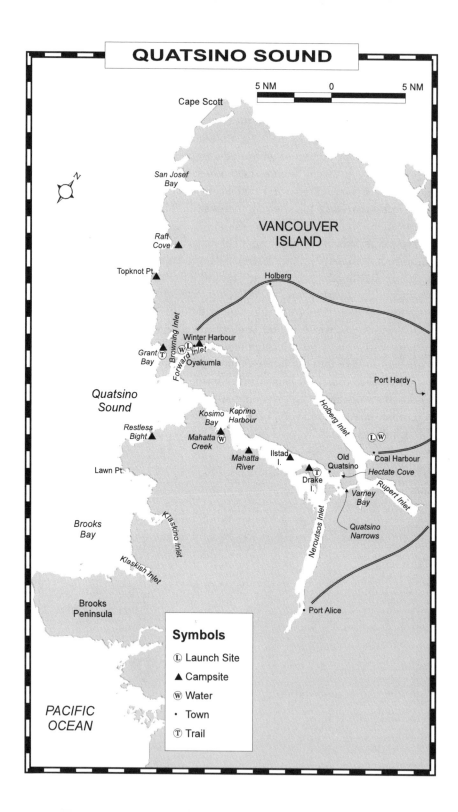

QUATSINO SOUND

5 NM   0   5 NM

Cape Scott

San Josef
Bay

VANCOUVER
ISLAND

Raft
Cove ▲

Topknot Pt.▲

Holberg

Browning Inlet

Winter Harbour ▲

Grant ▲
Bay Ⓣ   Ⓦ Ⓛ Forward Inlet
Oyakumla

Quatsino
Sound

Holberg Inlet

Port Hardy

Kosimo
Bay   Koprino
Harbour

Restless
Bight ▲

Mahatta Ⓦ
Creek

Ⓛ Ⓦ

Mahatta ▲
River   Ilstad
I. ▲

Lawn Pt.

Coal Harbour

Old
Quatsino • Hectate Cove

Drake Ⓣ
I. ▲

Brooks
Bay

Klaskino Inlet

Varney
Bay

Rupert Inlet

Quatsino
Narrows

Neroutsos Inlet

Klaskish Inlet

Brooks
Peninsula

• Port Alice

Symbols

Ⓛ Launch Site

▲ Campsite

Ⓦ Water

• Town

Ⓣ Trail

PACIFIC
OCEAN

Chapter Fourteen

Quatsino Sound
Fran Hunt-Jinnouchi

Despite the presence of major forestry and mining operations, the wild coastline and steep rockface in Quatsino Sound remain
much the same as they have for thousands of years. While the sound offers
both pristine wilderness and rigorous paddling, most interesting is that
Quatsino is still distinctly unpopulated by kayakers, and paddlers rarely
cross paths. With the rugged shoreline on one side and the brilliant, unre-
strained blue Pacific on the other, one cannot help but realize that the picturesque and tranquil sound will soon be discovered.

BACKGROUND

Quatsino Sound covers about 113 km (70 mi.) of waterways and has countless harbours of interest scattered along its shores. The most northern of
the five main sounds on the west coast of Vancouver Island, Quatsino
Sound has three arms: Neroutsos, Rupert and Holberg Inlets. Quatsino
has been interpreted to mean "people of the outside."

There were four native tribes throughout and to the north of Quatsino
Sound: the Koskimo, Giopino, Klaskino and Quatsino. Prior to the mid
1800s, there was also a tribe called the Hoyalas. Today, the main communities are Coal Harbour, Quatsino, Port Alice, Winter Harbour and Holberg
(Quatsino and Winter Harbour were important village sites of the Koskimo
people). During fishing season, the area is abuzz with activity, primarily in
and around Grant Bay and Winter Harbour. There are marinas at Coal Harbour, which has a government dock, and at Quatsino. Winter Harbour also
has a government dock.

On an unfortunate scenic note, major industries have developed in the

> Mahatta Creek. NORTH ISLAND KAYAK RENTALS

sound, such as the BHP Copper Mine in Rupert Inlet (closed in 1996) and the Western Forests Pulp Mill in Neroutsos Inlet. Logging activity has been extensive and ongoing, though somewhat scaled down today. Thankfully the birds don't seem to mind, and puffins, oystercatchers, murres, ducks, gulls, eagles and murrelets can be seen by those with a keen eye.

GETTING THERE

By land: You have to go through Port Hardy to reach Coal Harbour. Port Hardy is a community of 5,000 at the northern terminus of Highway 19 (the Island Highway). The drive from Nanaimo is approximately 4.5 hours. There is little in the way of amenities beyond Campbell River, especially if you are travelling in the evening, so be sure to have a full tank of gas. Securing accommodations can prove to be difficult without early reservations.

There are three First Nations in the immediate Port Hardy area: the Gwa'Sala-`Nakwaxda'wx, the Kwakwaka'wakw and the Quatsino. Calvin Hunt, a renowned Kwakwaka'wakw carver, owns and operates a native art gallery on the Kwakwaka'wakw reserve. The reserve is a 10-minute car ride from Port Hardy. Shops in Port Hardy carry almost everything you will need for your kayaking adventure including charts, groceries and camping gear. Coal Harbour is a tiny community approximately 18 km (11 mi.) or 15 minutes from Port Hardy. The road is paved and in good condition.

Winter Harbour is approximately 75 km (47 mi.) or 80 minutes from Port Hardy. The gravel road is usually kept in good shape though after heavy rains the potholes can be quite bad.

By air: The flight from Vancouver to Port Hardy on Pacific Coastal takes approximately 1 hour, and there is limousine service from the airport to town. It is possible to fly to Coal Harbour by float plane, but it is better to fly to the Port Hardy airport and take the shuttle to town or Coal Harbour. North Island Kayak Rentals in Port Hardy provides renters with a complimentary pick-up from the airport.

WEATHER AND HAZARDS

The weather in the Quatsino area is more or less typical of the west coast of Vancouver Island. Summer temperatures are mild, from a low of 8–10°c (46–50°F) at night to 16–20°c (61–68°F) during the day. May can be wet while July and August are the best months to avoid rain. The prevailing winds are generally from the west and in the afternoon. Wind funnelling down the sound creates a bit of chop. Rounding the point into Forward Inlet can be hazardous because of its openness to the Pacific; this area should be approached with caution. In late summer and early September, fog can appear but will usually dissipate before noon. Kayakers are cautioned to negotiate Quatsino Narrows during slack tide only.

There are some bears in the region, but they tend to avoid humans. Nonetheless, you should always approach bears and camping in bear country with extreme caution, particularly in Winter Harbour and Ahwhichaolto Inlet. There is a local garbage dump not too far inland that seems to attract bears that are prone to disturb campers. Eight years ago at a Rediscovery Children's Camp near Winter Harbour, seven bears came into the camp and made off with some food, and a cub got into the outhouse and stole a roll of toilet paper. In the last three years, however, tours in the Winter Harbour area have had no bear encounters. Either we have been lucky or the sound of all the drumming, singing and dancing has been scaring them off.

SPECIAL CONSIDERATIONS

I had the privilege of growing up in Quatsino Sound. My childhood was spent in the isolated Indian village, Quattishe, more recently known as Old Quatsino. My family and community made seasonal migrations to Winter Harbour to halibut and salmon fish.

We have not lived in Old Quatsino since the early 1970s, and prior to that time many of our people began their journey to larger centres in search of modern life and employment. My family was the very last to leave the village. During our last few weeks, grave robbers began to enter our shores and desecrate the gravesites in search of valuables. It was disturbing to watch, especially through my 12-year-old eyes. My community's experience with people entering our land has not always been pleasant, so for this reason and because of common courtesy and respect, kayakers are encouraged not to enter Old Quatsino. If you feel strongly about going ashore, please contact the Quatsino Band Council in writing.

Trip 33 Quatsino Sound

Skill:	Intermediate to advanced
Time:	4–10 days
Hazards:	Winds, currents and open coast (optional)
Access:	Coal Harbour/Winter Harbour
Charts:	3679 Quatsino Sound 1:50,000

3681   Plans Quatsino Sound
        Various scales
3686   Approaches to Winter Harbour
        1:15,000
Tide Book: Vol. 6

With Quatsino Sound as your destination, you can depart from Coal Harbour and paddle west to Winter Harbour, or vice versa. Paddling the east to west route will sometimes place you in a head-on position with howling winds, but either direction works. If you are launching from Coal Harbour, make sure your departure coincides with slack tide so you can run with an ebb tide.

A return trip between Coal Harbour and Winter Harbour usually takes around a week at a relaxed pace. Eight to 10 days would allow for full exploration of the area; if you are paddling one way, 3 to 4 days is sufficient. The main factor that can slow you down is the wind.

Launching

You can easily launch from Coal Harbour right off the beach or government dock; parking is nearby on the main road. You can also launch from the boat launch for $5 per kayak; there is a small fee for parking. The person who arranges parking and launching works inside the huge hanger that was once used to cut up whales. Coal Harbour also has a small store with a limited supply of goods, a post office and a restaurant. Fuel and water can be obtained at the dock.

In Winter Harbour, you can launch from the beach at the campsite just before town. Parking is inside the camping area, no charge. You can also go another mile into town and launch off the docks, or go to the end of the road and launch off the beach at "C" Scape B&B where Helen and "Winter Harbour" Bob will put you up for the night and keep your car safe. You can also park in and around the small village as long as you are not impeding the commercial fishing operations.

The following trip describes the route from Coal Harbour to Winter Harbour.

Sites

The whaling ramp and gigantic whalebone in the centre of town are testament to the whaling station that was active in Coal Harbour right up till the 1960s. DH Timber Towing and Salvage now operates chartered runs from the dock. You would be wise to talk to their very capable employees as to weather conditions, emergency channels and procedures; you can also advise them of your route—they are very helpful.

Departing from Coal Harbour, Quatsino Narrows quickly sets the tone for what lies ahead. Most paddlers do not venture off to Neroutsos or Holberg Inlets, though both inlets offer interesting exploration points. Day trips may be considered for these destinations.

Just prior to entering Quatsino Narrows is Varney Bay, on the south side of Rupert Inlet. This is where the Marble River enters the inlet. Varney Bay is an excellent site for bird- and otter-watching enthusiasts and a popular crabbing area. To enter the river, paddle through the narrow, attractive gorge in the bay; if time permits, you can follow the gorge to the bottom end of Marble River.

Quatsino Narrows   Quatsino Narrows is approximately 150-m (500-ft.) wide and 3.2-km (2-mi.) long, with steep rock walls on both sides. The rip tides and eddies at the northern entrance of the narrows are treacherous. Currents can run as fast as 8 knots and even the most experienced paddler is cautioned not to paddle the narrows during running tides. However, paddling during slack tide or a slow-moving tide provides you with one of the most enjoyable and attractive sites in Quatsino Sound. With eagles perched on low craggy trees, you may chance to pass just metres under one of these magnificent creatures. Be sure to have your camera in reach: it is not unusual to spot up to 50 bald eagles while paddling the relatively short narrows.

Coal Harbour is a former Royal Canadian Air Force base and a gun was once mounted at the narrows to restrict access. The warring aspect of the narrows goes back even further: as you pass through, look up the steep cliffs and try to imagine the Koskimo people luring their enemies to the harbour only to roll heavy logs down on them, smashing their canoes and drowning the paddlers. You can sometimes hear their cries if you paddle close enough to the cliffs' jagged walls.

If you are fond of cod or black bass, you are almost guaranteed a catch. Just toss your hook in along the steep wall and troll as you paddle. Black bass sizzled in soy sauce and garlic is extremely tasty. On the beaches of Hectate Cove you will find wild sea asparagus in abundance.

Old Quatsino was once a thriving community but has been reduced to a place of memories that sits eerily quiet. One small house remains along with a few hints of the people who inhabited the land not too long ago. As mentioned above, kayakers are asked not to enter Old Quatsino.

Drake and Ildstad Islands   A little farther west is the formidable Drake Island. Drake was once inhabited, and there are remnants of a homestead and meadow in the middle of the island. Pamphlet Cove sits in the centre of Drake Island on the north side and is a great place to stop overnight, as it provides protection from the winds. For those inclined to hike, a short trail leads to the south side of the island. Berries are plentiful and you are likely to stumble upon planted mistletoe. Drake Island has no fresh water. A small portion of Drake Island, approximately 8 ha (20 a.), is a Provincial Recreation Reserve. Do not camp on the exposed eel grass beach unless tides are very low.

Kayakers will find a good picnic spot on Ildstad Island. There is no major water source, but you can access a limited water supply at the creek on the north bank of the inlet behind Ildstad. You can camp in between the two small islands but only during extreme low tidal periods.

Cleogh Creek should be avoided. It is a noisy area with logging activity and waste is emitted into the ocean here. Mahatta River, or more specifically, the knoll just beyond Mahatta River, offers a nice campsite though the nearby generator hums constantly. A bonus feature of this area, however, is that there is usually plenty of fresh water. Koprino Harbour should be avoided because it is a busy log-booming site.

Mahatta Creek   Mahatta Creek is magnificent, truly breathtaking on a warm summer night when the moon glistens overhead. There is an excellent campsite to the east of Mahatta Creek, and the vast sandy beach and grassy areas provide plenty of camping spots, especially for large groups. Driftwood is usually at your disposal, and there is a fresh stream in the east corner of the beach. (Obtaining the water can be difficult, however, because the creek ends in a waterfall that tumbles into the sea.) Nonetheless, Mahatta Creek is an ideal spot. Berries of all varieties are bountiful, and the salmon fishing is excellent. Take a few minutes to paddle to the falls—the clear, icy water is beautiful and offers a refreshing cleanse. You will have to wait for high tide but the wait is worth it.

Try to arrange an early departure from Mahatta Creek because Forward Inlet can be difficult to negotiate. When you depart, be sure to immediately cross to the north side. The paddle to Forward Inlet can involve some large swells; there are also interesting rock formations along the wall. There are no places to stop except for emergency landings, so be prepared. Combine the swells with afternoon winds, and this area can spell trouble for less experienced paddlers. Expect to paddle for a few hours to reach your next destination, Oyakumla.

Oyakumla   Oyakumla is beautiful and offers fantastic camping. Known locally as Picnic Beach, Oyakumla is located on the northeast side of Forward Inlet as you make your way to Winter Harbour. It is discernable by its pebble beach. This is Quatsino Band reserve land, and permission to visit should be confirmed in writing with the band. If you haven't received advanced permission from the band, don't ruin the experience for others by camping illegally. You are only about 1.5 hours from Winter Harbour where campsites are available. On the east side of Oyakumla is a river with a great waterfall at the top. You can go for a day paddle to Grant Bay from here.

Grant Bay   An easy route to Grant Bay is to make the approximately 1-hour paddle from Oyakumla to Browning Inlet. Entry into Browning must occur at high tide or else the marsh area at the end of the inlet will be difficult to navigate. There is a path on the left side of the marsh indicated by a float tied to the branch of a tree. The hike into Grant Bay is about 35 minutes and not too difficult to manoeuvre. (This trail to Grant Bay also starts in Winter Harbour.) Grant Bay is splendid with its virgin white sand, high rushing waves, vast amounts of driftwood, berries and the odd glass ball.

Winter Harbour   The first houses in Winter Harbour date to the early 1930s when settlers lived on floats, fishing in the summer and hand logging in the winter. The harbour historically provided shelter for ships waiting out Pacific storms, and it continues to house a large commercial fishing fleet in the summer. Camping is available at the campsite just before town where there is a memorial pole in memory of my grandparents, who were lost at sea: Jessie and Billy George.

You can pull out at the beach by the campsite or at the docks in town.

ADDITIONAL ROUTES

Heading north and south: Both directions offer some of the most challenging paddling along the entire coast. The stretches from Winter Harbour around the Brooks Peninsula and from Winter Harbour around Cape Scott should be attempted by very experienced paddlers only. While it is usually possible to tuck in behind a point or a rock to avoid the swells, always be prepared for surf landings and, before you go, read the section on the open coast in Chapter 1.

If heading north, look for camping just past Topknot Point and at the north end of Raft Cove. If heading south, look for camping just north of Restless Bight and on the beaches of Brooks Bay.

CENTRAL COAST

Symbols

- Ⓛ Launch Site
- ▲ Campsite
- Ⓦ Water
- • Town

BRITISH COLUMBIA MAINLAND

Klemtu •
Ⓦ Ⓛ

Swindle I.

Finlayson Channel

Jackson Pass

Mathieson Channel

Dowager I.

Price I.

Milbanke Sound

Yeo I.

Ocean Falls
• Ⓦ
Ⓛ

Dean Channel

Seaforth Channel

Chatfield I.

Dufferin I.

Hose Pt. ▲

Cunningham I.

Bella Coola

King Island

Athlone I.

Cree Pt. ▲

Horsfall I.

Bella Bella/ McLoughlin Bay
Ⓦ
Ⓦ Ⓛ

Ⓦ • Ⓛ
Shearwater

Denny I.

Potts I. ▲

Campbell Island

Burke Channel

McMullin Group ▲

Soulsby Pt. ▲

Hunter Channel

Hunter I.

Queens Sound

▲

McNaughton Group

Kildidt Lagoon

Goose I.

▲

▲

Cultus Sound ▲

Kildidt Sound

Ⓛ Ⓦ
Namu

Hakai Recreation Area

Spider I.

▲ Ⓦ

Triquet I. ▲

Nalau Passage

Stirling I.

Koeye River

Fitz Hugh Sound

Hakai Passage

Hecate I.

Choked Passage

Pruth Bay

N

PACIFIC OCEAN

Calvert Island

5 NM   0   5 NM

Chapter Fifteen

The Central Coast
Frank Brown and John Nelson

The Central Coast is the ancient and contemporary home-land of the Heiltsuk, Kitasoo, Oweekeno and Nuxalk First Nations. For thousands of years, these peoples have derived their sustenance from the land and sea, with marine resources forming an integral part of their diet and economy. An intimate knowledge of these resources and environment is the basis of their survival and unique cultural achievements. Others have joined them more recently in their traditional territories, which are blessed with an amazing diversity of landscapes and wildlife. From tower-ing inland fiords to spectacular white sandy beaches, this largely unpopu-lated area will feed your soul with the sights and sounds of the unspoiled Pacific and the power of ancient cultures that live on today.

BACKGROUND

The Central Coast has just seven towns with 3,500 permanent residents in a 3 million-ha (7,410,000-a.) area. Most residents are native and live at the villages of Bella Bella, Bella Coola, Klemtu and Oweekeno. Ocean Falls, Shearwater and Hagensborg are the other communities in the area.

The Central Coast is bound by Tweedsmuir Provincial Park to the east, the Fiordland Recreation Area to the north and the Hakai Recreation Area to the west. Tweedsmuir is one of B.C.'s largest parks but is landlocked and of not much interest to paddlers. Fiordland Recreation Area is located northeast of Klemtu and occupies 76 500 ha (189,000 a.). Hakai Recreation Area, located on the outer coast south of Bella Bella, is an archipelago of small islands, well suited to exploration by kayak. Its 123 000 ha (304,000 a.) of ocean and islands make it the largest marine park on B.C.'s coast.

The Central Coast also contains five small marine parks, selected for their values as strategic anchorages and safe havens: Penrose Island, Codville Lagoon, Oliver Cove, Jackson Narrows and Green Inlet. A Central Coast Land Resource Management Plan (LRMP) is currently being developed and will take about two years to complete. While recreation areas have less formal protection than provincial parks, the LRMP is tasked with reviewing recreation area status and deciding whether these two areas should receive full park status or none at all. Both Hakai and Fiordland Recreation Areas are the subject of outstanding land claims, and the First Nations of the Central Coast are very concerned that the LRMP will be completed before their issues are properly resolved.

The Central Coast, however, is not just a place of politics. It is also a place of celebration, and in the summer of 1993 the Heiltsuk people hosted what may be the greatest gathering ever on this coast. Thousands of participants converged on Waglisla (Bella Bella) in ocean-going cedar canoes to celebrate indigenous maritime nations. The event was *Qatuwas*, "people gathered together in one place," and it renewed much of the cultural energy of communities up and down the coast.

GETTING THERE

By land: Bella Coola is the only community on the Central Coast that can be reached by road. From Vancouver, the journey starts with either Highway 99 (via Whistler) or Highway 1 (via Lytton) and goes to Cache Creek where the roads meet Highway 97 to Williams Lake. From Williams Lake, it is a 456 km (288 mi.) drive to Bella Coola along Highway 20, which is only paved for the first 221 km (137 mi.) and in the Bella Coola valley. Be careful when driving through Tweedsmuir Provincial Park and its notorious descent known as "the hill." With very steep grades and numerous switchbacks along a narrow gravel road, you must drive slowly, keeping a watchful eye for oncoming traffic and wildlife.

Sailing the coast. NORTH ISLAND KAYAK RENTALS

In Bella Coola, you can either take the ferry to your paddling destination (see below) or start your trip at the end of the road. Potential routes are only limited by time, ability and expectations (fiord routes versus outer coastal routes). There is pay parking at the Bella Coola launch site.

The Central Coast can also be reached via the Discovery Coast Ferry from Port Hardy on Vancouver Island. Port Hardy is 500 km (310 mi.) from Victoria or 391 km (242 mi.) from Nanaimo along Highway 19 (the Island Highway). Currently, you can park free of charge just outside the ferry compound at Port Hardy though this policy may change. Pay parking is available 2 km (1.25 mi.) away at Wildwoods campsite for $2 a day. Overnight camping is prohibited on B.C. Ferries property, so stay at a local hotel or campground the night before as most sailings depart early in the morning.

By water: The Discovery Coast Ferry, the newest addition to the B.C. Ferries fleet, leaves from Port Hardy and stops in Namu, McLoughlin Bay, Bella Bella, Shearwater, Klemtu, Ocean Falls and Bella Coola. Check the ferry schedule very carefully to determine when and where the ferry arrives and departs at each spot. Some ports are not available on all sailings though the ferry can launch kayaks directly from the ship without docking. Mid-channel launches or recoveries are at the discretion of the captain, subject to weather, and must be requested prior to sailing. Those kayakers wishing to do mid-channel launches or pick-ups should have a vhf radio. Contact the ferry on channel 11 north of Cape Caution and on channel 71 south of Cape Caution.

You can park your vehicle in Bella Coola or Port Hardy and take your kayak on board. Kayak wheels are handy. Ferry facilities include a licensed bar, storage lockers, a cafeteria, showers and a gift shop. Seats in the lounge recline to a sleeping position; you can also pitch a tent on the deck. Tents and binoculars are available for on-board use only. Water is also available.

Whether you are loading the ferry at Port Hardy or at Bella Coola, be sure to arrive at least 1 hour before departure, preferably 2 hours if your gear is disorganized. You will need the time to unload your gear, park your car and place your kayaks on the luggage racks. The length of voyage varies from 8 hours between Port Hardy and Namu, to as long as 33 hours between Port Hardy and Bella Coola. People taking a vehicle from Port Hardy to Bella Coola will need a reservation.

For information on the launching conditions at the ferry stops, see the section below on launching.

By air: A number of small airlines service the Central Coast including Wilderness Air, Timberline Air, Pacific Coastal and Air B.C.

WEATHER AND HAZARDS

The Central Coast is the home of the world's largest continuous area of intact coastal temperate rainforest. It has a generally wet and mild climate, and winds are predominately westerlies in the summer and easterlies in the winter. During the summer, sea breezes occur in most of the mainland inlets and fjords, beginning in the morning and often increasing to 20–25 knots in the afternoon. Winds typically decrease in the early evening though occasional gusty drainage winds can develop at night. Summer winds should not be taken lightly as many of the west to southwest winds funnelled into Milbanke Sound and other east-west channels along the Central Coast generate rough seas on ebbing tidal currents.

Visibility in the Central Coast is best in the spring. In late summer and fall, sea fog spreads over the area from the west and occasionally lowers visibility to less than 3.2 km (2 mi.). This fog can persist for several days until stronger, dryer winds flush it out of the area.

The Central Coast also has many localized hazards that directly affect kayakers. Currents often create tidal rapids in narrow passages, and tide rips occur where the waters of Fitz Hugh Sound drain into the open ocean such as at the western end of Hakai Passage. Open ocean swells can create boomers when they hit a submerged rock or reef, surf can make for dangerous landings, and campsites are few and far between. Be particularly cautious about the boat traffic in Fitz Hugh Sound, Hunter Channel and Milbanke Sound, and the potentially vicious water of Queens Sound.

Many of the offshore islands have black bears, and many of the mainland rivers, like the Koeye, have an ample supply of grizzly bears and the occasional wolf.

Help is often very far away, and passing fishing boats and pleasure craft may be your only chance for human contact. Do not attempt any journey if you cannot handle these conditions. None of the trips on the Central Coast are for beginners, and they should only be attempted by experienced sea kayakers who have done similar trips in wilderness areas. Kayak guiding companies provide excursions to this area for people who lack the necessary experience.

SPECIAL CONSIDERATIONS

Kayakers should be sensitive to the challenges their increasing numbers present to the Central Coast and be respectful of their potential impact on its natural and cultural sites. Regardless of whether these sites are on or off Indian Reserves, they are protected by law and very important to First Nations. Please avoid camping on any midden sites in the area unless you have the approval of the Heiltsuk.

Coastal First Nations have a long history of extensive trade networks and family ties up and down the coast and into the interior. The Heiltsuk have always welcomed visitors into their territory as long as they, and the resources and landscape that have sustained them for countless generations, are treated with respect. Local residents hope that mutual respect and reciprocity between themselves and visitors will be established. We

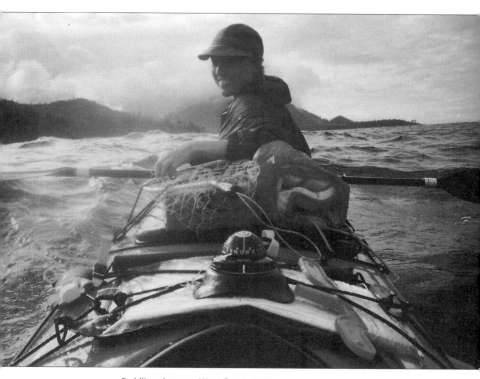

Paddling the open West Coast. NORTH ISLAND KAYAK RENTALS

would like to acknowledge and thank the Heiltsuk Cultural Education Centre (Jennifer Carpenter, director) and the Heiltsuk Fisheries Co-Management Program (John Bolton, director) for the information and perspectives they contributed to this chapter.

As always, try not to disturb any wildlife you may encounter on your travels. Be particularly cautious around Princess Royal Island, home to the Kermodei bear, a white black bear. This distinct coloration of the black bear is not albino, but a genetically distinct subspecies. These bears are unique, so it is important that they are not disturbed or harassed in any way. Pick kayaking routes that avoid Princess Royal Island; if you must camp on the island, be sure to hang your food, properly dispose of your dishwater and pack out all your garbage—as always!

Fecal contamination has been found in clam beds around Bella Bella. In association with the development of the Heiltsuk commercial clam fishery, Environment Canada has monitored water quality at commercial beaches since 1993. Beaches that tested clean in the past—and are today popular with kayakers—were found to be contaminated. The correlation is compelling, so you are asked to be very conscious of how you dispose of your waste. Clam beds are a source of both food and much needed employment for local residents.

One way kayakers can help reduce their impact is by supporting the construction of outhouses and composting toilets. Currently, no sites have outhouses except those in the Hakai Recreation Area. The Heiltsuk have expressed their support for constructing waste facilities as part of long-term management of recreational tourism in their traditional territory. Contact the Heiltsuk Tribal Council or the B.C. Marine Trail Association if you would like to contribute to this cause. (The BCMTA is currently pursuing a protocol agreement with the Heiltsuk Tribal Council.)

CENTRAL COAST TRIP (34)

There is no shortage of kayak trips in the waters of the Central Coast. From the surf beaches of Cape Caution, to the intricate island archipelagos of Hakai Passage, your options are only limited by your skill and imagination. The trip described in this chapter is based around Discovery Coast Ferry stops (described below) and covers a mere fraction of what the region has to offer. Feel free to explore the other paddling possibilities that exist throughout this isolated and wild stretch of the Pacific.

Launching

Namu Namu is an ancient village and processing site of the Heiltsuk and the oldest dated location on the coast. More recently it was a cannery site, and evidence of the old outbuildings can still be seen today. The Heiltsuk are currently seeking to regain this property and have it designated as a Canadian and World Heritage Site. In its current condition, don't expect much in the way of services when you arrive. The ferry ties up to a large floating dock where kayaks are simply walked off the ferry and launched. For those interested in trout fishing or simply walking through a very beautiful forest, Namu Lake is a 10-minute walk from the dock. Cold Creek, just south of Namu, has a long pebble beach suitable for camping and a source of fresh water.

Bella Bella/McLoughlin Bay Bella Bella, also known as Waglisla, is the home of the Heiltsuk First Nation and the largest native community on the Central Coast. With a population of 1,800, the present-day community of Waglisla is located on the east coast of Campbell Island, just north of the Discovery Coast Ferry stop at McLoughlin Bay (Old Bella Bella). The Bella Bella band store can be accessed from the government dock and offers dry goods, souvenirs and groceries. Waglisla also has a post office, fuel station, hospital, clinic and RCMP detachment. Be sure to visit the Heiltsuk Cultural Centre, located in the Bella Bella Community School just up from the wharf; you will find a wealth of information about Heiltsuk history, language, culture and community. A number of B&BS and charter operations are also located in Waglisla. The Bella Bella Coast Guard Auxiliary is on stand-by for marine emergencies.

At McLoughlin Bay, kayaks are unloaded from the ferry on special carts that can be walked directly to the shore. There is a commercial waterfront campsite with a few rustic cabins, and fresh water can be obtained from outdoor hoses at the fish plant and at the Bella Bella wharf. An interpretive centre offers Heiltsuk cultural sharing, traditional arts and crafts as well as guided nature walks and ocean canoe tours or expeditions. Most of these activities are offered through SeeQuest Adventures though a number of different charter companies will provide pick-up and drop-off service for kayakers.

Shearwater   Shearwater is a community of 75 people with two hotels, a restaurant pub and a small marine store. The community is located across from Bella Bella on Denny Island, and a sea bus runs on a regular schedule between the two towns. Kayak carts are off-loaded at the head of the ferry wharf. You then simply walk your kayak down the adjacent boat launch right into the water. There is water at the pub, and kayak rentals are available. Note: Shearwater is sometimes referred to as Bella Bella (due to its role as the Bella Bella postal drop).

Klemtu   Klemtu, located on the east coast of Swindle Island, is home to the Kitasoo First Nation. There are 450 residents, two grocery stores, a post office, a commercial campground, a B&B and a medical clinic. The Discovery Coast Ferry docks next to the government wharf. The ferry crew is happy to bring your kayak cart either to a float beside the ferry ramp or to the adjacent beach, which is a little rocky. There is water at the fuel dock.

Ocean Falls   Ocean Falls, a community of 50 people if you include the nearby town of Martin Valley, is located at the head of Cousins Inlet. There is a grocery store, post office, pub, restaurant, café and accommodation. For those looking for a new kayak, check out Rain Raven Kayaks, which sells locally made hand-built kayaks and canoes. Please note that Ocean Falls has no medical facilities. Martin Valley is located 3 km (2 mi.) from Ocean Falls. Your kayak cart will be left at the top of the wharf when unloaded from the ferry. To launch, walk down to the adjacent government wharf.

Bella Coola Bella Coola is the main town for the Nuxalk First Nation and has numerous hotels, B&Bs, restaurants, grocery stores, a post office, an RCMP detachment and a hospital. The Bella Coola Valley has 2,500 permanent residents, including the community of Hagensborg, located 18 km (11 mi.) from Bella Coola. You can launch from the government wharf immediately adjacent to the ferry dock. There are pay phones here but no other facilities; the actual town of Bella Coola is 3 km (2 mi.) away. Water can be obtained from the gas station in town or you can try the fuel dock.

Trip 34 Bella Bella and the Hakai Recreation Area

Skill:	Intermediate to advanced
Time:	7–21 days
Hazards:	Open ocean, tidal currents and boat traffic
Access:	Discovery Coast Ferry/Bella Coola
Charts:	3744 Queen Charlotte Sound 1:365,100
	3784 Kwakshua Channel to Spider Island and Namu 1:36,800
	3786 Queens Sound and Approaches 1:36,500
	3787 Queens Sound to Seaforth Channel 1:36,400
Tide Book:	Vol. 6

This trip to the Hakai Recreation Area starts in Bella Bella and is located entirely within Heiltsuk traditional territory. The journey begins at the ferry stop in McLoughlin Bay and heads west up Seaforth Channel.

Rounding Horsfall, Dufferin or Athlone Islands places you in the north end of Queens Sound and provides great access for those looking to camp in the McMullin Group or, for the truly adventurous, the Goose Group. Farther south, campsites in Cultus Sound and on Triquet and Stirling Islands create ideal bases for venturing into the surrounding lagoons. For people with more time, camping on the wind-swept beaches of Calvert Island or the rugged coast of the mainland offers a chance to get off the beaten path. At least this is usually true; you may find yourself on the doorstep of a fishing lodge—such is the West Coast. Paddling back to Bella Bella via Hunter Channel provides you with a change in scenery and a sheltered last leg to your journey.

Please note that unless you are prepared for outer coastal conditions, including surf landings and launches, as well as open ocean swell, you should avoid paddling the western end of Seaforth Channel and any shorelines exposed to the full force of Queens Sound. If you are unsure of your abilities, limit your paddling to the waters easily accessed from Hunter Channel. Be prepared to carry an ample supply of water, as there are few water sources in this region. Use vhf channel 2 for continuous weather broadcasts. Residents use channel 6, so this is a good channel to listen to for local chatter or to call for assistance. There is also a BC Parks headquarters at Pruth Bay from May to September; visitors are encouraged to drop in for information.

Sites

Hose Point   Leaving from McLoughlin Bay, you will briefly enter Lama Passage heading north and pass Dryad Point before heading west up Seaforth Channel. Just past Hose Point, at the north end of Horsfall Island, is a gently sloping gravel beach. There is room for three tents just up from the beach and a small creek at each end. Please note that clam digging is prohibited, and there is no toilet. Also, avoid camping on any shell middens in the area.

Cree Point   If you paddle south on the west or east side of Dufferin Island and have your timing quite right, you will likely encounter tidal rapids. Don't let these be a deterrent, however, as rapids often mark the presence of island lagoons and exploring in these parts is bound to uncover some gems. The campsite at Cree Point is in a sheltered cove at the extreme southern tip of Dufferin Island. The boulders that cover the beach at low tide have been moved to make for easy landing and launching on the sand. There is room for three tents but no water or outhouse. Please do not realign any of the rocks as this can disturb the Heiltsuk historical record and the pattern of traditional use sites.

The clam fishery in nearby Gale Creek is very sensitive, and kayakers should avoid the area completely if possible. Camping is off limits as is any discharge of waste in transit.

Louise Channel   There is a great white sand beach located on the east shore of a very small island at the southwest end of Louise Channel, just south of Potts Island. Hazards include currents, surf and reefs as you approach the island. The waters outside the basin are exposed to the pounding seas of Queens Sound, but a ring of islets protects the bay, and the landing is relatively easy. Look for the short trail that leads up from the beach to the tent spots. Once again, there is no drinking water or outhouse.

McMullin Group   For paddlers prepared to venture the perils of Queens Sound, the beaches of the McMullin Group will be your just reward. These small islands sit just north of the Goose Group and often appear as an oasis, fading in and out of the haze of the horizon. Exposed to the full brunt of the open Pacific, they are rugged, isolated and incredibly beautiful. Head for the lee side of the largest island if you want to land and camp. The beach is large, with a couple of different approaches, and you should have no trouble avoiding surf. There is no water, and weather can keep you pinned here for a few days. Be prepared.

If you are not comfortable with this sort of exposed paddling, work your way south and through the maze of intricate islands that border Queens Sound to the east. For a place to camp, try North McNaughton; the site has an easy landing at high tide. There is no toilet or water but there is room for a few tents.

Goose Group   A short hop from the McMullin Group, and even more exposed, is the Goose Group. So far from the rest of the Hakai Recreation Area, these islands truly have a character all to themselves. Their bogs, beaches and lagoons can keep you occupied for days while the stunning vistas of the distant Coast Range act as a reminder of where you must ultimately return.

There is camping at Snipe Island (often called Little Gull), just west of Gull Island, and on the outside of Goose Island, just below the northern tip. Please do not use the beach right at the north end of Goose: it is a Heiltsuk Rediscovery Camp. The Indian Reserves on the south end of Goose Island and the north end of Duck Island are private property and also off limits to the public. Bring your own water—sources on the islands are questionable.

Cultus Sound   Heading east from the Goose Group towards Cultus Sound is an exposed 9-km (5.5-mi.) crossing. Check the weather forecasts and time your crossing carefully. As you approach Cultus Sound, be cautious of tidal activity and rebounding waves. The sea can be extremely tricky in these parts, often rocking your boat in one direction and throwing it in another. Thankfully, the campsite in Cultus Sound, on the west side of Hunter Island, is well protected with an easy landing.

As you enter the sound, look for a beautiful sand beach flanked by two rocky shores. There is great beach camping here, as well as six tent spots in the woods and a box toilet. Fishing in the surrounding area is excellent and exploring the nearby lagoons reveals a whole new coastal environment. Take some time and study the amazing intertidal life that flourishes at the entrance to these lagoons. If possible, paddle in and drift about the serene waters. A few of the streams that flow into the lagoons lead to lakes, and a short hike can often bring the reward of a fresh-water bath. Don't forget, however, that as the tide drops, your doorway to this world will quickly close, only to open again at the next high water slack.

The paddle south to Triquet Island is delightful. Around headlands the waters can get a little tricky, particularly at the mouth of Cultus Sound, but for the most part you are protected from the raging Pacific and are free to enjoy the charms and passages of the many islets. If fog rolls in, these islets can quickly transform into a harrowing maze, so use care as there are not a lot of landing sites. On the way south, you might want to stop at Spider Island to explore the wooden road, remnants of a World War II military base, and fill your water bottles in the creek at the northeast end of the island.

Triquet Island   If the sun is shinning when you reach Triquet Island, the scene will be blissfully tropical. On the northern side of the island, there are a number of large, sandy beaches and plenty of room for camping. Landing is easy as the island is protected from the surf and southerly winds, though a few of the beaches become muddy, even quicksand-like, at low tide. There is no fresh water, but BC Parks has provided a box toilet.

Please avoid the shell midden at the north end. There is plenty of camping on the adjacent beaches.

Stirling Island   Plan carefully when you head west across Kildidt Sound. Not only is the area exposed, but the seas can get nasty at the western edge of Nalau Passage and Hakai Passage. Try to avoid the combination of strong west winds and a falling tide. Also, keep your distance from the schools of sport-fishing boats in the area. When $500 per day is the going rate, the last place you want to be is between a fisher and his catch. Although BC Parks lists Stirling Island as a campsite, there are a number of shell middens on the eastern shore that should be avoided.

Choked Passage Beaches   Farther south, the west coast of Calvert Island offers little shelter but many rewards for the intrepid paddler. At the northwest tip, beaches line the shores of Choked Passage and provide great camping just above the high tide mark. On the downside, there is a large fishing lodge nestled in the nearby woods; on the upside, the lodge is actually quite nice. Nonetheless, you will likely want to camp a good distance away. There is a hiking trail across private land to Pruth Bay and a BC Parks ranger station staffed during the summer. While there is no drinking water, there is a pit toilet at the Wolf Beach site.

At this point, you may want either to continue south to Port Hardy via the wild and stunning waters of Cape Caution or to cross over to the magnificent Koeye River en route to Namu and the Discovery Coast Ferry. For those heading back to Bella Bella, your best bet is to retrace your strokes to the site at Cultus Sound. From here, heading up Hunter Channel offers the most direct route to McLoughlin Bay and gives you a chance to try one more campsite before heading home.

Soulsby Point   Graced with spring wildflowers, the small island off Soulsby Point has a white shell beach and room for two or three tents. There is no water or outhouse on the island but you are now in a great position for the final leg of your journey. Of course, this might just be the starting point to a whole new paddling adventure . . .

ADDITIONAL ROUTES

Heading north: Paddling towards Klemtu puts you in Kitasoo territory. Until the Kitasoo Nation develops a tourism policy, the band council has asked that their area not be promoted in this book. Nonetheless, visitors are welcome and will not be turned away. Please check with the band office on arrival. You can also check with the BCMTA or the band office to find out the status of the Kitasoo tourism policy.

Heading northeast: Paddling towards Mussel and Kynoch Inlets and the fiords on the mainland puts you in the Fiordland Recreation Area. This area is known for its very steep cliffs that soar hundreds of feet above the ocean. Mountain goats grace the cliffs, while grizzly bears roam the rivers pouring into the inlets. A handful of kayakers paddle this route each year, a difficult trip due to the very few camping spots. BC Parks prohibits camping on estuaries within the recreation area because of the danger of bear encounters. This leaves only two small beaches where you can camp, but for paddlers up to the challenge, the scenery is the reward.

Look for the pebble beach east of David Bay, where a small creek flows into the south side of Mussel Inlet. There are a couple of rough tent spots in the woods and no facilities. The view is amazing when you wake up in the morning to look at the large waterfall flowing out of Lizette Lake amid the towering fiord walls that surround you. David Bay and Oatswish Bay are two delightful places to explore in Mussel Inlet. The estuaries of Mussel River and Poison Cove Creek will yield trout as well as bear sightings.

The small pebble beach at Heathorn Bay is the only other place we know of where you can camp in the Fiordland Recreation Area. Be aware that there can be currents and turbulence at Matheison Narrows. Heathorn Bay has a couple of rough tent spots in the woods but lacks any facilities, including water.

Take time to explore Kynoch Inlet, which has amazing views, including a large waterfall flowing directly into the ocean. Pick Desbrisay Bay as a lunch spot but not a campsite—bears.

Heading south: Paddling towards Port Hardy is one of the most enjoyable and challenging trips on the coast. If you decide to paddle south from Namu along the mainland, as opposed to the outside of Calvert Island, you will quickly encounter the magnificent Koeye River. The estuary of the river is prime grizzly habitat and must be approached with caution; camping is currently available near the river mouth. Farther south, camps at Penrose Island/Fury Island Marine Park and Cranston Point allow the paddler to rest up before attempting Cape Caution. Camping can be found at Burnett Bay and many of the smaller beaches near Cape Caution though it is likely you will have to execute a surf landing. For those mentally and physically prepared for such conditions, you won't be disappointed: the massive sand beaches are some of the most impressive in the Pacific Northwest and home to many gray whales during the summer. Please keep in mind that the weather and exposure on this stretch of the coast is severe and should only be attempted by advanced paddlers. Be sure to leave yourself plenty of time. Continuing south will place you in the waters described in Chapter 9.

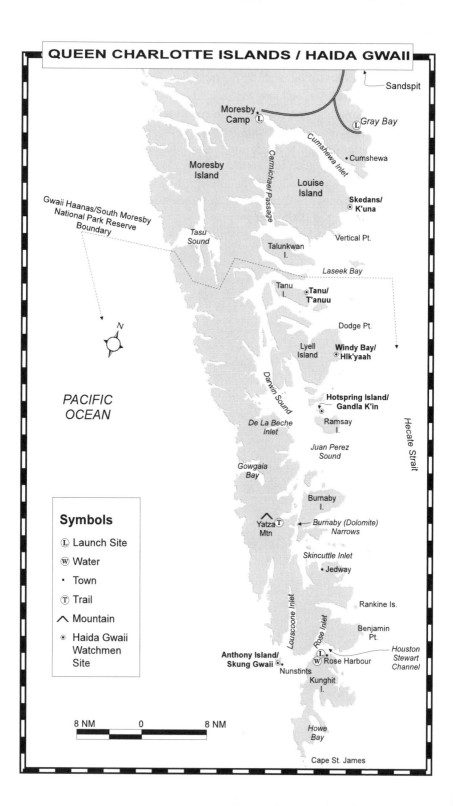

QUEEN CHARLOTTE ISLANDS / HAIDA GWAII

Sandspit

Moresby Camp Ⓛ

Ⓛ Gray Bay

Cumshewa Inlet

• Cumshewa

Moresby Island

Carmichael Passage

Louise Island

Skedans/ ⊙ K'una

Gwaii Haanas/South Moresby National Park Reserve Boundary

Tasu Sound

Talunkwan I.

Vertical Pt.

Laseek Bay

Tanu I.

⊙ Tanu/ T'anuu

Dodge Pt.

N

Lyell Island

Windy Bay/ ⊙ Hlk'yaah

PACIFIC OCEAN

Darwin Sound

Hotspring Island/ Gandla K'in ⊙

De La Beche Inlet

Ramsay I.

Juan Perez Sound

Hecate Strait

Gowgaia Bay

Burnaby I.

Yatza Ⓣ Mtn

Burnaby (Dolomite) Narrows

Symbols

Ⓛ Launch Site

ⓦ Water

• Town

Ⓣ Trail

⋀ Mountain

⊙ Haida Gwaii Watchmen Site

Skincuttle Inlet

• Jedway

Rankine Is.

Louscoone Inlet

Rose Inlet

Benjamin Pt.

Ⓛ •

ⓦ Rose Harbour

Houston Stewart Channel

Anthony Island/ Skung Gwaii ⊙•

Nunstints

Kunghit I.

8 NM   0   8 NM

Howe Bay

Cape St. James

Chapter Sixteen

Queen Charlotte Islands/Haida Gwaii

Peter McGee and Michele Deakin

Not long ago the notorious stretch of water known as Hecate Strait was paddled by the Haida during raids on mainland tribes. Legend has it that following an attack, the Haida canoes would turn and head towards Haida Gwaii, the Queen Charlotte Islands, leaving their less seaworthy adversaries bound to the mainland for fear of crossing the strait. Times have changed, but even today the isolation of the islands continues to preserve their natural and cultural wealth. Nowhere is this more apparent than in Gwaii Haanas/South Moresby National Park Reserve and Haida Heritage Site in the southern third of the archipelago. Here the paddler can travel through sheltered bays and inlets, explore ancient forests and Haida villages, and gain a sense of the wilderness and society that have lived together since time began. Gwaii Haanas is an area so distinctive, both culturally and biologically, it is often referred to as the Canadian Galapagos. It is truly one of the world's great paddling destinations.

BACKGROUND

A variety of cultures and nationalities has recently shaped the history of the Queen Charlotte Islands/Haida Gwaii, but the culture that has truly reigned is that of the Haida. At points in their 10,000-year history, it is estimated that the Haida population on the islands was upwards of 20,000; by 1870, however, smallpox epidemics had come close to decimating them. The Haida who survived, roughly 1,500 people, left their traditional villages and congregated in Skidegate and Old Massett. Since then, the Haida have regained their political voice, though Spanish, French, British, American and Canadian influences have forever altered many of the 140 islands.

As elsewhere in the province, the logging industry thrived in the Queen Charlotte Islands for the better part of this century, largely unchecked by environmental concerns. In 1974, a small but dedicated group contested the logging plans of Burnaby Island, situated 120 km (75 mi.) south of Sandspit, and the struggle to save South Moresby began.

Fourteen years later, following a preservation campaign that reached people around the world, the provincial government signed a deal with the federal government that transferred the rights of the land from the province to Ottawa and established the national park reserve in South Moresby. The total cost to the federal government for the preservation of Lyell Island to Cape St. James, a wild and remote area that stretches 90 km (56 mi.), was $106 million.

Although native land claims have yet to be resolved and ultimate authority over the land yet to be determined, the area is currently co-managed by Parks Canada as a national park reserve and by the Council of the Haida Nation as a Haida Heritage Site. The legal agreement that creates Gwaii Haanas as a cooperatively managed/protected area recognizes that long-term protective measures are essential to safeguard the archipelago as one of the world's great natural and cultural treasures. Gwaii Haanas also reflects the desire to sustain Haida culture and provides for the continuation of cultural activities and traditional renewable resource harvesting activities.

GETTING THERE

There are two considerations when going to the Queen Charlotte Islands: how much time you've got and how much money you want to spend. In general, getting to the islands is neither quick nor inexpensive.

You can either drive to Port Hardy or Prince Rupert and take a B.C. ferry to Skidegate Landing, with or without your vehicle, or you can fly to Sandspit. It is possible to rent a car on the islands, but this tends to be quite expensive. However, getting around the Charlottes without a vehicle is difficult, so you should make arrangements for the appropriate transportation. A third option for reaching the islands is to take an Alaska Marine Highway ferry, from either Washington State or Alaska to Prince Rupert, and then board a B.C. ferry.

By land: It is about a 20-hour drive to Prince Rupert from Vancouver, along Highways 1 and 97 to Prince George, and then through the pic-

East coast of Louise Island. PETER McGEE

turesque interior of the province on Highway 16 (the Yellowhead). With a car full of people, this is by far the cheapest way to go. Once in Prince Rupert, follow the signs to the B.C. Ferries terminal and catch the sailing to Skidegate Landing.

If you are on Vancouver Island (or want to spend more time on a boat than in a car), your best bet is to drive to Port Hardy and catch the ferry to Prince Rupert. See Chapter 15 for information about the ferry terminal at Port Hardy. Often people will take the ferry one way and drive the other— a good way to mix up the scenery.

If you have extra time, you can also try the train; VIA Rail leaves Vancouver three times a week for Prince Rupert. The trip takes three days, with overnights in Jasper and Prince George at your own expense. Greyhound Bus Lines operates a two-day service between Vancouver and Prince Rupert.

By water: B.C. Ferries sails from Port Hardy to Prince Rupert, then from Prince Rupert to Skidegate Landing. Alaska Marine Highway ferries sail from Washington State and Alaska to Prince Rupert. These trips are a great way to see the coast and meet people. You must have advance reservations for all ferry rides, and reservations should be made for both directions, even though stand-by spots do come available.

By air: Canadian Regional Airlines flies twice daily to Sandspit from Vancouver. The flight time is approximately 1.5 hours. Once in Sandspit, Harbour Air and South Moresby Air can fly you into Gwaii Haanas. Both

Canadian Airlines and Air B.C. offer daily flights to Prince Rupert from Vancouver; again, flight time is approximately 1.5 hours.

WEATHER AND HAZARDS

The climate of the Queen Charlottes is typical of B.C.'s West Coast: cool and wet at virtually any time of year. May, June and July are generally the driest months. The rainy season can begin as early as mid-August. The east side of the islands is considerably drier than the west, which can receive 500–800 cm (200–315 in.) of rain a year. Northwest and westerly winds prevail in summer and can blow hard for lengthy periods of time. These winds often funnel over Moresby Island and down the inlets of the east coast creating sudden gusty conditions that can be a hazard to kayakers. Storms associated with the passage of a frontal system hammer the islands from the southeast and southwest. These occur frequently throughout the winter and are not uncommon in the summer. There are no guarantees here, but, in general, the best months for paddling are from mid-June through mid-August. As always, make sure you build enough time into your plans for the days you may be "weathered in" and unable to travel.

Use caution travelling around exposed points of land as there are often strong tidal currents, swells and winds. Tidal currents occur elsewhere throughout the islands so be sure to check the charts and tide tables, especially in the Houston Stewart Channel area. Sea fog occurs frequently during the summer along the West Coast and throughout the Houston Stewart Channel area.

You should also use proper bear etiquette in Gwaii Haanas (see Chapter 1). Although there are no grizzlies on the islands, the black bears here are among the largest in North America: their snouts tend to be longer, their jaws and teeth heavier. In the event of problem encounters between bears and people, the park's policy is to close areas to public use. They will not remove any bears. Don't ruin the experience for others—be sure to bear-proof your camp. Please be particularly careful around Burnaby Narrows and Rose Inlet.

Please note: Although Gwaii Haanas is a managed park reserve, it is also extremely isolated and help may be a long way off.

SPECIAL CONSIDERATIONS

Reservations, registrations and orientations: Gwaii Haanas is in the midst of introducing several visitor management systems for reservations, registrations and orientations. These are intended to reduce crowding during the peak season, increase public safety and ensure environmental impacts are reduced in the protected area. User fees will be introduced in 1998.

If you are planning a trip into Gwaii Haanas as an independent traveller, contact the Gwaii Haanas office for information on how to make an advance reservation. If you choose not to make an advance reservation, you and the members of your group must travel into Gwaii Haanas using daily walk-in space; there is no guarantee that space will be available. Reservations are highly recommended, and group size is limited to 12 people.

Everyone travelling into Gwaii Haanas *must* take the orientation session and register each trip they take. Registration provides information that is essential to managing the protected area. The orientation is also a means for you to get updates, the latest safety or closure information and interesting new research findings that will make your trip safer and more enjoyable. Visitors travelling with an operator will receive their orientation from that operator.

The information on campsites in this chapter is limited, as requested by Parks Canada and the Council of the Haida Nation, to ensure that the necessary exchange between paddlers and Gwaii Haanas personnel occurs. We all believe this will allow the area to be managed in the best possible way.

The Haida Gwaii Watchmen: The Haida Nation started the Watchmen program in 1981 when the number of visitors to the area started to increase. Parks Canada began funding the program in 1990 and continues to work jointly with the Haida Gwaii Watchmen.

Haida Watchmen live at five of the village sites in Gwaii Haanas during the visitor season. There are usually two to four people at each site, including one elder. The Watchmen are not there as attendants or servants but as guardians and hosts who provide basic assistance to visitors. The village sites are K'una (Skedans, which is actually outside Gwaii Haanas), T'anuu (Tanu), Hlk'yaah (Windy Bay), Gandla K'in (Hotspring Island) and Skung Gwaii (Anthony Island). The village of Nunstints (formerly Ninstints) on Skung Gwaii is considered to have the world's finest display of Haida mortuary poles, all of which are more than 100 years old. In consultation with the Haida people, UNESCO declared Skung Gwaii/Anthony Island a World Heritage Site in 1981.

Trip 35   Gwaii Haanas

Skill: Intermediate to advanced
Time: 7 days and up
Hazards: Isolation and frequent weather changes
Access: Moresby Camp/Gray Bay/boat and plane charters
Charts: 3807   Atli Inlet to Selwyn Inlet 1:37,500
3808   Juan Perez Sound   1:37,500
3809   Carpenter Bay to Burnaby Island 1:37,500
3825   Cape St. James to Houston Stewart Channel   1:40,000
3853   Cape St. James to Cumshewa Inlet and Tasu Sound   1:50:000
3855   Houston Stewart Channel 1:20,000
Tide Book: Vol. 6

Most of the paddling that occurs in the Queen Charlotte Islands takes place in the Gwaii Haanas park reserve. From Sandspit you can paddle to the beginning of Gwaii Haanas, but conditions can be quite treacherous and most people choose to launch from Moresby Camp. A one-way trip from Moresby Camp to Skung Gwaii (at the south end of Gwaii Haanas) can take as little as a week, but allow at least two so you have time to enjoy yourself. The ultimate journey is a trip from Moresby Camp to Skung Gwaii and back, paddling both inside and outside the smaller islands on the east coast of Moresby.

However, laying out an agenda is not true wilderness travel in Gwaii Haanas, and some careful spontaneity is encouraged. When too many people follow a pre-determined, predictable itinerary, the results are over-crowding at Watchmen sites and campsites, and heavy user impacts. Paddlers looking to experience the real Gwaii Haanas should pick an area based on the charts and explore it. Slow down to the rhythm of the tides, poke in and out of the little bays and be open to the "whole" of Gwaii Haanas. To travel the area and check sites off a list is to miss the connection between humans and the land. Let Gwaii Haanas define you.

Paddlers who do not have time to cover the whole Gwaii Haanas tend to focus trips either around Hotspring Island and the centre of Gwaii Haanas or around Skung Gwaii and the village of Nunstints. It is also worth noting that, though more expensive, customizing your trip to Gwaii Haanas is relatively easy, and boat and plane charters can make drop-offs and pick-ups at the destination of your choice. The northern boundary of Gwaii Haanas lies a good 2 days' paddle (under reasonable conditions) from the closest road access at Moresby Camp, so arranging a charter makes sense if you are short on time. The boundary for Gwaii Haanas begins near Talunkwan Island. Some options:

- Explore Tanu, Juan Perez Sound, Hotspring Island and Burnaby Narrows, with put-in and pick-up sites to be determined by your charter.
- Explore the southern end of Gwaii Haanas, visiting Skung Gwaii and using Rose Harbour as a put-in and pick-up site.
- To limit your charter costs, paddle one way from Moresby Camp to Juan Perez Sound, or vice versa. Another possibility is to take a commercial trip, many of which are only a week in length and simplify the logistics of dealing with charters and rentals.
- With two weeks, your options open up a little. One possibility is to simply take more time to paddle one of the trips described above. For those who want to cover a little more ground, consider launching from the north end of Gwaii Haanas, around Tanu, and paddling to Skung Gwaii, or vice versa. If you want to cut down your charter costs, you can always put in or pull out from Moresby Camp or Gray Bay.

If you have three weeks or more, paddling from Moresby Camp to Skung Gwaii and back will give you the best sense of the area. Ironically, though this is the longest trip, it is also the cheapest as there are no charter costs involved. This is the trip described below.

Launching

Moresby Camp is the closest road access to Gwaii Haanas and the preferred launching spot for independent paddlers. Most tour companies have designated drop-off and pick-up spots within the park reserve. Other options include launching at Gray Bay or taking a boat or plane into Gwaii Haanas to the launch site of your choice.

To reach Moresby Camp or Gray Bay, you need to travel on active logging roads. Moresby Camp is about 32 km (20 mi.) from the ferry terminal. To reach the camp, turn right as you leave the terminal and drive for about 10 km (6 mi.) to South Bay. Continue for 7 km (4.5 mi.) along the Main Line and turn right onto the Moresby Main. Another 11 km (7 mi.) will take you to the Moresby Camp recreation site. There is an outhouse, dock and creek, but the site is quite industrial so you are advised to bring your own water.

To reach Gray Bay from Sandspit, drive south past the golf course and along the gravel Main Line. At the 14-mile marker (22.5 km), turn left and drive another 11 km (7 mi.) until you reach the sand beach of Gray Bay. There are a number of Forest Service campsites and a small creek, but the water is not drinkable.

From May to the beginning of September, check with the visitor information centre upon arrival for further information on the state of the logging roads. In the off-season you can call TimberWest in Sandspit. It is also possible to paddle directly from Sandspit, but the seas here are shallow and confused, creating hazardous conditions.

Sites

Random camping is practised in Gwaii Haanas. You camp where you please though there are exceptions: camping is not permitted at T'anuu Village or on Gandla K'in (Hotspring Island), Ata Naa (House Island), Rankine Island, Copper Island, Jeffrey Islands, Slug Islet, Skung Gwaii (Anthony Island) or Burnaby Narrows. Maximum group size is 12, and you are asked to limit your stay at any one campsite to a maximum of 4–5 days. Although not at every campsite, water is plentiful throughout the islands.

Launching from Moresby Camp puts you at the head of Cumshewa Inlet, an area of active logging. You will probably want to head south around the exposed side of Louise Island or through Carmichael Passage as quickly as possible. Try to catch the ebb tide from Moresby Camp and, if taking the outside route, exercise caution as you pass over the shoal and kelp bed near Skedans Point.

Skedans/K'una   If you have chosen the outside route, don't miss the chance to visit the village of Skedans/K'una. Traditionally a Raven Crest site, it is estimated that Skedans had upwards of 30 houses and 738 inhabitants prior to 1890 when, aside from seasonal use, it was abandoned for a site on Maude Island and then Skidegate. Most of the totems at Skedans that were not taken to museums or private collections have fallen, but dramatic carvings can still be detected amidst the moss and decay. According to George F. MacDonald's *Haida Monumental Art: Villages of the Queen Charlotte Islands*, the head chief of Skedans, Gida'nsta, was friends with Chief Tsebassa of Kitkatla, which led to the introduction of many new crests and stories from the mainland. The three dominant Raven families shared the same crests, with the exception of the moon, which was the exclusive right of the chief. The shared crests included the mountain goat (a crest obtained from the Tsimshian as a result of the relationship with Kitkatla), the grizzly bear, the killer whale, the rainbow, the sea-grizzly and the child of Property Woman.

The village faces south onto Skedans Bay and, though north of the park reserve, is a Haida Watchmen site. The small peninsula is bordered by a high rocky bluff at one end and a rocky prominence on the other. There is no camping at Skedans.

Vertical Point Continuing along the outside of Louise Island, you will come across Vertical Point and a narrow spit connecting the impressive limestone bed of the point with Louise Island. The area has been used consistently over the years, first as a site of a Xa'lanit village and then during the Depression as a refuge for handloggers. The people who chose to make the spit their home left a legacy of apple trees, honeysuckle and rose trees. The remains of log cabins lie nearby as does a fine well.

If you want to camp, check out the cabin on the south side of the spit. According to author Kathleen Dalzell, it was built by Benita Saunders, a young artist from New York, in the early 1970s. Head for the meadow where the point narrows and tuck your boats in behind the kelp. The cabin is only a few hundred feet from the shore, and its logbook provides some great reading to get you ready for the remainder of your trip.

Farther south you will still see many logging scars until you enter Gwaii Haanas, just south of Talunkwan Island. From here on, aside from Lyell Island and Jedway Bay, signs of recent logging and mining are virtually nonexistent, and the ancient history of the islands slowly begins to envelope you.

Tanu/T'anuu *T'anuu* means sea-grass town in Haida. The village site is the next Watchmen camp you will encounter and a hauntingly beautiful place. Moss and time have disguised much of its greatness, but the remaining house-pits, numbering over 20, are signs that Tanu was one of the most flourishing villages on the islands. Like most Haida villages, Tanu was struck by the smallpox epidemics. Over the course of 10 years, begin-

Anthony Island / Skung Gwaii. PETER McGEE

ning in 1880, the population dwindled from over 500 to less than 80. When approaching Tanu, paddlers should land on the southeastern beach. There is a posted map of the house-pit sites at the landing area and great camping on the nearby islands and beaches.

Windy Bay/Hlk'yaah   If you continue taking the outside route, you will come across Windy Bay/Hlk'yaah near Gogit Point. The 1985 stand-off between the Haida and Western Forest Products occurred nearby and, as a result, the bay is still home to one of the most spectacular watersheds on the coast. Although the B.C. minister of forests gave the go-ahead to log Lyell Island after the arrests of 1985, the blockade was considered a success since it created a wave of international support for the Haida cause and led to the direct involvement of the federal government, a critical step in the ultimate creation of Gwaii Haanas. Images of Haida elders being arrested for non-violent protest struck a chord with people around the world and shamed the provincial government for their actions. Windy Bay is a joyous place to visit these days, with the beauty and spiritual forces of the streams and the forests of immense Sitka spruce, hemlock and cedar.

If you do visit Windy Bay, and it is highly recommended, keep in mind that camping is only allowed if weather conditions create a dangerous situation for paddlers to continue on their trip. Even in the best of weather, the access to Windy Bay is exposed and not appropriate for beginners. Be particularly cautious of the winds and waves near Dodge Point. Windy Bay is a Watchmen site. A little farther south is the beloved Hotspring Island.

Hotspring Island/Gandla K'in   Names like Smoke Bay, Volcanic Island, Island of Fire and now Hotspring Island leave little doubt as to what makes this one of the most precious spots in Gwaii Haanas. Francis Poole, a civil and mining engineer with the Queen Charlotte Mining Company, was told by Chief Klue of T'anuu that soaking in the miracle waters would cure him of every ailment. The year was 1862. How much of that claim is true is difficult to verify, but the numerous pools on the island continue to work wonders on the aching muscles of paddlers and fishers alike.

Popularity has a price, and it is quite likely you'll be sharing your bliss with people from around the world. Please be considerate of their experience. The Watchmen huts are located near the pools as are the new solar-composting toilets. The pools are on the southwest corner of the island, but landing is also possible at the north end as a trail runs across the island. There is no alcohol allowed in or around the pools, and you should refrain from using soap in anything but the bathing hut. There are great campsites on many of the surrounding islands, so you won't have to travel far to set up for the night.

Paddling in Juan Perez Sound gives you access to some stunning scenery but also exposes you to some extreme weather. When a southeaster is blowing, it is best to sit it out for the day. A little less predictable are the gap winds that funnel over the San Cristoval Range on Moresby (see Chapter 1). Some afternoons you will encounter ferocious headwinds and steep waves paddling west from Hotspring Island. These winds should always be treated with respect, no matter how short your passage.

If you have the time and desire, hiking through the open alpine of the San Cristovals provides a fantastic view of the remote west coast of Moresby and gives your arms a break from the daily grind. One of the more popular day hikes begins in Island Bay, across from the northern tip of Burnaby Island, and summits the 707-m (2330-ft.) Yatza Mountain. Sections of the hike are difficult, but the biggest concern is a quick change in the weather. Be prepared and don't assume the sun (if you are so lucky) will hold for the whole day.

Burnaby Narrows Continuing south, you will soon find yourself in a 50-m- (164-ft.-) wide passage that cuts between Moresby and Burnaby Islands. Burnaby Narrows is called Dolomite Narrows on the charts and is one of the most significant intertidal areas in North America. Less than 10 per cent of all coastlines support intertidal life such as that found here. The seabed is reputed to contain more protein per square metre than anywhere else in the world, and it is virtually impossible to walk here at low tide without stepping on living creatures of many kinds. As a result, visitors are asked to float through the narrows to see the intertidal life. However tempting, rearranging intertidal life for photographic purposes is strongly discouraged; photos are possible through the water even with normal camera equipment. Camping is not permitted in the narrows, but you won't have a problem finding suitable spots at either end.

At this point in the trip, you are making a big commitment if you choose to continue south. Rounding Benjamin Point, and heading into Houston Stewart Channel, puts you in an area of incredible beauty that is also extremely rugged and isolated. Weather and currents in this part of Gwaii Haanas can have you shorebound for several days so be sure to leave ample time in your trip planning. Cautions aside, however, visiting the village site of Skung Gwaii is a highlight that should not be missed.

As you paddle south, be very careful of the wave action caused by the shallows off Benjamin Point and the current and wind interaction entering Houston Stewart Channel. Camping is a little tough between Skincuttle Inlet and Kunghit Island, but there are a number of possible sites in and around the channel. For those interested in some luxury, consider making arrangements to spend a few nights in Rose Harbour.

Rose Harbour   Rose Harbour is a beautiful little community located on the north shore of Kunghit Island, the last remaining vestige of privately held land in Gwaii Haanas. The site was originally purchased by G. A. Huff of Alberni for a syndicate of businessmen from Vancouver and Victoria in 1910; the Queen Charlotte Whaling Company began operations that summer. By late fall, Rose Harbour had already put through 80 whales and employed 150 men. Over time, the station's annual catch went from 300 whales to 150, and operations were eventually shut down in 1941.

Rose Harbour is now owned by 14 shareholders but only 3 families live here. The harbour is relatively busy during the summer and has a number of facilities that might interest paddlers including a guest house, kayak rentals, boat tours and organic meal services. Visitors are welcome to explore the old boilers and digesters of the whaling station but should call ahead if they plan on staying or using any of the facilities.

Anthony Island/Skung Gwaii   Perched at the southern tip of Moresby Island, and exposed to the full force of the Pacific Ocean, lies the secluded island of Skung Gwaii and the magical village of Nunstints (formerly Ninstints). While the Kunghit Haida have moved, they are still very much connected to this village, and their legacy continues as the totems watch over the village in silence, slowly succumbing to the climate of the North Coast.

Due to the popularity of the site, please ensure that you radio ahead to arrange access with the Watchmen. You may have to wait at another point (e.g., Louscoone Inlet) until enough people have left to allow you to go. The result will be a better experience for all once you get to Skung Gwaii.

Visitors to Skung Gwaii should enter the village site from the back end of the island, either at the small pocket beach on the island's southern tip or at the larger, more protected bay to the north. The experience from the back of the island is one of discovery—beaching the kayaks, walking through the quiet forest and coming out upon the village site. Please don't approach via the front of the village. This results in crowding and interference with the solitary experience most visitors are looking for at Nunstints. And please: no camping in the village site.

ADDITIONAL ROUTES

For the more adventurous, the Queen Charlotte Islands/Haida Gwaii offer stunning paddling on the west coast of both Moresby and Graham Islands, but the shore is typically steep and rocky with pounding surf. For huge stretches landing may be impossible or, at best, very difficult, and exploring this region should be attempted only by experienced paddlers and even then, only with extreme caution. For more information, contact the BCMTA. If you are looking for less intense alternatives, try the following areas:

- Skidegate Inlet is an extensive area that can be explored for a couple of hours, a day or several days. There are islands to visit, fascinating geology and the company of oystercatchers, pigeon guillemots, herons, harlequin ducks, bald eagles, loons and other water birds. The adventurous, and experienced, can opt for several day trips out through Skidegate Narrows for a taste of the islands' west coast.
- Rennel Sound, accessible by logging road, offers the west coast in a relatively sheltered setting.
- North Beach on Graham Island is for paddlers who like fun in the surf.
- Masset Inlet is where the waters of Dixon Entrance penetrate right into the heart of Graham Island.
- Mayer Lake is probably the most accessible of the islands' larger lakes.

NORTH COAST

Zayas I.

Dundas Island

Edith Harbour

Island #50

Baron I.

Dunira I.

Island #42

Melville I.

Island #35

Dixon Entrance

Brown Passage

Tugwell I.

Lucy Is.

Hecate Strait

Tree Nob Group

Rushton I.

Bell Passage

Stephens I.

Chatham Sound

China Islet

Skiakle Bay

Phillips Cone

Joyce I.

Prescott I.

Prescott Passage

Arthur I.

Edye Pass

Oval Bay

Welcome Harbour

Porcher Island

Porcher Inlet

Cape George

Goschen I.

Kitkatla

BRITISH COLUMBIA MAINLAND

Tsimpsean Peninsula

Metlakatla

Salt Lakes

Seal Cove

Fairview Floats

Prince Rupert

Digby I.

Kaien I.

Butze Rapids

Ridley I.

Port Edward

McNeil River

16

Inverness Passage

Skeena River

Kitson I.

Smith I.

Port Essington

Kennedy I.

Lewis I.

Oona River

Pitt Island

Ogden Channel

Grenville Channel

PACIFIC OCEAN

Symbols

Ⓛ Launch Site

▲ Campsite

ⓦ Water

• Town

Browning Entrance

Petrel Channel

McCauley Island

6 NM   0   6 NM

Chapter Seventeen

The North Coast

Charles Justice

The extreme north end of British Columbia's Inside Passage comprises the islands that border Chatham Sound on their east and Hecate Strait and Dixon Entrance on their west. Located only 32 km (20 mi.) miles south of the Alaskan border at their northernmost point, these islands are largely uninhabited and pristine. Their western coastlines are beautiful, rugged and irregular, affording shelter in small bays as well as the occasional sandy beaches. Although exposed and not for the faint of heart, islands such as Porcher, Stephens and Dundas provide some of the best paddling B.C. has to offer.

BACKGROUND

The nearest access point for all these trips is Prince Rupert, a deep-water port located near the mouth of the Skeena River with a population of 18,000. Prince Rupert was created in the early decades of this century as the Pacific terminus of the now defunct Grand Trunk Pacific Railway. Its founder, Charles Hays, died aboard the *Titanic*.

There are three permanent Tsimshian villages in the area. Kitkatla is the southernmost, situated in a protected area close to the south end of Porcher Island. Port Simpson is the oldest European settlement in the area; it started out as a Hudson's Bay trading post in 1834 and is now an Indian Reserve. Metlakatla, at the outer limits of Prince Rupert Harbour, was started in 1862 as a utopian native community by the lay Anglican minister, William Duncan. It once had the largest church north of San Francisco but that has since burnt down. In 1887, due to a dispute with the

Ogden Channel, south coast of Porcher Island. PETER McGEE

Anglican hierarchy, Duncan and half the population moved to Alaska and established a second Metlakatla just outside Ketchikan.

The Tsimshian are currently involved in a major land claim that could affect any or all of the islands situated off Prince Rupert. As always, we ask that you treat any cultural sites you come across with the utmost respect.

GETTING THERE

Please see the Getting There section of Chapter 16 for information about reaching Prince Rupert, the gateway to paddle routes of the north coast.

Once in Prince Rupert, you will likely launch either from the Fairview floats, located about 15 minutes from the town centre, or from the Port Edward boat launch. If you do not feel like paddling Chatham Sound's exposed crossing, a boat charter company can take you from Prince Rupert to the starting point of your choice. Prices usually begin at around $200, depending on the number of people.

WEATHER AND HAZARDS

Northwesterlies are the prevailing winds in the region from July to September. Southeasterlies are common for the remainder of the year though they also occur during the summer. Gusty winds are found in Prince Rupert Harbour during southeast gales produced by airflow over the local mountains. A heavy build-up of seas occurs in the entrance to the harbour with strong northwesterly winds.

Prince Rupert is an active port, and there is considerable boat traffic in and around the area. Of particular concern are Alaskan tugs towing barges at 18 knots, ocean liners and the Alaskan and B.C. ferries. Because of this traffic, crossing Chatham Sound in the fog is not advised.

Close to the mouth of the Skeena you will encounter the effects of the river and the tides, which can create difficult seas particularly when there is an ebbing tide and a westerly or northwesterly wind. Numerous commercial fishers work the mouth of the Skeena so beware of boats and nets. As always, watch for enraged sea lions.

During gales, seas can be quite hazardous on the west coast of the outer islands; fortunately there are a number of bays and smaller islands that afford shelter.

SPECIAL CONSIDERATIONS

When paddling on the North Coast, you are in Tsimshian territory. *Tsimshian* means "going into the river of mists" and refers to the mighty Skeena River. Seven Tsimshian communities currently occupy the lower portions of the Skeena and much of the coast on either side of the river mouth. Tsimshian history is well documented in the middens that abound in this part of the coast as well as in the Tsimshian science of the past, the *adawx,* or oral record of events. Please respect this history and the Tsimshian territories in your travels by following the guidelines on cultural impacts outlined in Chapter 1. As with any other First Nations traditional territory, visitors should include seeking permission to visit the area as part of your trip planning process. See Useful Contacts at the back of the book or contact the BCMTA for more information.

NORTH COAST TRIPS (36–38)

The North Coast is an enormous area with unlimited paddling potential. If you have at least five days, heading almost due west from Prince Rupert to explore Stephens Island and the Tree Nobs provides spectacular views and puts you on the edge of Hecate Strait. With a bit more time, it is worthwhile to head south and explore Porcher Island or to venture to the northern extremes of the B.C. border and the waters surrounding Dundas Island. Recommended times are based on fair weather, and it is best to leave a buffer of a few days. If the following trips are beyond your skill level, consult Additional Routes at the end of the chapter for a few beginner and intermediate trips that occur in the sheltered bays and inlets surrounding Prince Rupert.

Because some of the sites overlap on these trips, they have been arranged from south to north, not from shortest to longest. All these trips require crossing Chatham Sound. This is an exposed crossing through a shipping corridor, so be prepared, listen to the weather reports and exercise good judgement and caution. Avoid crossing in the fog.

Please note that Porcher, Stephens, the Tree Nobs, Dunira and Dundas Islands have small Indian Reserves and the occasional unoccupied fisherman's cabin. Please respect the owner's privacy. Camping on reserves or occupying cabins should not be done without permission.

Trip 36 Porcher Island

Skill:	Intermediate to advanced	
Time:	7–14 days	
Hazards:	Winds, currents and boat traffic	
Access:	Port Edward boat launch	
Charts:	3717	Approaches to Skeena River 1:25,000
	3761	Kitkatla Inlet 1:36,500
	3773	Grenville Channel, Baker Inlet to Ogden Channel 1:36,500
	3956	Malacca Passage to Bell Passage 1:40,000
	3957	Approaches to Prince Rupert Harbour 1:40,000
	3958	Prince Rupert Harbour 1:20,000
	3927	Bonilla Island to Edye Passage 1:77,800
Tide Book:	Vol. 6	

To reach the northern tip of Porcher Island, the best route is to depart from the Port Edward boat launch, paddle to Kitson Island Marine Park and then cross the southern end of Chatham Sound. From here you can continue to Edye Pass, Welcome Harbour, Oval Bay on the west coast of Porcher, past Fan Point and on to Cape George at the southern tip of the island. At this point, you can either double back or circumnavigate Porcher Island, passing the communities of Kitkatla and Oona River as you go.

Launching

To reach the Port Edward boat launch from Prince Rupert, take Highway 16 across the bridge from Kaien Island to the mainland and take the first right. Follow the signs to Port Edward, then continue down the road for just under a mile to the big fish plant. Look for a sharp right turn just before the plant and take that road down to the boat launch. You can park your vehicle in the big lot across from the plant for free.

Sites

Kitson Island Marine Park   A provincial park, this little island is less than an hour's paddle from the Port Edward boat launch. There is a nice sand beach at its eastern end, behind which there is room for about six tents. Beach camping is possible though space is limited. At the far eastern end of the beach is a short trail leading to a very small, and possibly temporary, outdoor toilet. Although close to Port Edward, the beach affords complete privacy because, apart from other paddlers, any boat traffic passes at a distance. The view to the south of Porcher Island is beautiful. Unfortunately, there is no fresh water. Take note of the shoal to the north of the island, which can create some steep waves when the wind is blowing.

Welcome Harbour   Across Chatham Sound, you will likely be able to see the profile of Porcher Island. Head for its northern tip and work your way along its northwestern shore. The west coast of Porcher Island forms a long, narrow, bifurcating peninsula. Welcome Harbour, a popular sailboat anchorage, is nestled in the east side of the northern end of the peninsula. It is a picturesque lagoon with a maze of protected islets. The Forest Service and the Prince Rupert Sailing Club maintain a small site at the beach with a picnic table and outhouse. There is room in the woods for several tents. A short trail connects the two sides of the peninsula. There is no fresh water.

Oval Bay   This is a beautiful 6-km- (4-mi.-) long gently curving sand beach on the west cost of Porcher Island. There are a few small creeks along the beach except during extended dry spells, and good beach camping on virtually the entire stretch. You may have to camp in the woods during an extreme high tide; otherwise the beach is plenty wide. It is exposed to Hecate Strait, however, and has surf with any strong wind except an easterly. Some protection is afforded by the extensive kelp beds along the coast.

Cape George   There is a sandy bay with rock outcroppings just east of Cape George at the extreme south end of Porcher Island. Exposed to the south, the site has ample room above the high tide level for tents, as well as a small creek with questionable water. A shipwreck is in the bay.

Porcher Island (East Side)   If you are circumnavigating Porcher Island, be forewarned that camping on the east side is quite tough and finding sites should not be left for the end of the day. The community of Oona River is very friendly, with a government wharf and pay phone. At time of writing there was talk of opening a paddler's B&B. A little farther north, just outside the harbour, a few of the islands have gravel beaches and some room for tents.

Trip 37   Stephens Island and the Tree Nobs

Skill:	Intermediate to advanced
Time:	5–10 days
Hazards:	Winds, currents and boat traffic
Access:	Port Edward boat launch

Charts:		
	3717	Approaches to Skeena River 1:25,000
	3956	Malacca Passage to Bell Passage 1:40,000
	3957	Approaches to Prince Rupert Harbour 1:40,000
	3958	Prince Rupert Harbour 1:20,000
	3927	Bonilla Island to Edye Passage 1:77,800

Tide Book:	Vol. 6

This trip takes you from the Port Edward boat launch across Chatham Sound to the north end of Porcher Island. From here you cross Edye Pass to Arthur Island and continue, via Prescott Passage, around Joyce Island to the south coast of Stephens Island. You can then follow the shoreline to the northwest tip of Stephens or to the Tree Nobs and back. It is possible to accomplish this trip in as little as 4 days though a week is recommended; the Chatham Sound crossing is quite exposed and dependent on favourable weather.

Launching

For directions on how to reach the Port Edwards boat launch, see the Porcher Island trip (above).

Sites

Kitson Island Marine Park If you plan to visit Kitson Island, see the Porcher Island trip. If you have experience in exposed crossings, you can avoid Kitson Island and head directly from the Port Edward boat launch to Porcher Island. The crossing usually takes between 2–4 hours, but should be approached with caution.

Arthur Island Arthur Island forms the north side of Edye Passage. There is a small beach on the east end of the island facing Prescott Passage, but the best camping spot is farther up the passage on the northwest tip of Arthur. This is a well-protected sand beach with a beautiful view of Prescott Island. Beach camping is not practical but there are level spaces behind the fringe of trees. There is no fresh water.

Phillips Cone Paddling northwest brings you to Stephens Island. Just west of Phillips Cone is a narrow inlet that mostly dries at high tide. Good water can be obtained at the creek at the head of this inlet, and good camping can be had at a tiny beach just west of the inlet, virtually around the corner. There is thick salal at the edge of the beach but behind are lots of fairly level tent spaces.

Skiakle Bay Skiakle Bay is a lagoon on the south side of Stephens Island. It can be divided into two parts: a wide part forming the mouth of the bay, which is exposed to waves from Hecate Strait, and the head of the bay, which is much more protected. About five creeks flow into the bay. The more placid part of Skiakle Bay is best explored at high tide as is the case with all lagoons. Cloudy days, when the mists are partially obscuring the forested hills, are a magical experience.

Near the mouth of Skiakle Bay, at the north end of Skiakle Island, is a small oval island adjoining Skiakle by a white sand beach. The sand gives way easily and even at low tide you sink at least a foot while walking here. The beach is well protected from wind and waves and is mostly sand with a few barnacle-covered rocks. Behind the beach there is a small area thick with moss with enough space for several tents. There is no fresh water at the site, but water is available from numerous creeks at the head of Skiakle Bay.

China Islet   China Islet is a superb camping site in fair weather with its spectacular view of the Tree Nobs. However, it is exposed to north and south winds. China Islet sticks out into Hecate Strait more than any other part of the Stephens Island complex. It is very rugged and forms a contrast to nearby Philips Island. The sand beach that joins these two islands is flat and exposed to the south. About 1.2 m (4 ft.) above the beach is a small, level wildflower meadow with plenty of room for tents. Avoid damaging the vegetation and tie your tents down well.

Tree Nobs   A photogenic spread of small islands off the north end of Stephens Island, the Tree Nobs form a kind of boundary between Chatham Sound and North Hecate Strait. These charming little islands give the illusion of being tropical. There are so many of them, they afford some protection from Hecate Strait. Unfortunately, there are not many good campsites here. The best one is on a white sand beach adjoining Rushton Island. Rushton Island is an Indian Reserve, so you must receive permission to camp from the Metlakatla Indian Council.

Getting to the Tree Nobs is easiest from the north end of Stephens Island, though you need to watch the strong current between Chatham Sound and Hecate Strait.

Trip 38   Dundas and Melville Islands

Skill:	Advanced	
Time:	7–14 days	
Hazards:	Winds, currents and boat traffic	
Access:	Fairview floats	
Charts:	3957	Approaches to Prince Rupert Harbour 1:40,000
	3958	Prince Rupert Harbour 1:20,000
	3959	Hudson Bay Passage 1:40,000
	3960	Approaches to Portland Inlet 1:40,000
Tide Book:	Vol. 6	

Launching

To reach the Fairview floats in Prince Rupert, drive west along Highway 16 as though you were heading to the B.C. and Alaskan ferry docks. As you approach the terminals, keep in the left lane and head for the Coast Guard trailer and the fish plant. Between those two buildings is the government wharf. If you are unloading a lot of gear, be sure not to get in the way of the commercial traffic. Free parking can be found along the road or at the ferry terminal.

Launch from the Fairview floats, cross the harbour and continue through Venn Passage past Metlakatla over to Tugwell Island. From Tugwell, head to Lucy Island.

From the Fairview floats to Tugwell Island typically takes 3–4 hours in these relatively protected water. The crossing from Tugwell to Lucy Island puts you in the middle of Chatham Sound and takes about 2–3 hours.

Sites

Lucy Island   Lucy Island is a small island halfway between Tugwell and Melville Islands in the middle of Chatham Sound. It is narrow with a white sand beach at one end and an automated lighthouse at the other; a boardwalk connects the two ends. The campsite is just off the beach. It has an outhouse, which is a rarity in these parts, and is frequented by powerboats during the summer. Nevertheless, Lucy Island is an excellent stopping-off point for kayakers paddling to or from Melville Island. There is no fresh water on the island.

From here you will cross Chatham Sound to Melville Island. This should be done with caution; the passage takes about 2 hours, weather permitting.

Melville Island and Dunira Island Lagoon   The west side of Melville and Dunira Islands forms a complex maze of small islands and spacious lagoons that is wonderful for exploring in kayaks. Because of the variety of seacoasts all in one place, this area is bound to become a popular spot for kayak charters and groups. A number of these islands have suitable camping spots, both for large and small groups, and fresh water is available from creeks on both islands.

Island #42 (chart 3959) offers a superb campsite that is often frequented by powerboaters in the summer. There is a rock fireplace and beaten trails as well as cleared space for a number of tents. The beach is white sand, shell and gravel and very protected. There is no fresh water.

Island #35 (chart 3959) offers a well-protected, flat sand beach that is accessible at any tide. A couple of places behind the beach are suitable for tents though there are lots of deadfalls and thick devil's club. There is a small stagnant creek to the south that can be reached by walking or paddling along the shore.

From these islands you will cross Hudson Bay Passage and head to Edith Harbour on Dundas Island, preferably within a few hours of high tide slack.

Dundas Island Although the west coast of Dundas is exposed to the swells of Dixon Entrance, Edith Harbour, a tidal narrows at the southwestern tip of Dundas, is a peaceful sanctuary. It is so protected by topography that even if there were a gale out in Dixon Entrance, you would never know it. The harbour has several reversing rapids, fascinating rock formations and a beautiful painted cliff—a wonderful place to kayak.

Just south of Edith Harbour on the west side of Dundas is Island #50 (chart 3959). A small beach with rock outcroppings connects this island to Dundas. The beach is well protected with lots of room for tents behind it.

From here you can double back and head north along the spectacular west coast of Dundas, continuing as far as the island's north coast, just east of the White Islands. The east coast of Dundas is not recommended paddling: it is monotonous and affords no shelter. Dundas Island is best visited in the spring or fall when the mosquitoes are not so ferocious.

ADDITIONAL ROUTES

Prince Rupert is surrounded by beautiful islands, channels and inlets that are accessible to a wide range of kayaking abilities. Prince Rupert Harbour, Tuck Inlet, Venn Passage, Koiya Bay and Dodge Cove are all suitable trips for beginner paddlers, as are the trips to the Salt Lakes and Butze Rapids described below. In contrast, the trip to Port Essington requires intermediate level skills.

Salt Lakes: Most people who have lived in Prince Rupert for more than a few years know Salt Lakes as the old local swimming hole for Ruperites. Formerly connected to the ocean, it was dammed to keep it warmer than the ocean. The float, changing house and boardwalk have all deteriorated but the lakes are still worth a visit. To get here, depart from Fairview floats (see above) and paddle straight across to the north side of Rupert Harbour. Have a chart handy so you know which of those inlets leads to the Salt Lakes; you will know you've reached the right inlet when you see a group of funky shacks lining both sides. A footpath to Salt Lakes can be reached from the end of the inlet to the right of the rapids. The tidal rapids at the head of Salt Lakes are only navigable at high water slack.

Seal Cove to Butze Rapids: One of the most pleasant, protected and picturesque paddles in the region is along Fern Channel from Seal Cove to Butze Rapids. The rapids, at full force, are impossible to miss so it is easy to keep your distance while you admire this raw force of nature. At high water slack, however, they are no more than flat water with ripples. To get there, leave from the Seal Cove floats, which are located at the north end of Prince Rupert. There is a place to launch kayaks right alongside the on-ramp to the floats. Keep well clear of any float planes landing or taking off. Bring charts and a tide table. It is best to leave towards the end of a flooding tide so the current will be with you as you round the Coast Guard base to your right. With mountains all around, this is a spectacular paddle not unlike being in a fiord. Butze is reached just beyond the new sawmill.

Near Prince Rupert: For those with a bit more experience, Ridley Island to Kinahans, Ridley Island to Digby and circumnavigating Digby are all good possibilities. Avoid these in strong southerlies, however, as it can really kick up. It will take at least 6 hours to circumnavigate Digby so you better be in shape. Port Edward to Osland is also a great paddle as long as you do it with the tides. Inverness Channel is almost always windy and choppy and an inexperienced kayaker can easily be tipped—be careful.

Port Essington and Ecstall River: Port Essington is a ghost town located on the nearly uninhabited south side of the Skeena River, at the mouth of the Ecstall. It was originally a stopping-off point for native people on the way up and down the Skeena. In the 1870s, Robert Cunningham put up a store and way station. In its heyday at the turn of the century, Port Essington had a hotel, two canneries and a multinational population. It died in the 1960s after a series of fires levelled most of the town. Nearby Ecstall is a very picturesque tidal river with steep sides and magnificent waterfalls.

To get to Port Essington from Prince Rupert, head east on Highway 16 (the Yellowhead). After passing Rainbow Summit, the highway descends. At the bottom of the long hill, the highway turns to the left and crosses

McNeil River, a sluggish tidal river that flows into the Skeena. The bank is steep, but it is possible to launch here just before or at high water. It takes about 10 minutes to reach the Skeena. Once there, head straight across to Port Essington. The crossing should take 1–2 hours but may be longer depending on the current.

Crossing the Skeena River is not for beginners. Very strong outflow and inflow winds can whip up big standing waves. The best time to cross is at high water slack. Low water slack is not a good time unless you enjoy slogging through the mud and dragging your kayak over sandbars. Overcast days are preferable as the wind is usually calm.

After arriving at Port Essington, be prepared for a lot of bushwhacking—a machete would be handy. There are houses, a church and a schoolhouse buried in the bush, and good beachcombing for old bottles at low tide. Be sure to visit the mayor of Port Essington, which presently has a population of one. Len Croteau also runs the Port Essington Museum.

Heading south: If you decide to go south of Prince Rupert down Grenville Channel, you will find camping spots at Stuart Bight and Nabannah Bay. If you go down Petrel Channel, there is some camping near the creek on the south side of the large elbow bend. For more information, check with the B.C. Marine Trail Association.

Heading north: Crossing the border to Alaska requires that you pass through U.S. Customs. If possible, call the Ketchikan office before you go: tel.: (907) 225-8373. Once in Alaska, there is a lifetime of paddling opportunities including the wild experience of paddling in glacial ice. One of the highlights of the area is the fishing town of Petersburg. Located on Mitkof Island near the mouth of the Stikine River, the Le Conte Glacier and the humpback feeding grounds of Frederick Sound, Petersburg is a playground of natural delights.

If you are looking for campsites directly north of the border, try Nakat Bay on Tongass Island or the lighthouse at Tree Point.

This guidebook now ends, perched on the Alaskan border. Beyond is a region where the landscape begins to overwhelm humans and the drama of the north takes over. One day, the marine trail that passes through Washington and B.C. will be joined to Alaska and beyond. That, however, is for another time and book.

GENERAL CONTACTS (BRITISH COLUMBIA)

Emergencies

Canadian Coast Guard, Victoria Rescue Centre: Toll free 1-800-567-5111 or cellular *311 B.C. Tel/Cantel. The Victoria Rescue Centre coordinates emergency responses for the entire B.C. coast.

Canadian Coast Guard, Pacific Region, 350-555 W. Hastings St., Vancouver, B.C. V6B 5G3. Tel. (604) 631-3702, fax (604) 631-3704. Webpage: www.ccg-gcc.gc.ca/main.htm/. The Pacific regional webpage (www.pacific.ccg-cc.gc.ca/epages/home/home.htm) includes marine weather forecasts and information on marine communication and search and rescue.

Weather

Environment Canada. Manager, Commercial Services, Suite 120-1200 W. 73rd Ave., Vancouver, B.C., V6P 6H9 Tel. (604) 664-9080, fax (604) 664-9081. Webpage: www.weatheroffice.com. For purchase of *Marine Weather Hazards Manual* and other products.

Weather One-on-One. Tel. 1-900-565-5555. Talk directly to a weather forecaster for $1.95/minute, 2-minute minimum. Using a cellular phone, dial 0-955-656-5555. Credit card needed.

Environment Canada Weather: Tel. (604) 664-9010. Free recorded marine forecasts for Howe Sound, Strait of Georgia, Haro Strait and Juan de Fuca Strait.

Marine Weather Radio (VHF): WX1 (162.55 MHzx), **WX2** (162.40 MHz), **WX3** (162.475 MHz) and **21B** (161.65 MHz).

Marine Charts, Tide Tables, Maps & Books

Canadian Hydrographic Service, Chart Sales and Distribution, Institute of Ocean Sciences, 9860 West Saanich Rd., Sidney, B.C., V8L 4B2. Tel. (250) 363-6358, fax (250) 363-6841.

Coastal Waters Recreation, Suite 547, 185-911 Yates St., Victoria, B.C., V8V 4Y9. Tel./fax (250) 383-5555. Recreation kayaking maps of Nootka Sound, Kyuquot Sound, Esperanza Inlet and Clayoquot Sound. Others available in the future.

Crown Publications Inc., 521 Fort St., Victoria, B.C., V8W 1E7. Tel. (250) 386-4636, fax (250) 386-0221. Webpage: vvv.com/crownpub/. Specializes in government publications, nautical

charts, topographical maps, marine books, natural history books and First Nations culture books.

Ecomarine, 1668 Duranleau St., Vancouver, B.C., V6H 3S4. Tel. (604) 689-7575, fax (604) 689-5926. Kayaking books, laminated nautical charts, etc.

Field Naturalist, 1126 Blanshard St., Victoria, B.C., V8W 2H6. Tel. (250) 388-4174, fax (250) 388-9236. Specialty books for naturalists.

Nanaimo Maps and Charts, 8 Church St., Nanaimo, B.C., V9R 5H4. Toll-free 1-800-665-2513, tel. (250) 754-2513, fax 1-800-553-2313. One of the largest selections of Canadian and American nautical charts, from the West Coast to the Arctic.

World Wide Books and Maps, 736A Granville St., Vancouver, B.C., V6Z 1G3. Tel. (604) 687-3320, fax (604) 687-5925. Extensive selection of books and nautical charts.

Getting There

Ferries

B.C. Ferries Corporation. Head Office: 1112 Fort St., Victoria, B.C., V8V 4V2. Tel. (250) 386-3431 or (604) 669-1211 in Vancouver. For 24-hour pre-recorded schedule information on major routes, tel. (250) 381-5335 (in Victoria or outside B.C.) or toll-free 1-888-223-3779 (within B.C.). Webpage: www.bcferries.bc.ca. Includes all schedules, fare information, etc.

To make vehicle reservations (no charge) for Discovery Coast Passage (Port Hardy to the Central Coast), Inside Passage (Port Hardy to Prince Rupert), or Tsawwassen to the Gulf Islands, tel. (250) 386-3431 (in Victoria or outside B.C.) or toll-free 1-888-223-3779 (within B.C.), fax (250) 381-5452. For vehicle reservations from the Lower Mainland to Nanaimo or Swartz Bay (fee for service), tel. (604) 444-2890 (outside B.C.) or toll-free 1-888-724-5223 (within B.C.).

Air

Air B.C., Box 2375, Airport Postal Outlet, Richmond, B.C., V7B 1Y7. Reservations: Toll-free in B.C. 1-800-663-3721, toll-free in U.S. 1-800-776-3000. Scheduled destinations include Campbell River, Courtenay/Comox, Nanaimo, Prince Rupert, Vancouver and Victoria.

Baxter Aviation Ltd., 52 Anchor Way, Seaplane Terminal, Box 1110, Nanaimo, B.C., V9R 6E7. Tel. (250) 754-1066, toll-free 1-800-661-5599, fax (250) 754-1075. Destinations include the Gulf Islands, Nanaimo, Victoria, Bamfield, Tofino, Ucluelet, Alert Bay, Campbell River, Comox/Courtney, Gold River, Port Alberni, Pender Harbour, Powell River, Sechelt, Tahsis and Vancouver.

Canadian Regional Airlines, 321-5400 Airport Rd., Richmond, B.C., V7B 1B4. Reservations: Toll-free in B.C.: 1-800-665-1177, toll-free in U.S. 1-800-426-7000. Scheduled destinations include: Campbell River, Comox/Courtenay, Nanaimo, Port Hardy, Prince Rupert, Sandspit, Vancouver and Victoria.

Coval Air, (mailing address) Box 1451, Campbell River, B.C., V9W 5C7. Street address: 3050 Spit Rd. Tel. (250) 287-8371, fax (250) 287-8366. Float plane charters and scheduled flights, including Campbell River, Cortes, Rivers Inlet, Vancouver and numerous coastal destinations.

Harbour Air, 4760 Inglis Dr., Richmond, B.C., V7B 1W4. Vancouver: tel./fax (604) 688-1277. Victoria: tel. (250) 385-2203, fax (250) 385-2234. Toll-free 1-800-665-0212. Webpage: www.harbour-air.com/. Scheduled flights, charters and sightseeing by float plane;

serving Victoria, Vancouver, the Gulf Islands, Nanaimo, Pender Harbour, Masset, Prince Rupert and Sandspit. **Kenmore Air,** Box 82064, Kenmore, WA 98028-006. Tel. (425) 486-1257, fax (425) 485-4774, toll-free 1-800-543-9595. Webpage: www.kenmoreair. com/. Serving Seattle, Victoria, and San Juan Islands by float plane. Adventure packages for kayaking and grizzly bear viewing in B.C. are also available.
Pacific Coastal Airline, 117-4440 Cowley Cres., Richmond, B.C., V7B 1B8. Tel. (604) 273-6864, toll-free 1-800-663-2872. Serving Bella Bella, Powell River, Rivers Inlet, Port Hardy and Vancouver.
Pacific Spirit Air, 3rd floor, Bellevue Centre, 235-15th St., West Vancouver, B.C., V7T 2X1. Toll-free tel./fax 1-800-665-2359. Scheduled flights and charters throughout coastal B.C.
Sound Flight, Inc., Box 812, Renton, WA 98057. Tel. (425) 255-6500, toll-free 1-800-825-0722. Webpage: www.sound flight.com/. Scheduled flights (floats and wheels) from Seattle. Destinations include Barkley Sound, Ucluelet, Tofino, Johnstone Strait, the Gulf Islands, the San Juan Islands, Desolation Sound and the Discovery Islands.
Vancouver Island Air, Box 727, Campbell River, B.C., V9W 6J3. Tel. (250) 287-2433, fax (250) 286-3269. Scheduled flights on wheels and floats, serving Vancouver Island and mainland destinations.
West Coast Air, Box 48197, Bentall Centre, Vancouver, B.C., V7X 1N8. Toll-free 1-800-347-2222, fax (604) 688-7042. Scheduled flights between Vancouver and Victoria, and charter services to the Gulf Islands by float plane.

Bus
Greyhound Canada, 850 16th St. SW, Calgary, AB, P3B 3V8. Toll-free in

Canada 1-800-661-8747, tel. (403) 260-0877. Webpage: www.grey hound.ca/. Servicing mainland British Columbia, including Prince Rupert.
Island Coach Lines (Gray Line of Victoria), 700 Douglas St., Victoria, B.C., V8W 2B3. Tel. (250) 385-4411, fax (250) 388-9461, toll-free 1-800-318-0818 (within B.C.). Webpage: www.victoriatours.com/. Servicing Vancouver Island.
Maverick Coach Lines, 1150 Station St., Vancouver, B.C., V6A 2X7. Tel. (604) 662-8051. Webpage: www.maverick coachlines.bc.ca/lines.html. Servicing the Sunshine Coast, Squamish, Whistler and Nanaimo.
Pacific Coach Lines, 1150 Station St., Vancouver, B.C., V6A 4C7. Tel. (604) 662-8074, fax (604) 681-1515. tel. Victoria (250) 385-4411. Webpage: www.pacificcoach. com/index.html. Servicing Victoria to Vancouver, and connecting to Vancouver International Airport.

Railway
B.C. Rail, Box 8770, Vancouver B.C., V6B 4X6. Toll-free 1-800-663-8238. Webpage: ww.bcrail.com/bcrpasss/index. htm/. Serving North Vancouver to Prince George.
E&N (VIA) Rail, 450 Pandora Ave., Victoria, B.C., V8W 3L5. Toll-free 1-800-561-8630. Webpage: www.viarail.ca/. Servicing Victoria to Courtenay.
VIA Rail Canada, 1150 Station St., Vancouver, B.C., V6A 4C7. Toll-free 1-800-561-8630. Webpage: www.viarail.ca/ Servicing Vancouver, Prince Rupert and points in between.
British Columbia Passenger Rail Services webpage: www.mcs.net/~dsdawdy/Canpass/provinces/bc.html. This handy webpage connects you to train schedules for VIA, E&N and B.C. Rail.

Parks

BC Parks, Ministry of Environment, Lands and Parks, 800 Johnson St., 2nd floor, Victoria, B.C., V8V 1X4. Tel. (250) 387-5002, fax (250) 387-5757. Webpage: www.env.gov.bc.ca. To make reservations for provincial parks, toll-free 1-800-689-9025 (March 15–September 15).

Parks Canada Pacific Region, 300-300 W. Georgia St., Vancouver, B.C., V6B 6C6. Tel. (604) 666-0176, fax (604) 666-350. Webpage: parkscanada. pch.gc.ca/np/np_e.htm/. For information and reservations in national parks.

Tourism & Accommodation

B.C. Adventure Network: www.bcadventure.com/. A comprehensive website on tourist services, accommodation and transportation in B.C. An excellent source for vacation planning.

Hostelling International Canada, B.C. Region, 402-134 Abbott St., Vancouver, B.C., V6B 2K4. Tel. (604) 684-7111, toll-free 1-800-661-0020.

Tourism B.C., 812 Wharf St., Victoria, B.C., V8W 1T3. Tel. (604) 663-6000, fax (604) 801-5710 (Vancouver), toll-free 1-800-663-6000. Webpage: www.tbc.gov.bc.ca. Tourism B.C. makes reservations for hotels, motels and bed & breakfasts and distributes tourism guides, free of charge, including *B.C. Accommodations*, *B.C. Bed & Breakfast Directory* and *Outdoor & Adventure Guide*.

Vancouver Island webpage: www.axxe.com/onsite/. Information on businesses, accommodation, transportation, tourist services, including the Broken Islands.

Kayaking & Outdoor Associations

B.C. Marine Trail Association, Box 36046, 1156 Esquimalt Rd., Victoria, B.C. V9A 3N7 Tel./fax (250) 383-1100.

Outdoor Recreation Council, 334-1367 W. Broadway Ave., Vancouver, B.C., V6H 4A9. Tel. (604) 737-3058, fax (604) 737-3666. Webpage: home.istar.ca/ ~orcbc/. Advocacy body for outdoor recreational interests, with over 40 affiliates.

Pacific International Kayaking Association, 2415 Aladdin Cres., Abbotsford, B.C. V2S 5K7. PIKA organizes an annual sea kayaking symposium at Thetis Island, where paddlers can build their paddling skills.

Sea Kayak Association of B.C., Box 751, Stn. A, Vancouver, B.C., V6C 2N6.

Other Contacts

Ministry of Aboriginal Affairs, Communications Branch, 1st Floor, 908 Pandora Ave., Victoria, B.C., V8V 1X4. Tel. (250) 356-0330, fax (250) 387-1785. Webpage: www.aaf.gov.bc.ca/aaf/. For information or to request a copy of *A Guide to Aboriginal Organizations and Services in B.C.*

Department of Fisheries and Oceans, Communications Branch, Pacific Region, 412-555 W. Hastings St., Vancouver, B.C. V6B 5G3. Tel. (604) 666-0384, fax: (604) 666-1847. For general enquiries, tel. (604) 666-3545; for shell fish information (red tide warnings), tel. (604) 666-2828; for recreational fishing, tel. (604) 666-3271. Pacific Region webpage: www.pac. dfo.ca/comm/pages/commhome.htm/.

Enquiry B.C. Tel. (604) 387-6121 (Victoria), tel. (604) 660-2421 (Vancouver), toll-free 1-800-663-7867 (elsewhere in B.C.). Provides any provincial government phone or fax number and connects you free of charge.

Ministry of Small Business, Tourism and Culture. Archaeology Branch, Box 9817, Stn. Prov. Govt., Victoria, B.C.,

V8W 9W3. Tel. (250) 356-0882, fax (250) 387-4420.

PUGET SOUND (WASHINGTON STATE)

Emergencies

U.S. Coast Guard: Bellingham, tel. (360) 734-1692; Everett, tel. (425) 252-5281; and Port Angeles, tel. (360) 452-2342 or (360) 457-2226 or (360) 457-2200. To contact the Coast Guard on a cellular phone, tel. *CG.

Weather & Marine Radio

National Oceanic and Atmospheric Administration (NOAA) National Weather Forecast Service Office: Seattle, tel. (206) 526-6087; Olympia NOAA broadcast: VHF WX3 (162.475 MHz); Seattle NOAA broadcast: VHF WX1 (162.55 MHz).

Seattle Time Information Line, tel. (206) 464-2000, bin 9900. Webpage: www.seawfo.noaa.gov/. Excellent source of weather forecasts for Washington State.

Marine Charts & Tide Tables

Captain's Navigation Supplies, Inc., 2500 16th Ave. W., Seattle, WA 98119. Toll-free 1-800-448-2278, tel. (206) 283-7242, fax (206) 261-4921.

NOAA Distribution Branch, N/CG33, National Ocean Service, Riverdale, MD 20737-1199. Tel. (301) 436-6990, fax (301) 436-6829. Webpage: mapindex. nos.noaa.gov/. Phone or fax for a catalogue of nautical charts.

Getting There

Ferries

Black Ball Transport, 101 E. Railroad Ave., Port Angeles, WA 98362. Tel. (250) 386-2202 (Victoria), fax (250) 386-220;

tel. (360) 457-4491 (Port Angeles), fax (360) 457-4493. Vehicle ferry between Port Angeles and Victoria.

Clipper Navigation, Inc., 2701 Alaskan Way, Pier 69, Seattle, WA 98121. For reservations, tel. (250) 382-8100 (Victoria) or (206) 448-5000 (Seattle) or toll-free outside Seattle and Victoria 1-800-888-2535, fax: (206) 443-2583. Service between Victoria and Seattle: *Victoria Clipper* (passengers only) and *Princess Margurite* (car ferry).

Washington State Ferries, 801 Alaskan Way, Seattle, WA 98104-1487. Tel. (206) 464-6400 (Seattle) or (250) 381-1551 (Victoria) or (250) 656-1531 (Sidney) or toll-free within Washington 1-800-84-FERRY. Vehicle ferry from Anacortes to Sidney, B.C.; other routes available within Puget Sound.

Webpage links for ferry services in Washington State: www.wsdot.wa.gov/ferries/other-svcs/default.htm/.

Air

Baxter Aviation Ltd., 52 Anchor Way, Seaplane Terminal, Box 1110, Nanaimo, B.C., V9R 6E7. Tel. (250) 754-1066, toll-free 1-800-661-5599, fax. (250) 754-1075. Destinations include San Juan Islands and Seattle.

Kenmore Air, Box 82064, Kenmore, WA 98028-006. Tel. (425) 486-1257, fax (425) 485-4774, toll-free 1-800-543-9595. Webpage: www.kenmoreair. com/. Serving Seattle, Victoria and San Juan Islands by float plane. Adventure packages for kayaking and grizzly bear viewing in B.C. also available.

Sound Flight, Inc., Box 812, Renton, WA 98057. Toll-free 1-800-825-0722, tel. (425) 255-6500. Webpage: www.soundflight.com/. Scheduled flights (floats and wheels) from Seattle.

Destinations include Barkley Sound, Ucluelet, Tofino, Johnstone Strait, Gulf Islands, San Juan Islands, Desolation Sound and Discovery Islands.

Bus

Greyhound Bus Lines, toll-free 1-800-231-2222.

Gray Line Bus, tel. (206) 252-2143. Provides service between Seattle and Anacortes from May 1 to October 31.

Webpage for bus services in Washington State: www.wsdot.wa.gov/pubtran/getthere/bus.htm.

Parks & Tourism

Washington Water Trails Association, c/o The Good Shepherd Center, 305-4649 Sunnyside Ave. N., Seattle, WA 98103-6900. Tel./fax (206) 545-9161. Webpage: www.eskimo.com/~wwta.

Washington State Parks and Recreation Commission, Box 42650, Olympia, WA 98504-2650. Toll-free (information center) 1-800-233-0321 or toll-free (reservations) 1-800-452-5687. Webpage: www.parks.wa.gov.

Native American Contacts

Governor's Office of Indian Affairs. Tel. (360) 753-2411.

Equipment Rentals/Tours

Backpackers Supply, 5206 South Tacoma Way, Tacoma, WA 98409. Tel. (253) 472-4402, fax (253) 475-6575. Tours in the San Juan Islands and rentals.

Blue Moon Explorations, Box 2568, Bellingham, WA 98227. Tel./fax (360) 856-5622. Tours in the San Juan Islands and rentals.

Elakah Expeditions, Box 4092-B, Bellingham, WA 98227. Tel. (360) 734-7270 or toll-free 1-800-434-7270. Tours in the San Juan Islands.

Kayak Pursuits, 15145 NE 90th St., Redmond, WA 98052. Tel. (425) 869-7067, fax (425) 869-9014. Rentals.

Northwest Outdoor Center, 2100 Westlake Ave. N, Seattle, WA 98109. Tel. (206) 281-9694, fax (206) 282-0690. Tours in the San Juan Islands and rentals.

Olympic Outdoor Center, 18971 Front St., Poulsbo, WA 98370. Tel. (360) 697-6095, fax (360) 697-1102. Tours in the San Juan Islands and rentals.

Outdoor Odysseys, 12003 23rd Ave. NE, Seattle, WA 98125. Tel./fax (206) 361-0717 or toll-free 1-800-647-4621. Webpage: www.karuna.com/odyssey/. Tours in the San Juan Islands.

Shearwater Adventure, Box 787, Eastsound, WA 98245. Tel. (360) 376-4699. Webpage: www.pacificrim.net/~kayak/.Tours and classes in the San Juan Islands.

Vashon Island Kayak, 14326 Olympic Dr. SW, Vashon Island, WA 98070. Tel. (206)567-4398. Rentals.

GULF ISLANDS

Emergencies

Saltspring Island RCMP, tel. (250) 537-5555.

Gabriola Island RCMP, tel. (250) 247-8333.

Weather & Marine Radio

Environment Canada: Marine weather recording for Victoria, tel. (250) 656-2714 or (250) 656-7515. For Nanaimo, tel. (250) 245-8899.

Comox Weather Services, tel. (250) 339-5044,

Weather Radio Canada, Victoria, 1260 Khz AM band.

VHF Weather Radio: channel 21B

(161.65 MHz).

Getting There

See GENERAL CONTACTS (B.C.) for information about B.C. Ferries and air carriers.

Bus

Go Galiano Island Shuttle, 771 Georgeson Bay Rd., Galiano Island, B.C., V0N 1P0. Tel. (250) 539-5224, fax (250) 539-5544. Bus service on Galiano Island.

Water Taxi

Gulf Island Water Taxi Ltd., 2-100 Fulford-Ganges Rd., Saltspring Island, B.C., V8K 2S3. Tel. (250) 537-2510, fax (250) 537-9202. Servicing the Gulf Islands from Gabriola to Saturna.

Parks & Tourism

Canadian Gulf Islands Bed & Breakfast Reservation Service 637 Southwind Rd., Montague Harbour, Galiano Island, B.C., V0N 1P0. Tel. (250) 539-5390. Free of charge; kayak packages available.

Canada Customs, Bedwell Harbour on Pender Island. All foreign vessels and individuals entering the country must check in. Toll-free 1-800-222-4919 (to contact Customs upon arrival).

BC Parks, Southern Vancouver Island District, 2930 Trans-Canada Highway, R.R. #6, Victoria, B.C., V9B 5T9. Tel. (250) 391-2300, fax (250) 478-9211. For reservations at Sidney Spit, including group camping, tel. (250) 475-1341.

B.C. Forest Service, South Island District, 5785 Duncan St., Duncan, B.C., V9L 5G2. Tel. (250) 746-2700, fax (250) 746-2790.

Gabriola Travel Infocentre, 575 North Rd., Folklife Village, Gabriola Island, B.C., V0R 1X0. Tel. (250) 247-9332.

Saltspring Island Travel Infocentre, 121 Lower Ganges Rd., Saltspring Island, B.C. V8K 2T1. Tel. (250) 537-5252 or (250) 537-4223, fax (250) 537-4276. Webpage: www.saltspringisland.bc.ca.

Nanaimo Travel Infocentre, tel. (250) 754-8474.

Qualicum Travel Infocentre, tel. (250) 752-9532.

First Nations

Lyackson First Nation, tel. (250) 246-5019, fax (250) 246-5059. Traditional territory includes Valdes Island.

Penelakut Indian Band, Box 360, Chemainus, B.C., V0R 1K0. Tel. (250) 246-2321, fax (250) 246-2725. For permission to camp at Tent Island IR.

Qualicum Indian Band, 5850 River Rd., Qualicum Beach, B.C., V9L 1Z5. Tel. (250) 757-9337, fax (250) 757-9898. Operates a commercial campground (summer only) accessible by kayak.

Tsawout Indian Band, Box 121, Saanichton, B.C., V8M 2C3. Tel. (250) 652-9101, fax (250) 652-9114. For permission to camp on Saturna Island IR.

Equipment Rentals/Tours

Adventure Fitness, 1510 Duranleau St., Vancouver, B.C., V6H 3S4. Tel. (604) 687-1528, fax (604) 687-2769. Guided tours of the Gulf Islands, Johnstone Strait and Clayoquot Sound. Lessons, rentals and equipment sales.

Coastal Connections, 1027 Roslyn Rd., Victoria, B.C., V8S 4R4. Tel. (250) 480-9560, toll-free 1-800-840-4453 (North America), fax (250) 598-7043. Webpage: www.islandnet.com/~coast com/. Guided kayaking, hiking or sailing tours in the Gulf Islands.

Comox Valley Kayaks Ltd., 2020 Cliffe Ave., Courtenay, B.C., V9N 2L3. Tel. (250) 334-2628, toll-free 1-888-545-5595. Webpage: www.island.net/~seakayak/.

Rentals and tours on Vancouver Island.

Denman Island Sea Kayak, Box 52, Denman Island, B.C., V0R 1T0. Tel. (250) 335-2505, fax (250) 335-2221, cel. (250) 897-2552. Webpage: www.island. net/~salal/. Rentals and lessons.

Ecosummer Expeditions, 1516 Duranleau St., Vancouver, B.C., V6H 3S4. Toll-free 1-800-465-8884, fax (604) 669-3244. Webpage: www.ecosummer.com. Guided tours.

Gabriola Cycle and Kayak Ltd., 910 Clarendon Rd., Site 1, C-23, Gabriola Island, B.C., V0R 1X0. Tel. (250) 247-8277. Tours.

Galiano Island Sea Kayaking, 637 Southwind Rd., Galiano, B.C., V0N 1P0. Tel. (250) 539-2930, toll-free 1-888-539-2930. Guided day trips, rentals and accommodation; overnight kayaking trips with catamaran sailboat.

Gulf Island Kayaking, S-24, C-34, Galiano Island, B.C., V0N 1P0. Tel./fax: (250) 539-4224. Webpage: www.sea kayak.bc.ca/tour/. Tours and rentals.

Hornby Ocean Kayaks, Box 1-11, Hornby Island, B.C., V0R 1Z0. Tel./fax (250) 335-2726. Tours, rentals and lessons.

Island Escapades, 118 Natalie Lane, S-20, A-5, Ganges, Saltspring Island, B.C., V0S 1E0. Tel. (250) 537-2571, toll-free 1-888-KAYAK-67. Webpage: www.global serve.net/~tnplh/ie/ie.html. Kayaking in the Gulf Islands and throughout Vancouver Island.

Mayne Island Kayak & Canoe Rentals, 359 Maple Rd., Mayne Island, B.C., V0N 2J0. Tel. (250) 539-2667. Free pick-up from ferries.

Mouat Point Kayaks, 1615 Storm Cres., R.R. #2, Pender Island, B.C., V0N 2M2. Tel. (250) 629-6767.

North Island Water Sports, 2755 Departure Bay Rd., Nanaimo, B.C., V9S 3W9. Tel./fax (250) 758-2488. Tours,

lessons and rentals.

Ocean River Sports, 1437 Store St., Victoria, B.C., V8W 3J6. Tel. (250) 381-4233, fax (250) 361-3536. Webpage: www.oceanriver.com/. Tours, lessons and kayaking supplies. Rentals in downtown Victoria and Sidney.

Ocean West Expeditions Ltd., 40450 Cheakamus Place, Garibaldi Highlands, B.C., V0N 1T0. Tel. (604) 898-4979, fax (604) 898-4980. Webpage: www.ocean-west.com. Rentals (English Bay Beach) and lessons. Tours in Gulf Islands, Johnstone Strait and Desolation Sound.

Raven Adventures, Box 143, 4B-1533 Estevan Rd., Nanaimo, B.C., V9S 3Y3.

Sage Wilderness Experiences Ltd., Box 16082, 3017 Mountain Hwy., North Vancouver, B.C., V7J 3S9. Tel. (604) 983-3108, fax (604) 988-7791. Guided tours.

Saltspring Kayaking Ltd, 2935 Fulford-Ganges Rd., Saltspring Island, B.C., V0S 1C0. Tel. (250) 653-4222. Rentals and tours.

Seadog Kayaking, Box 45, R.R. #1, Nanoose Bay, B.C., V0R 2R0. Tel./fax (250) 468-5778 Webpage: nanaimo.ark. com/~seadog/. Tours, lessons and rentals, including Jedediah Island and Ballenas/Winchelsea Islands.

Sea Otter Kayaking, 1186 North End Rd., Saltspring Island, B.C., V8K 1M1. Tel. (250) 537-5678.

Sea Trek Sports, 9813-3rd St., Sidney, B.C., V8L 3A6. Tel. (250) 656-9888. Lessons and rentals.

Silver Seas Adventure Tours, 4034 Gulfview Dr., Nanaimo, B.C., V9T 6B4. Tel. (250) 751-8613, fax (250) 751-8628. Webpage: vvv.com/vtourist/ silver.html. Tours and lessons.

Tree Island Kayaking Co., 3025 Comox Rd., Courtenay, B.C., V9N 3P7. Tel. (250) 339-0580. Lessons, tours and rentals.

Water's Edge Kayaking, 3726 West

Island Hwy., Qualicum Beach, B.C.,
V9K 2G7. Tel. (250) 752-6345.
Wildheart Adventures, 2774 Barnes Rd.,
Nanaimo, B.C., V9R 5K2. Tel. (250)
722-3683, fax (250) 722-2175.
Webpage: www.island.net/~wheart.
Tours throughout the Gulf Islands and
Vancouver Island.
Wilderness Kayaking Co., 1130 Bazett
Rd., Duncan, B.C., V9L 5S8. Tel./fax (250)
746-0151. Tours, rentals and lessons.
Windrunner Ocean Adventures, Box
2575, Sidney, B.C., V8L 4C1. Tel. (250)
216-2628. Webpage: www.windrunner.
bc.ca/~windrun/. Kayaking and sailing
tours in the Gulf Islands.

IN AND AROUND VANCOUVER

Emergencies
Tel. 911 for non-marine emergencies.

Weather & Marine Radio
Canadian Coast Guard Weather Report,
tel. (604) 666-3655. Continuous marine
recording.
Vancouver Coast Guard Radio, tel. (604)
666-6617. For weather information or to
file a float plan.
VHF Weather Radio: channel WX3
(162.475 MHz).

Getting There
See GENERAL CONTACTS (B.C.) for information about B.C. Ferries and air carriers.

Parks & Tourism
Travel Infocentre, 200 Burrard St.,
Vancouver, B.C., V6C 3L6. Tel. (604)
683-2000, fax (604) 282-6839.
**BC Parks, Lower Mainland Parks
District,** 1610 Mt. Seymour Rd., North
Vancouver, B.C., V7G 1L3. Tel. (604)
924-2200, fax (604) 924-2244.

Greater Vancouver Regional Parks,
4330 Kingsway, Burnaby, B.C., V5H 4G8.
Tel. (604) 432-6355, fax (604) 432-6296.
B.C. Forest Service, Vancouver Region,
2100 Labieux Rd., Nanaimo, B.C., V9T 6E9.
Tel. (250) 751-7001, fax (250) 751-7190.

First Nations
Musqueam Nation, 6370 Salish Dr.,
Vancouver, B.C., V6N 2C6. Tel. (604)
263-3261, fax (604) 263-4212.
Semiahmoo First Nation, 16049 Beach
Rd., Surrey, B.C., V4B 5A8. Tel. (604)
536-3101, fax (604) 536-6116.
Squamish Nation, 320 Seymour Blvd.,
North Vancouver, B.C., V7L 2J3, Tel. (604)
980-4553, fax (604) 980-4523.
Tsleil-Waututh First Nation, 3082 Ghumly
Dr., North Vancouver, B.C., V7H 1B3. Tel.
(604) 929-3454, fax (604) 929-4714.

Equipment Rentals/Tours
Adventure Fitness, 1510 Duranleau St.,
Vancouver, B.C., V6H 3S4. Tel. (604)
687-1528, fax (604) 687-2769. Rentals,
lessons, tours and rental.
Boundary Bay Water Sports, 1-15531
24th Ave., White Rock, B.C., V4A 2J4.
Tel. (604) 541-9191, fax (604) 541-9192.
Lessons, day tours, rentals and retail.
Deep Cove Canoe & Kayak Centre, 2007
Rockcliff Rd, North Vancouver, B.C., V7G
1X3 (mailing address). 2156 Banbury Rd.,
North Vancouver (street address). Tel.
(604) 929-2268, fax (604)929-2662. Web-
page: www.vancouver-bc.com/DeepCove
CanoeKayak/index.html. Rentals, tours
and lessons; open spring through fall.
Ecomarine Ocean Kayak Centre, 1668
Duranleau St., Vancouver, B.C., V6H 3S4,
Tel. (604) 689-7575 (store), tel. (604)
689-7520 (school), fax (604) 689-5926.
Webpage: www.ecomarine.com/kayak/.
Extensive retail selection, including lami-
nated charts, books, kayaking gear, signal

devices, etc. Tours, rentals and lessons.
Natural West Coast Adventures, 1308 Everall St., White Rock, B.C., V4B 3S6, Tel./fax (604) 535-7985. Instruction, tours, and rentals.
Ocean West Expeditions Ltd., 40450 Cheakamus Place, Garibaldi Highlands, B.C., V0N 1T0. Tel. (604) 898-4979, fax (604) 898-4980. Webpage: www.ocean-west.com. Rentals (English Bay beach) and lessons. Tours in Gulf Islands, Johnstone Strait and Desolation Sound.
Sage Wilderness Experience, 2607 Hoskins Rd., Box 16082, North Vancouver, B.C., V7J 3S9. Tel. (604) 983-3108. Tours.
Western Canoeing & Kayaking, Box 115, 1717 Salton Rd., Abbotsford, B.C., V2S 4N8. Tel. (604) 853-9320, fax (604) 852-6933. Rentals and sales.

HOWE SOUND

Emergencies
Squamish RCMP, tel. (604) 898-9611.

Weather & Marine Radio
Canadian Coast Guard Weather Report, tel. (604) 666-3655. Continuous marine recording.
Vancouver Coast Guard Radio, tel. (604) 666-6617. For weather information or to file a float plan.
VHF Weather Radio: channel WX3 (162.475 MHz).

Getting There
See GENERAL CONTACTS (B.C.) for information about B.C. Ferries and air carriers.

Water Taxis
Cormorant Marine Water Taxi, R.R. #1 A-4, Bowen Island, B.C., V0N 1G0. Cel. (604) 250-2630 , tel. (604) 947-2243,

fax 947-9615.
Gambier Island Water Taxi, R.R. #3 Gibsons B.C., V0N 1V0. Cel. (604) 740-1133, tel. (604) 886-8321. Will also tow kayaks.
Squamish Marine Service, Box 1099, Squamish, B.C., V0M 3G0. Tel. (24 hrs) (604) 898-3733, fax (604) 898-9177.

Parks & Tourism
Squamish/Howe Sound Visitor Information Centre, 37950 Cleveland Ave., Box 1009, Squamish, B.C., V0N 3G0. Tel. (604) 892-9244, fax (604) 892-2034.
BC Parks, Garibaldi/Sunshine Coast District, Box 220, Brackendale, B.C., V0N 1H0. Tel. (604) 898-3678, fax (604) 898-4171.
B.C. Forest Service, Squamish District, 42000 Loggers Lane, Squamish, B.C., V0N 3G0. Tel. (604) 898-2100, fax (604) 898-2191.

First Nations
Squamish Nation, 320 Seymour Blvd., North Vancouver, B.C., V7L 2J3. Tel. (604) 980-4553, fax (604) 980-4523.

Equipment Rentals/Tours
Bowen Island Sea Kayaking, Box 87, Bowen Island, B.C., V0N 1G0. Tel. (604) 947-9266, toll-free 1-800-60-KAYAK, fax (604) 947-9717. Tours, instruction and rentals.
See also GULF ISLANDS and IN AND AROUND VANCOUVER.

SUNSHINE COAST

Emergencies
Gibsons RCMP, tel. (604) 886-2245.
Sechelt RCMP, tel. (604) 885-2266.

Weather & Marine Radio

Canadian Coast Guard Weather Report, Vancouver, tel. (604) 666-3655. Continuous marine recording.

Vancouver Coast Guard Radio, tel. (604) 666-6617. For weather information or to file a float plan.

VHF Weather Radio: channels WX1 (162.550 MHz) or 21B (161.65 MHz).

Getting There

See GENERAL CONTACTS (B.C.) for information about B.C. Ferries and air carriers.

Water Taxis

Coastal Water Taxi, R.R. #1, S-4, C-118, Gibsons, B.C., V0N 1V0. Cel. (604) 740-1912, fax (604) 886-3016. Serving Howe Sound, Sunshine Coast, Desolation Sound and Gulf Islands.

Gibsons Water Taxi, R.R. #4, S-19, C-76, Gibsons, B.C., V0N 1V0. Tel. (604)886-0226, cel. (604) 740-2000.

Egmont Water Taxi, Box 66, Dearheart St., Madeira Park, B.C., V0N 2H0. Tel./fax (604) 883-2092. Serving Desolation Sound and Sunshine Coast.

Parks & Tourism

Gibsons Travel Infocentre, Box 1190, 668 Sunnycrest Rd., Gibsons, B.C., V0N 1V0. Tel. (604) 886-2325, fax (604) 886-2379.

Sechelt Travel Infocentre, Box 360, #45-5755 Cowrie St., Sechelt, B.C., V0N 3A0. Tel. (604) 885-0662, fax (604) 885-0691.

B.C. Parks, Garibaldi/Sunshine Coast District, Box 220, Brackendale, B.C., V0N 1H0. Tel. (604) 898-3678, fax (604) 898-4171.

B.C. Forest Service, Sunshine Coast District, 7077 Duncan St., Powell River, B.C., V8A 1W1. Tel. (604) 485-0700, fax (604) 485-0799.

First Nations

Sechelt Indian Band, Box 740, Sechelt, B.C., V0N 3A0. Tel. (604) 688-3017, fax (604) 885-3490.

Equipment Rentals/Tours

Pedals & Paddles, Box 2601, Tillicum Bay Marina, Sechelt, B.C., V0N 3A0. Tel. (604) 885-6440, fax (604) 885-3064. Webpage: www.sunshine.net/paddle/. Rentals, lessons and trip planning.

Rising Sun Kayak Adventures, R.R. #1, S-6, C-29, Garden Bay, B.C., V0N 1S0. Tel. (604) 883-2062, toll-free 1-800-632-0722, fax (604) 883-2298. Webpage: www.sportsx.com/raisingsun/. Rentals, tours, instruction and lodging.

Sunshine Kayaking, R.R. #4, S-12, C-18, Gibsons, B.C., V0N 1V0. Tel. (604) 886-9760. Webpage: www.sunshine.net/www/100/sn0156/. Day tours, instruction and rentals.

Seadog Kayaking, Box 45, R.R. #1, Nanoose Bay, B.C., V0R 2R0. Tel./fax (250) 468-5778. Webpage: nanaimo.ark.com/~seadog/. Tours, lessons and rentals, including Jedediah Island and Ballenas/Winchelsea Islands in the Nanaimo area.

Tzoonie Ventures Ltd., Box 157, Sechelt, B.C., V0N 3A0. Tel. (604) 885-9802, fax (604) 885-9826. Webpage: http://www.sunshine.net/tzoonie/. Operates Narrows Inlet Wilderness Camp.

DESOLATION SOUND

Emergencies

Powell River RCMP, tel. (604) 485-3400.

Weather & Marine Radio

Environment Canada, tel. (250) 339-0748. Continuous weather recording, Johnstone Strait to Nanaimo.

North Island Marine Report, Campbell River, tel. (250) 286-3575.

Comox Coast Guard Radio, tel. (250) 339-3613. For weather information or to file a float plan.

VHF Weather Radio: channel WX1 (162.550 MHz).

Getting There

See GENERAL CONTACTS (B.C.) for information about B.C. Ferries and other air carriers.

Air

Rush Air, Box 704, Campbell River, B.C., V9W 6J3. Tel. (250) 287-7555, fax (250) 287-7760. Can provide drop-off service to remote areas; 2 hard-shelled boats maximum per trip.

Water Taxis

Coast Mountain Expeditions, Box 25, Read Island, Surge Narrows, B.C., V0P 1W0. Tel. (250) 287-0635. Webpage: www.vquest.com/coastmtn/. Tours, instruction, lodge and water taxi.

Discovery Launch Water Taxi, Box 164, Campbell River, B.C., V9W 5A7. Tel. (250) 287-7577, fax (250) 923-7700.

Lund Water Taxi, General Delivery, Lund, B.C., V0N 2G0. Tel. (604) 483-9749, fax (604) 483-8078, cel. (604) 483-1129. Service from Lund to Cortes Island.

Sutil Charters, Box 82, Heriot Bay, Quadra Island, B.C., V0P 1H0. Tel. (250) 285-3689.

Parks & Tourism

Powell River Travel Infocentre, 4690 Marine Ave., Powell River, B.C., V8A 2L1. Tel. (604) 485-4701, fax (604) 485-2822.

BC Parks, Garibaldi/Sunshine Coast District, Box 220, Brackendale, B.C., V0N 1H0. Tel. (604) 898-3678, fax (604) 898-4171.

B.C. Forest Service, Sunshine Coast District, 7077 Duncan St., Powell River,

B.C., V8A 1W1. Tel. (604) 485-0700, fax (604) 485-0799.

First Nations

Homalco Indian Band, 1218 Bute Cres., Campbell River, B.C., V9H 5G1. Tel. (250) 923-4979, fax (250) 923-4987. Discovery Islands, Desolation Sound and Bute Inlet.

Klahoose Indian Band, Box 9, Squirrel Cove, Cortes Island, B.C., V0P 1K0. Tel. (250) 935-6536, fax (250) 935-6997.

Sliammon Native Council, R.R. #2, Sliammon Rd., Powell River, B.C., V8A 4Z3. Tel. (604) 483-9646, fax (604) 483-9769.

Equipment Rentals/Tours

Coast Mountain Expeditions (see Water Taxis, above).

Powell River Sea Kayaks, tel. (604) 483-2410, fax (604) 483-2388. Webpage: www.prcn.org/kayak/. Rentals. Closed in winter.

T'Ai Li Lodge, Cortes Island, B.C., V0P 1K0. Tel. (250) 935-6749, toll-free 1-800-939-6644. Rentals, sales, lessons, tours, food, lodging and camping.

Wolfson Creek Canoe Rentals, 9537 Nassichuk Rd., Powell River, B.C., V8A 5C1. Tel. (604) 487-1699, fax. (604) 487-4445. Lessons and guiding.

DISCOVERY ISLANDS

Emergencies

Campbell River RCMP, tel. (250) 286-6221.

Quadra Island RCMP, tel. (250) 285-3631.

Weather & Marine Radio

Environment Canada, tel. (250) 339-0748. Continuous weather recording, Johnstone Strait to Nanaimo.

North Island Marine Report, Campbell River, tel. (250) 286-3575.
Comox Coast Guard Radio, tel. (250) 339-3613. For weather information or to file a float plan.
VHF Weather Radio: channel WX1 (162.550 MHz).

Getting There

See GENERAL CONTACTS (B.C.) for information about B.C. Ferries and air carriers. For water taxis, see DESOLATION SOUND.

Parks & Tourism

Campbell River Visitor Infocentre, 1235 Shoppers Row, Box 400, Campbell River, B.C., V9W 5B6. Tel. (250) 287-4636, fax (250) 286-6490.
BC Parks, Strathcona District, Box 1479, Parksville, B.C., V9P 2H4. Tel. (250) 954-4600, fax (250) 248-8584.
B.C. Forest Service, Campbell River District, 370 S. Dogwood St., Campbell River, B.C., V9W 6Y7. Tel. (250) 286-9300, fax (250) 286-9490.

First Nations

Cape Mudge Indian Band, Box 220, Quathiaski Cove, B.C., V0P 1N0. Tel. (250) 285-3316, fax (250) 285-2400. Quadra Island and area. Cape Mudge Museum and Cultural Centre, tel. (250) 285-3733.
Homalco Indian Band, 1218 Bute Cres., Campbell River, B.C., V9H 5G1. Tel. (250) 923-4979, fax (250) 923-4987. Discovery Islands, Desolation Sound and Bute Inlet.
Kwakiutl District Council, Box 2490, Port Hardy, B.C., V0N 2P0. Tel. (250) 949-9433, fax (250) 949-9677. Council of nine bands on northeast Vancouver Island, from Comox to Port Hardy.
Klahoose Indian Band, Box 9, Squirrel Cove, Cortes Island, B.C., V0P 1K0. Tel. (250) 935-6536, fax (250) 935-6997. Cortes Island and area.

Equipment Rentals/Tours

Coast Mountain Expeditions, Box 25, Read Island, Surge Narrows, B.C., V0P 1W0. Tel. (250) 287-0635. Webpage: www.vquest.com/coastmtn/. Tours, instruction, lodge and water taxi service.
Comox Valley Kayaks Ltd, 2020 Cliffe Ave., Courtenay, B.C., V9N 2L3. Tel. (250) 334-2628, toll-free 1-888-545-5595. Webpage: www.island.net/~seakayak/. Sales, lessons, tours and rentals.
Strathcona Outfitters, 888 Island Hwy., Campbell River, B.C., V9W 2C3. Tel. (250) 287-4453, fax (250) 287-7354. Retail sales and rental of camping and kayaking gear.
Strathcona Park Lodge, Jamie Boulding, Box 2160, Campbell River, B.C., V9W 5C9. Tel. (250) 286-3122.
T'Ai Li Lodge, Cortes Island, B.C., V0P 1K0. Tel. (250) 935-6749, toll-free 1-800-939-6644. Rentals, sales, lessons, tours, food, lodging and camping.

JOHNSTONE STRAIT

Emergencies

Port McNeill RCMP, tel. (250) 956-4441.
Albert Bay RCMP, tel. (250) 974-5544.

Weather & Marine Radio

Environment Canada. Continuous weather recording, tel. (250) 974-5305, northeast Vancouver Island; (250) 339-0748, Johnstone Strait to Nanaimo.
North Island Marine Weather Office, Port Hardy, tel. (250) 949-7148.
Comox Coast Guard Radio. In Comox, tel. (250) 339-3613; in Alert Bay, tel. (250) 974-5293. For weather information or to file a float plan.
Weather Radio Canada, Port Hardy, 130.7 Mhz.

VHF Weather Radio: channel 21B (161.65 MHz).

Getting There

See GENERAL CONTACTS (B.C.) for information about B.C. Ferries and other air carriers.

Air

Air Rainbow, 1514 Broughton Blvd., Port McNeill, B.C., V0N 2R0. Tel. (250) 956-2020, fax (250) 956-2025. Float plane service.

Water Taxis

Rainbow Express Water Taxi, Box 97, Port McNeill, B.C., V0N 2R0. Tel. (250) 956-2999, cel. (250) 974-8025.

Viking West Charters, Box 113, Port McNeill, B.C., V0N 2R0. Tel./fax (250) 956-3431, cel. (250) 974-8088.

Parks & Tourism

Port McNeill Travel Infocentre, tel. (250) 956-3131.

BC Parks, Strathcona District, Box 1479, Parksville, B.C., V9P 2H4. Tel. (250) 954-4600, fax (250) 248-8584.

BC Parks, Cape Scott Zone, Bag 11000, 8785 Gray St., Port Hardy, B.C., V0N 2P0. Tel. (250) 949-2800, fax (250) 949-6346. Responsible for Tsitika Valley Park and Robson Bight Ecological Reserve.

B.C. Forest Service, Port McNeill District, Box 7000, Port McNeill, B.C., V0N 2R0. Tel. (250) 956-5000, fax (250) 956-5005.

First Nations

Kwakiutl District Council, 2490, Port Hardy, B.C., V0N 2P0. Tel. (250) 949-9433, fax (250) 949-9677. Council of nine bands on northeast Vancouver Island, from Comox to Port Hardy.

Mamaleleqala Que'Qwa'Sot'Enox Band, 1400 Weiwaikum Rd., Campbell River, B.C., V9W 5W8. Tel. (250) 287-2955, fax (250) 287-4655. For permission to visit Village Island IR and Compton Island IR.

Musgamagw Tsawataineuk Tribal Council, Box 90, Alert Bay, B.C., V0N 1A0. Tel. (250) 974-5516, fax (250) 974-5466. A council of bands in the Alert Bay area, including the Tlowitsis-Mumtagila Band.

U'mista Cultural Centre, Alert Bay, tel. (250) 974-5403, fax (250) 974-5499. An excellent museum dedicated to First Nations culture.

Equipment Rentals/Tours

Adventure Fitness, 1510 Duranleau St., Vancouver, B.C., V6H 3S4. Tel. (604) 687-1528, fax (604) 687-2769. Rentals, lessons and tours (Gulf Islands, Johnstone Strait and Clayoquot Sound).

Alder Bay Resort, Box 1090 Port McNeill, B.C., V0N 2R0. Tel. (250) 956-4117, fax (250) 956-2552. Boat launching, camping and pay parking.

Cormorant Sea Kayaking Ltd., Box 17, Sointula, B.C., V0N 3E0. Tel./fax (250) 973-6033. Sea kayak rentals and B&B on Malcolm Island. Nautical chart sales.

Discovery Expeditions, 2755 Departure Bay Rd., Nanaimo, B.C., V9S 3W9. Tel./fax (250) 758-2488. Tours, lessons and rentals.

Ecosummer Expeditions, 1516 Duranleau St., Vancouver, B.C., V6H 3S4. Toll-free 1-800-465-8884, fax (604) 669-3244. Webpage: www.ecosummer.com. Guided tours.

Gabriola Cycle and Kayak Ltd., 910 Clarendon Rd., Site 1, C-23, Gabriola Island, B.C., V0R 1X0. Tel. (250) 247-8277. Tours.

Islands Sauvage, tel. (250) 282-3644,

toll-free 1 800-667-4354. Webpage:
oberon.ark.com/~sauvage/. Guided tours.
North Island Kayak Rentals, Box 291,
Port Hardy, B.C., V0N 2P0. Tel./fax (250)
949-7707. Rentals in Alder Bay, Port
Hardy and Quatsino, and kayak tours
with a First Nations cultural emphasis.
Northern Lights Expeditions Ltd,
113-1817 Campbell Way, Port McNeill,
B.C., V0N 2R0. Port McNeill: tel. (250)
956-2080 (summer only); Bellingham:
tel. (360) 734-6334, fax (360) 734-6150.
Toll-free 1-800-754-7402. Webpage:
www.bonsai.com/~indi/nle/. Guided
kayak tours.
Ocean West Expeditions Ltd., 40450
Cheakamus Place, Garibaldi Highlands,
B.C., V0N 1T0. Tel. (604) 898-4979,
fax (604) 898-4980. Webpage: www.
ocean-west.com. Tours in Gulf Islands,
Johnstone Strait and Desolation Sound.
Odyssey Kayaking, 9590 Scott St., Port
Hardy, B.C., V0N 2P0. Tel./fax (250)
902-0565. Rentals, instruction and tours.
Pacific Rim Paddling Company, Box
1840, Victoria, B.C., V8W 2Y3. Tel. (250)
384-6103, fax (250) 361-2686. Guided
tours.
Silver Seas Adventure Tours, 4034
Gulfview Dr., Nanaimo, B.C., V9T 6B4.
Tel. (250) 751-8613, fax (250)
751-8628. Webpage: vvv.com/vtourist/
silver.html. Tours and lessons.
Telegraph Cove Resorts, Box 1, Telegraph
Cove, B.C., V0N 3J0. Tel. (250) 928-3131,
toll-free 1-800-200-4665, fax (250)
928-3105. Boat launching, car parking,
camping, café and fishing charters.
Tofino Expeditions Ltd., Box 15280, Seattle, WA 98115-0280. Tel. (206)
517-5244, fax (206) 517-5203. Webpage:
www.tofino.com/. Guided tours throughout B.C., including Johnstone Strait.
Wildheart Adventures, 2774 Barnes Rd.,
Nanaimo, B.C., V9R 5K2. Tel. (250)

722-3683, fax (250) 722-2175.
Webpage: www.island.net/~wheart.
Tours throughout the Gulf Islands and
Vancouver Island.

BARKLEY SOUND

Emergencies
Ucluelet RCMP, tel. (250) 726-7773.
Tofino RCMP, tel. (250) 725-3242.

Weather & Marine Radio
**Vancouver Island (west coast) Marine
Weather Forecast,** tel. (250) 726-3415.
Tofino Coast Guard Radio, tel. (250)
726-7312. For weather information and
to file a float plan.
VHF Weather Radio: channel 21B (161.65
MHz).

Getting There
See GENERAL CONTACTS (B.C.) for information about B.C. Ferries and other air carriers.

Air
Klitsa Air Ltd, 4855 Johnston Rd., Port
Alberni, B.C. V9Y 5M2. Tel. (250)
723-2375, fax (250) 724-7188. Float
plane charters.

Bus
Western Bus Lines, 4521 10th Ave., Port
Alberni, B.C., V9Y 4X9. Tel. (250) 723-
3341, fax (250) 723-8115. June to
October, between Port Alberni and
Bamfield.
West Coast Trail Express, 3954 Bow Rd.,
Victoria, B.C., V8N 3B1. Tel./fax (250)
477-8700. Between Victoria and Bamfield.

Water Taxis
Alberni Marine Transport, Box 188,
Port Alberni, B.C., V9Y 7M7. Tel. (250)
723-8313, toll-free 1-800-663-7192

(Apr.–Sept.), fax (250) 723-8314. For travel on the MV *Lady Rose* and MV *Frances Barkley*; also kayak rentals and Sechart Lodge.

Bamfield Express Water Taxi, General Delivery, Bamfield, B.C., V0R 1B0. Tel. (250) 728-3001, cel. (250) 720-9246. For accommodation at Kildonan Cannery Lodge, kayak rentals and water taxi.

Subtidal Adventures, tel. (250) 726-7336. Transportation to the Broken Group from Ucluelet.

Parks & Tourism

Alberni Valley Visitor Information, S-215, C-10, Port Alberni, B.C., V9Y 7L6. Tel. (250) 724-6535, fax (250) 724-6560.

Ucluelet Visitor Information, Box 428, Ucluelet, B.C., V0R 3A0. Tel. (250) 726-4641, fax (250) 726-4611.

BC Parks, Strathcona District, Box 1479, Parksville, B.C., V9P 2H4. Tel. (250) 954-4600, fax (250) 248-8584.

Parks Canada, Pacific Rim National Park Reserve, Box 280, Ucluelet, B.C., V0R 3A0. Tel. (250) 726-7721, fax (250) 726-4720.

B.C. Forest Service, Port Alberni District, 4227 6th Ave., Port Alberni, B.C., V6Y 4N1. Tel. (250) 724-9205, fax (250) 724-9261.

First Nations

Huu-ay-aht First Nation, Box 70, Bamfield, B.C., V0R 1B0. Tel. (250) 728-3414, fax (250) 728-1222.

Nuu-chah-nulth Tribal Council, Box 1383, Port Alberni, B.C., V9Y 7M2. Tel. (250) 724-5757, fax (250) 723-0463.

Equipment Rentals/Tours

Alberni Marine Transport. See Water Taxis (above).

Bamfield Express Water Taxi. See Water Taxis (above).

Majestic Ocean Kayaking, Box 287, Ucluelet, B.C., V0R 3A0. Toll-free 1-800-889-7644. Guided tours.

Pacific Rim Paddling Company, Box 1840, Victoria, B.C., V8W 2Y3. Tel. (250) 384-6103, fax (250) 361-2686. Guided tours.

Pristine Adventures, Box 795, Ucluelet, B.C., V0R 3A0. Tel. (250) 726-4477. Guided canoe tours, bear watching, birdwatching and fly-fishing.

Sage Wilderness Experiences Ltd., Box 16082, 3017 Mountain Hwy., North Vancouver, B.C., V7J 3S9. Tel. (604) 983-3108, fax (604) 988-7791. Guided tours.

Seabird Kayaking and Tours, 151 Lombard St., Bamfield, B.C. Tel. (250) 728-2341.

Wilderness Kayaking Co., 1130 Bazett Rd., Duncan, B.C., V9L 5S8. Tel./fax (250) 746-0151. Tours, rentals and lessons.

Wildheart Adventures, 2774 Barnes Rd., Nanaimo, B.C., V9R 5K2. Tel. (250) 722-3683, fax (250) 722-2175. Webpage: www.island.net/~wheart. Tours.

CLAYOQUOT SOUND

Emergencies

Tofino RCMP, tel. (250) 725-3242.

Weather & Marine Radio

Vancouver Island (west coast) Marine Weather Forecast, tel. (250) 726-3415.

Tofino Coast Guard Radio, tel. (250) 726-7312. For weather information and to file a float plan.

Weather Radio Canada, Tofino, 1260 Khz AM.

VHF Weather Radio: channels WX1 (162.55 MHz), WX3 (162.475 MHz) or 21B (161.65 MHz).

Getting There

See GENERAL CONTACTS (B.C.) for information about B.C. Ferries and other air carriers.

Air

Atleo River Air, 106 Ahousaht Reserve, Ahousaht, B.C., V0R 1A0. Tel. (250) 670-9633, fax (250) 670-9519. Serving Clayoquot Sound, Nootka Sound and Kyuquot Sound.

North Vancouver Air, 311-5260 Airport Rd. S., Richmond, B.C., V7B 1B4. Toll-free 1-800-228-6608, tel. (604) 278-1608, fax (604) 278-2608. Scheduled destinations include Ucluelet, Tofino, Port Alberni, Victoria and Vancouver.

Tofino Air, Box 99, Tofino, B.C., V0R 2Z0. Tel. (250) 725-4454, fax: (250) 725-4421. Float plane charters for sightseeing and drop off.

Water Taxis

Matlahaw Water Taxi, VHF channel 66. Contact Hesquiaht Band Office for information: tel. (250) 724-8570, fax (250) 724-8570.

Spirit of Marktosis (sea bus to Ahousaht). Contact Ahousaht Band Office for information: tel. (250) 670-9563.

Vargas Island Inn, Box 267, Tofino, B.C., V0R 2Z0. Tel. (250) 725-3309. Water taxi service. Also, an excellent kayak-friendly hostel in the middle of the Clayoquot Sound wilderness.

Parks & Tourism

Tofino Visitor Infocentre, Box 249, 380 Campbell St., Tofino, V0R 2Z0. Tel. (250) 725-3414, fax (250) 725-3296.

BC Parks, Strathcona District, Box 1479, Parksville, B.C., V9P 2H4. Tel. (250) 954-4600, fax (250) 248-8584.

Parks Canada, Pacific Rim National Park Reserve, Box 280, Ucluelet, B.C.,

V0R 3A0. Tel. (250) 726-7721, fax (250) 726-4720.

B.C. Forest Service, Port Alberni District, 4227 6th Ave., Port Alberni, B.C., V6Y 4N1. Tel. (250) 724-9205, fax (250) 724-9261.

First Nations

Ahousaht Band Office, General Delivery, Ahousaht, B.C., V0R 1A0. Tel. (250) 670-9563, fax (250) 670-9531,

Hesquiaht Band Office, Box 2000, Tofino, B.C., V0R 2Z0. Tel. (250) 724-8570, fax (250) 724-8570.

Nuu-chah-nulth Tribal Council, Box 1383, Port Alberni, B.C., V9Y 7M2. Tel. (250) 724-5757, fax (250) 723-0463.

Tla-o-qui-aht First Nation, Box 18, Tofino, B.C., V0R 2Z0, Tel. (250) 725-3233, fax (250) 725-4233

Walk the Wild Side, Box 150, Ahousaht, B.C., V0R 1A0. Toll-free 1-888-670-9586, fax (250) 670-9696. First Nations tourism resource centre; water taxis, accommodations and hiking guides.

Equipment Rentals/Tours

Hot Springs Lodge, tel. (250) 670-1106.

Majestic Ocean Kayaking, Box 287, Ucluelet, B.C., V0R 3A0. Toll-free 1-800-889-7644. Guided tours.

Remote Passages, Box 624, Tofino, B.C., V0R 2Z0. Tel. (250) 725-3330, fax (250) 725-3360. Toll-free 1-800-666-9833. Webpage: www.island.net/~remote/. Guided day tours and instruction.

Tofino Expeditions Ltd., Box 15280, Seattle, WA 98115-0280. Tel. (206) 517-5244, fax (206) 517-5203. Webpage: www.tofino.com/. Guided tours throughout B.C., including Clayoquot Sound.

Tofino Sea Kayaking Company/ Paddler's Inn, Box 620, Tofino, B.C., V0R 2Z0 (mailing address); 320 Main St. (street

address).Tel. (250) 725-4222, fax (250) 725-2070, toll-free 1-800-TOFINO-4. Webpage: www.island.net/~paddlers/. Lessons, B&B, tours, rentals and kayaking gear sales. Also a great little bookstore.
Wilderness Kayaking Co., 1130 Bazett Rd., Duncan, B.C., V9L 5S8. Tel./fax (250) 746-0151. Tours, rentals and lessons.

NOOTKA SOUND

Emergencies
Gold River RCMP, tel. (250) 283-2227.
Tahsis RCMP, tel. (250) 934-6363.

Weather & Marine Radio
Vancouver Island (west coast) Marine Weather Forecast, tel. (250) 726-3415.
Tofino Coast Guard Radio, tel. (250) 726-7312. For weather information and to file a float plan.
VHF Weather Radio: channel WX2 (162.40 MHz).

Getting There
See GENERAL CONTACTS (B.C.) for information about B.C. Ferries and other air carriers.

Air
Air Nootka, 777 Mill Rd., Box 19, Gold River, B.C., V0P 1G0. Tel. (250) 283-2255. Scheduled stops in Nootka and Kyuquot Sounds.
Atleo River Air, 106 Ahousaht Reserve, Ahousaht, B.C., V0R 1A0. Tel. (250) 670-9633, fax (250) 670-9519. Serving Clayoquot, Nootka and Kyuquot Sounds.

Water Taxis
Maxi's Water Taxi, government wharf, Gold River, B.C., V0P 1G0. Tel. (250) 283-2282, fax (250) 283-2335.
Nootka Sound Service, Box 57, Gold River, B.C., V0P 1G0. Tel. (250)

283-2325, fax (250) 283-2515. Transportation aboard the MV *Uchuck III.*

Parks & Tourism
Ahaninaquus Tourist Centre, 100 Owatin Rd., Tsaxana Reserve, Gold River, B.C., V0P 1G0. Tel. (250) 283-2015, toll-free 1-800-238-2933, fax (250) 283-2335.
Gold River Travel Infocentre, Box 610, Gold River, B.C., V0P 1G0. Tel. (250) 283-2418, fax (250) 283-7500. Open May 15 to Sept. 25.
BC Parks, Strathcona District, Box 1479, Parksville, B.C., V9P 2H4. Tel. (250) 954-4600, fax (250) 248-8584.
B.C. Forest Service, Campbell River District, 370 S. Dogwood St., Campbell River, B.C., V9W 6Y7. Tel. (250) 286-9300, fax (250) 286-9490.

First Nations
Mowachaht/Muchalaht Band, Box 459, Gold River, B.C., V0P 1G0. Tel. (250) 283-2015.

Equipment Rentals/Tours
Nootka Sound Kayaking Adventures Ltd, Merville, B.C., V0R 2M0. Tel. (250) 337-5292 toll-free 1-800-661-9393. Webpage: hhtp://comox.island.net/~kayak/. Summer only.
Sage Wilderness Experiences Ltd., Box 16082, 3017 Mountain Hwy., North Vancouver, B.C., V7J 3S9. Tel. (604) 983-3108, fax (604) 988-7791. Guided tours.
Tuta Marina and Campgrounds, Box 765, Gold River, B.C., V0P 1G0. Tel. (250) 283-7550. Launching and parking.
Wilderness Kayaking Co., 1130 Bazett Rd., Duncan, B.C., V9L 5S8. Tel./fax (250) 746-0151. Tours, rentals and lessons.
Wildheart Adventures, 2774 Barnes Rd., Nanaimo, B.C., V9R 5K2.

Tel. (250) 722-3683, fax (250) 722-2175.
Webpage: www.island.net/~wheart.
Guided tours.

KYUQUOT SOUND

Emergencies
Tahsis RCMP, tel. (250) 934-6363 (inquiries are routed to Kyuquot detachment).

Weather & Marine Radio
See NOOTKA SOUND.

Getting There
See GENERAL CONTACTS (B.C.) for information about B.C. Ferries and other air carriers.

Air
Air Nootka, 777 Mill Rd., Box 19, Gold River, B.C., V0P 1G0. Tel. (250) 283-255. Scheduled stops in Nootka and Kyuquot Sounds.
Atleo River Air, 106 Ahousaht Reserve, Ahousaht, B.C., V0R 1A0. Tel. (250) 670-9633, fax (250) 670-9519. Serving Clayoquot, Nootka and Kyuquot Sounds.

Water Taxis
Nootka Sound Service, Box 57, Gold River, B.C., V0P 1G0. Tel. (250) 283-2325, fax (250) 283-2515. Transportation aboard the MV *Uchuck III*.
Perseverance Charters, General Delivery, Kyuquot, B.C., V0P 1G0. Tel. (250) 332-5377.
QwaQwath (Hilda Hansen) Water Taxi, General Delivery, Kyuquot, B.C., V0P 1J0. Tel. (250) 332-5232.
Slam Bang Lodge, General Delivery, Kyuquot, B.C., V0P 1J0. Tel. (250) 332-5313. Kayak rentals and water taxi.

Parks & Tourism
BC Parks, Strathcona District, Box 1479,

Parksville, B.C., V9P 2H4. Tel. (250) 954-4600, fax (250) 248-8584.
BC Parks, Cape Scott Zone, Bag 11000, 8785 Gray St., Port Hardy, B.C., V0N 2P0. Tel. (250) 949-2800, fax (250) 949-6346. Before you go to Kyuquot, please get a Checleset Bay Ecological Reserve brochure from this office.
B.C. Forest Service, Campbell River District, 370 S. Dogwood St., Campbell River, B.C., V9W 6Y7. Tel. (250) 286-9300, fax (250) 286-9490.
The Old Co-op B&B and **Miss Charlie's Restaurant,** Kyuquot, B.C., V0P 1J0. Tel. (250) 332-5293.
Kyuquot Environment and Economic Protection Society, tel. (250) 332-5287.

First Nations
Checleset Kyuquot First Nations, General Delivery, Kyuquot, B.C., V0P 1J0. Tel. (250) 332-5259, fax (250) 332-5210. You are asked to stop at the band office before heading into Kyuquot Sound.

Equipment Rentals/Tours
Islands Sauvage, tel. (250) 282-3644, toll-free 1 800-667-4354. Webpage: oberon.ark.com/~sauvage/. Guided tours.
Slam Bang Lodge. See Water Taxis (above).
West Coast Expeditions, Box 3733, Courtenay, B.C., V9N 7P1. Tel. (250) 338-9789, toll-free 1-800-665-3040. Guided kayak tours and water taxi service.
Wilderness Kayaking Co., 1130 Bazett Rd., Duncan, B.C., V9L 5S8. Tel./fax (250) 746-0151. Tours, rentals and lessons.

QUATSINO SOUND

Emergencies
Port Hardy RCMP, tel. (250) 949-6335.

Weather & Marine Radio
See NOOTKA SOUND.
VHF Weather Radio: channel 21B (161.65 MHz).

Getting There
See GENERAL CONTACTS (B.C.) for information about B.C. Ferries and other air carriers.

Air
North Vancouver Air, 311-5260 Airport Rd. S., Richmond, B.C., V7B 1B4. Tel. (604) 278-1608, toll-free 1-800-228-6608, fax (604) 278-2608.

Bus
North Island Transportation, Box 1074, Port Hardy, B.C., V0N 2P0. Tel. (250) 949-6300, fax (250) 949-6388. Passenger transportation from B.C. Ferries terminal and Port Hardy Airport into Port Hardy.

Water Taxi
D.H. Timber Towing, Box 69, Coal Harbour, B.C., V0N 1K0. Tel. (250) 949-6358, fax (250) 949-9886.

Parks & Tourism
Port Hardy Travel Infocentre, Box 249, Port Hardy, B.C., V0N 2P0. Tel. (250) 949-7622, fax (250) 949-6653.
BC Parks, Strathcona District, Box 1479, Parksville, B.C., V9P 2H4. Tel. (250) 954-4600, fax (250) 248-8584.
BC Parks, Cape Scott Zone, Bag 11000, 8785 Gray St., Port Hardy, B.C., V0N 2P0. Tel. (250) 949-2800, fax (250) 949-6346.
B.C. Forest Service, Port McNeill District, Box 7000, Port McNeill, B.C., V0N 2R0. Tel. (250) 956-5000, fax (250) 956-5005.

First Nations
Quatsino Band Council, Box 100,

Coal Harbour, B.C., V0N 1K0. Tel. (250) 949-6245, fax (250) 949-6249.

Equipment Rentals/Tours
North Island Kayak Rentals, Box 291, Port Hardy, B.C., V0N 2P0, Tel./fax (250) 949-7707. Rentals and tours with First Nations emphasis.
Odyssey Kayaking, 9590 Scott St., Port Hardy, B.C., V0N 2P0. Tel./fax (250) 902-0565. Rentals, instruction and tours.

CENTRAL COAST

Emergencies
Bella Bella RCMP, tel. (250) 957-2388.

Weather & Marine Radio
Environment Canada, tel. (250) 974-5305. Continuous weather recording.
Prince Rupert Coast Guard, tel. (250) 627-3081 or 627-3074. For weather information or to file a float plan.
VHF Weather Radio: channels WX1 (1162.55 Mh), **WX2** (162.40 MHz) or **WX3** (162.475 MHz).

Getting There
See GENERAL CONTACTS (B.C.) for information about B.C. Ferries and other air carriers.

Air
Mid Coast Air, Box 425, 718 North Rd., Gibsons, B.C. V0N 1V0. Tel. (250) 957-2529, fax (250) 957-2522. Scheduled and charter float planes between Bella Bella and Klemtu.
North Vancouver Air, 311-5260 Airport Rd. S., Richmond, B.C., V7B 1B4. Tel. (604) 278-1608, toll-free 1-800-228-6608, fax (604) 278-2608. Scheduled destinations include Port Hardy, Bella Bella, Victoria and Vancouver.

Timberline Air, Bella Bella. Tel. (250) 957-4228. Scheduled float plane service to Bella Bella.

Wilderness Air, 4540 Agar Dr., Richmond, B.C., V7B 1A4. Tel. (250) 982-2225, toll-free 1-800-665-9453, fax (604) 276-9586. Servicing Bella Bella, Bella Coola, Campbell River, Shearwater, Vancouver and Anahim Lake. Charters available; both float and wheels.

Bus

Gold Pan City Stage Lines, 1471 Quesnel-Hixon Rd., Quesnel, B.C., V2J 5Z3. Toll-free 1-888-992-6168. Bookings can be made with Tweedsmuir Travel in Bella Coola, tel. (250) 799-5638. Bus service between Williams Lake to Bella Coola; stops include Anahim Lake and Nimpo Lake.

North Island Transportation, Box 1074, Port Hardy, B.C., V0N 2P0. Tel. (250) 949-6300, fax (250) 949-6388. Passenger transportation from B.C. Ferries terminal and Port Hardy Airport into Port Hardy.

Water Taxis

AK Trips and Charters, Box 1620, Port Hardy, B.C., V0N 2P0. Tel. (250) 949-7952, fax (250) 949-6040. Serving Cape Scott and Cape Caution from Port Hardy.

Campbell Island Charters, Box 781, Waglisla, B.C., V0T 1Z0. Tel. (250) 957-2319, fax (250) 957-2710. Fishing and sightseeing charters.

Gistala Adventures, Box 78, Bella Bella, B.C., V0T 1B0. Tel./fax (250) 957-2652, toll-free (tel/fax) 1-800-642-7111. Rentals, guided tours and water taxi charter service to Hakai and Fiordland Recreation Areas.

Sea Going Excursions, Box 862, Waglisla, B.C., V0T 1Z0. Tel. (250) 957-2999, fax (250) 957-2601. Water taxi,

sightseeing and salmon fishing charters in the Bella Bella area.

SeeQuest Adventures, Box 155, Waglisla, B.C., V0T 1Z0. Tel. (250) 957-2611, fax (250) 957-2619. Webpage: www.seequest.com. Water taxi from Bella Bella to Hakai Pass.

Parks & Tourism

Port Hardy Travel Infocentre, Box 249, Port Hardy, B.C., Tel. (250) 949-7622, fax (250) 949-6653.

BC Parks, Cariboo District Office, 281 North 1st Ave., Williams Lake, B.C., V2G 1Y7. Tel. (250) 398-4414, fax (250) 398-4686. Write for a copy of the Hakai Recreation Area map/brochure.

BC Parks, Bella Coola Zone Office, Box 126, Bella Coola, B.C., V0T 1C0. Tel. (250) 799-5526, fax (250) 799-5568.

B.C. Forest Service, Mid Coast District, Box 190, Hagensborg, B.C., V0T 1H0. Tel. (250) 982-2000, fax (250) 982-2090.

First Nations

Heiltsuk Nation, Box 880, Waglisla, B.C., V0T 1Z0. Tel. (250) 957-2381, fax (250) 957-2544. Contact the Heiltsuk Cultural Centre at tel. (250) 957-2626, fax (250) 957-2780.

Kitasoo Indian Band, General Delivery, Klemtu, B.C., V0T 1L0. Tel. (250) 839-1255, fax (250) 839-1256.

Oweekeno Nation, Bag 3500, Port Hardy, B.C., V0N 2P0. Tel. (250) 949-2107, fax (250) 949-2112.

Equipment Rentals/Tours

Gistala Adventures, Box 78, Bella Bella, B.C., V0T 1B0. Tel./fax (250) 957-2652, toll-free (phone and fax) 1-800-642-7111. Guided tours, rentals (in Shearwater) and water taxi.

North Island Kayak Rentals, Box 291, Port Hardy, B.C., V0N 2P0. Tel./fax (250)

949-7707. Rentals in Port Hardy for use on Discovery Coast ferry route.

Odyssey Kayaking, 9590 Scott St., Port Hardy, B.C., V0N 2P0, B.C. Tel./fax (250) 902-0565. Rentals in Port Hardy.

Rain Raven Kayaks, Ocean Falls, B.C. V0T 1P0. Tel. (250) 289-3218. Retail sale of hand-built wooden canoe and kayaks, plus local information.

SeeQuest Adventures, Box 155, Waglisla, B.C., V0T 1Z0 Tel. (250) 957-2611, fax (250) 957-2619. Webpage: www.seequest.com. Canoe trips, camping, water taxi and other services.

Tofino Expeditions Ltd., Box 15280, Seattle, WA 98115-0280. Tel. (206) 517-5244, fax (206) 517-5203. Webpage: www.tofino.com/. Guided tours throughout B.C., including Cape Caution Beaches.

QUEEN CHARLOTTE ISLANDS/HAIDA GWAII

Emergencies

Masset and Port Clements RCMP, tel. (250) 626-3991.

Queen Charlotte Islands (Sandspit) RCMP, tel. (250) 559-4421.

Weather & Marine Radio

See CENTRAL COAST.

VHF Weather Radio: channels WX1 (1162.55 Mh), **WX2** (162.40 MHz), **WX3** (162.475 MHz) or **21B** (161.65 MHz).

Getting There

See GENERAL CONTACTS (B.C.) for information about B.C. Ferries and other air carriers.

Air

South Moresby Air, Box 969, Queen Charlotte City, B.C., V0T 1S0. Tel. (250) 559-4222, toll-free 1-888-551-4222.

Float plane charters; will carry hard-shell kayaks.

Water Taxis/Ferry

Alaska Marine Highway (Alaskan Ferries), Box 25535, Juneau, AK 99802-5535. Toll-free (for reservations) 1-800-642-0066, fax (Juneau) (907) 277-4829, toll-free (in Canada) 1-800-665-6414, tel. (Prince Rupert) (250) 627-1744. Webpage: www.dot.state.ak.us/external/amhs/home. Destinations include Bellingham, WA, Prince Rupert and Juneau. Please call to confirm ports of call.

Moresby Explorers, Box 109, Sandspit, B.C., V0T 1T0. Tel. (250) 637-2215, toll-free 1-800-806-7633. Webpage: www.cybersurf.net/~Moresby.

Queen Charlotte Adventures, Box 196, Queen Charlotte City, B.C., V0T 1S0. Tel. (250) 559-8990, toll-free 1-800-668-4288.

Parks & Tourism

Queen Charlotte Visitor Centre, Box 819, Queen Charlotte City, B.C., V0T 1S0. Tel. (250) 559-8316, fax (250) 559-8952. Open May 1 to Labour Day.

BC Parks, Skeena District, Bag 5000, Smithers, B.C., V0J 2N0. Tel. (250) 847-7320, fax (240) 847-7659.

BC Parks, Queen Charlotte Island Zone Office, Box 19, Tlell, B.C., V0T 1Y0. Tel. (250) 557-4390, fax (250) 557-4629.

Parks Canada, Gwaii Haanas National Park Reserve/Haida Heritage Site, Box 37, Queen Charlotte City, B.C., V0T 1S0. Tel. (250) 559-8818, fax (250) 559-8268. Webpage: http//parkscanada.pch.gc.ca.

Gwaii Haanas Office, Gwaii Haanas, Box 37, Queen Charlotte City, B.C., V0T 1S0. Tel. (250) 559-8818, fax (250) 559-8366, TDD (250) 559-8139. Webpage: http//fas.sfu.ca/canheritage.

B.C. Forest Service, Queen Charlotte Islands District, Box 39, Queen Charlotte City, B.C., V0T 1S0. Tel. (250) 559-6200, fax (250) 559-8324.

TimberWest, 453 Alliford Bay, Sandspit, B.C., V0T 1T0. Tel. (250) 637-5323, fax (250) 637-2219.

First Nations

Council of the Haida Nation, Box 589, Masset, B.C., V0T 1M0. Tel. (250) 626-5252, fax (250) 626-3493.

Skidegate Indian Band, Box 1301, Skidegate, Haida Gwaii, B.C., V0T 1S1. Tel. (250) 559-4496, fax (250) 559-8247.

Haida Gwaii Watchmen, VHF channel 6.

Equipment Rentals/Tours

Ecosummer Expeditions, 1516 Duranleau St., Vancouver, B.C., V6H 3S4. Toll-free 1-800-465-8884, fax (604) 669-3244. Webpage: www.ecosummer.com. Guided tours.

Gwaii Haanas Guest House and Kayaks, Box 578, Queen Charlotte City, B.C., V0T 1S0. Tel. (250) 559-8638, autotel (250) 624-8707. Webpage: www. gwaiihaanas.com/. Guest house and meals at Rose Harbour; kayak rentals and customized group trips.

Moresby Explorers, Box 109, Sandspit, B.C., V0T 1T0. Tel. (250) 637-2215, toll-free 1-800-806-7633. Webpage: www.cybersurf.net/~Moresby. Kayak rentals and transportation.

Pacific Rim Paddling Company, Box 1840, Victoria, B.C., V8W 2Y3. Tel. (250) 384-6103, fax (250) 361-2686. Tours.

Queen Charlotte Adventures, Box 196, Queen Charlotte City, B.C., V0T 1S0. Tel. (250) 559-8990, toll-free 1-800-668-4288. Webpage: Www.island.net/ ~infobus/qca/. Guided tours, kayak rentals and transportation.

Tofino Expeditions Ltd., Box 15280, Seattle, WA 98115-0280. Tel. (206) 517-5244, fax (206) 517-5203. Webpage: www.tofino.com/. Guided tours throughout B.C., including the Queen Charlotte Islands/Haida Gwaii.

NORTH COAST

Emergencies

Prince Rupert RCMP, tel. (250) 627-0700, **Port Simpson RCMP,** tel. (250) 624-2136.

Weather & Marine Radio

See CENTRAL COAST.

VHF Weather Radio: channels WX1 (1162.55 Mh), **WX2** (162.40 MHz), **WX3** (162.475 MHz) or **21B** (161.65 MHz).

Getting There

See GENERAL CONTACTS (B.C.) for information about B.C. Ferries, bus, train and air carriers.

Water Taxi/Ferry

Alaskan Marine Highway. See QUEEN CHARLOTTE ISLANDS/HAIDA GWAII.

Prince Rupert Water Taxi/Metlakatla Ferry Service, Box 224, Prince Rupert, B.C., V8J 3P4. Tel. (250) 624-3337 or (250) 628-3201. Charters.

Parks & Tourism

Tourist Bureau, Box 669, Prince Rupert., B.C., V9J 3S1. Tel. (250) 624-5637, fax (250) 627-8009.

BC Parks, Skeena District, Bag 5000, Smithers, B.C., V0J 2N0. Tel. (250) 847-7320, fax (240) 847-7659.

B.C. Forest Service, North Coast District, 125 Market Place, Prince Rupert, B.C., V8J 1B9. Tel. (250) 624-7460, fax (250) 624-7479.

First Nations

Kitkatla Indian Band, General Delivery, Kitkatla, B.C., V0V 1C0. Tel. (250) 848-2214, fax (250) 848-2238.

Metlakatla Indian Band, Box 459, Prince Rupert, B.C., V8J 3R2. Tel. (250) 628-3234, fax (250) 628-9205.

North Coast Tribal Council, 100 W. First Ave., Prince Rupert, B.C., V8J 1A8. Tel. (250) 624-4666, fax (250) 627-1602. Member bands include Hartley Bay, Metlakatla, Skidegate, Kincolith and Old Masset.

Equipment Rentals/Tours

Kaien Sports, 344 2nd Ave. W., Prince Rupert, B.C., V8J 1G6. Tel. (250) 624-3633, fax (250) 627-4502. Kayak rentals and water taxi information.

Seasport Marine, 295 1st Ave. E., Prince Rupert, B.C., V8J 1A7. Tel. (250) 624-5337. Retail kayaking gear.

ESSENTIALS

- ☐ kayak with secure buoyancy fore and aft, and decklines and webbing to assist with self-rescues
- ☐ paddle
- ☐ spare paddle
- ☐ properly fitted sprayskirt
- ☐ properly fitted lifejacket with a whistle
- ☐ pump or bailer that floats
- ☐ compass, charts and tide tables (current tables if appropriate)
- ☐ flares (for day and night use)
- ☐ repair kit
- ☐ weather radio or VHF in a waterproof case
- ☐ self-rescue aids
- ☐ tow line
- ☐ first aid kit
- ☐ matches or a lighter, and fire starter
- ☐ knife
- ☐ flashlight
- ☐ water bottle
- ☐ sunglasses with retainer straps (for eyeglasses too)
- ☐ sunscreen
- ☐ sponge
- ☐ watch

ADDITIONAL GEAR

- ☐ wet suit or dry suit (advised)
- ☐ helmet (for surf landings)
- ☐ paddling jacket
- ☐ rain gear and extra clothing in waterproof bags (avoid cottons if possible—always be prepared for cold water immersion)
- ☐ tent, sleeping bag and sleeping pad in waterproof bags
- ☐ stove, fuel and other cooking utensils
- ☐ personal items including toiletries
- ☐ fishing gear and licence

Recommended Reading

Blades, Michael. *Day of Two Sunsets: Paddling Adventures on Canada's West Coast.* Victoria: Orca Books, 1993.

Brower, Kenneth. *The Starship and the Canoe.* New York: Harper and Row, 1978.

Broze, Matt et al. *Sea Kayaker's Deep Trouble.* Camden, ME: Ragged Mountain Press, 1997.

Brunt, Douglas. *Paddle B.C.: The Broken Islands.* Delta: Summit Productions, 1995.

Burch, David. *Fundamentals of Kayak Navigation.* Chester, CT: Globe Pequot Press, 1993.

Campbell, Eileen, B.C. Waterfowl Society, et al. *Waterbirds of the Strait of Georgia.* Vancouver: Gordon Soules, 1994.

Cannings, Richard, and Sidney Cannings, *British Columbia: A Natural History.* Vancouver: Greystone Books/ Douglas & McIntyre, 1997.

Coull, Cheryl. *A Traveller's Guide to Aboriginal B.C.* Vancouver: Whitecap Books, 1996.

Daniel, Linda. *Kayak Cookery.* Chester, CT: Globe Pequot Press, 1997.

Day, Beth. *Grizzlies in Their Backyard.* Surrey: Heritage House Publishing, 1994.

Diaz, Ralph. *The Complete Folding Kayaker.* Camden, ME: Ragged Mountain Press, 1994.

Dorst, Adrian, and Cameron Young. *Clayoquot on the Wild Side.* Vancouver: Western Canada Wilderness Committee, 1990.

Douglass, Don. *Exploring Vancouver Island's West Coast.* Bishop, CA: Fine Edge Productions, 1996.

———. *Exploring the North Coast of British Columbia.* Bishop, CA: Fine Edge Productions, 1997.

———. *Exploring the South Coast of British Columbia.* Bishop, CA: Fine Edge Productions, 1997.

Dowd, John. *Sea Kayaking: A Manual for Long-Distance Touring.* Vancouver: Greystone Books/Douglas & McIntyre, 1997.

Drope, Bodhi, and Dorothy Drope. *Paddling the Sunshine Coast.* Madeira Park, B.C.: Harbour Publishing, 1997.

Dutky, Paul. *The Bombproof Roll and Beyond.* Birmingham: Menasha Ridge Press, 1993.

Dyson, George. *Baidarka.* Edmonds, WA: Alaska Northwest Publishing Company, 1988.

Ecomarine Coast Kayaking School. *Cultural Impacts.* Vancouver: Ecomarine, 1997.

Ford, John, et al. *Killer Whales: The Natural History and Genealogy of Orcinus orca in B.C. and Washington State.* Vancouver: UBC Press, 1994.

Forgey, William. *The Basic Essentials of Hypothermia.* Merrillville, IN: ICS Books, 1991.

———. *The Basic Essentials of First Aid for the Outdoors.* Merrillville, IN: ICS Books, 1991.

Foster, Nigel. *Nigel Foster's Sea Kayaking.* Chester, CT: Globe Pequot Press, 1997.

Gilbert, Jim, et al. *Drift Fishing.* Surrey: Heritage House Publishing, 1985.

Grescoe, Paul, and Audrey Grescoe. *Fragments of Paradise.* Vancouver: Raincoast Books, 1995.

Hampton, Bruce, and David Cole. *Soft Paths.* National Outdoor Leadership School. Harrisburg: Stackpole Books, 1988.

Harbo, Rick. *Shells and Shellfish.* Madeira Park, B.C.: Harbour Publishing, 1997.

Harbord, Heather. *Nootka Sound and the Surrounding Waters of Maquinna.* Surrey: Heritage House Publishing, 1996.

Harold, Hughina. *Totem Poles and Tea.* Surrey: Heritage House Publishing, 1996.

Harrison, David. *Kayak Camping.* New York: Hearst Marine Books, 1995.

———. *Sea Kayaking Basics.* New York: Hearst Marine Books, 1993.

Herrero, Stephen. *Bear Attacks: Their Causes and Avoidance.* New York: Lyons & Burford, 1985.

Horwood, Dennis, and Tom Perkin. *Islands for Discovery: An Outdoors Guide to B.C.'s Queen Charlotte Islands.* Victoria: Orca Books, 1996.

Hoyt, Erich. *Orca: The Whale Called Killer.* Buffalo: Camden House, 1995.

Hutchinson, Derek. *The Complete Book of Sea Kayaking.* Chester, CT: Globe Pequot Press, 1995.

———. *Derek Hutchinson's Guide to Expedition Sea Kayaking.* Chester, CT: Globe Pequot Press, 1995.

Ince, John, and Hedi Kottner. *Sea Kayaking Canada's West Coast.* Vancouver: Raxas Books, 1982.

Keller, Betty, and Rosella Leslie. *Sea-Silver: Inside B.C.'s Salmon Farming Industry.* Victoria: Horsdal & Schubart Publishers, 1996.

Lawrence, Iain. *Far Away Places.* Victoria: Orca Books, 1995.

Maine Island Trail Association. *The Maine Island Trail Guidebook.* Portland, ME: MITA, 1996.

May, Elizabeth. *Paradise Won.* Toronto: McClelland & Stewart, 1990.

MacDonald, George. *Ninstints: Haida World Heritage Site.* Vancouver: UBC Press, 1992.

McAllister Ian, et al. *The Great Bear Rainforest.* Madeira Park, B.C.: Harbour Publishing, 1997.

McConnaughey, et al. *National Audubon Society Nature Guides: Pacific Coast.* New York: Knopf, 1988.

McFarlane, John et al. *Official Guide to Pacific Rim National Park Reserve.* Calgary: Blackbird Naturgraphics, 1996.

McKinnon, Andy, and Jim Pojar. *Plants of Coastal British Columbia.* Vancouver: Lone Tree, 1994.

Merry, Wayne. *St. John's Ambulance Official Wilderness First-Aid Guide.* Toronto: McClelland & Stewart, 1994.

Ministry of Forests. *Safety Guide to Bears in the Wild.* Victoria: Queen's Printer, 1997.

Ministry of Small Business, Tourism and Culture. *Middens.* Victoria: MSBTC, 1997.

National Outdoor Leadership School. *Leave No Trace: Temperate Coastal Zones.* Lander, WY: NOLS, 1996.

Outdoor Recreation Council. *Back Country Sanitation.* Vancouver: ORC, 1996.

———. *Water Recreation Code of Ethics.* Vancouver: ORC, 1996.

———. *A Wilderness Code of Ethics.* Vancouver: ORC, 1996.

Paine, Stefani. *Beachwalker: Sea Life of the West Coast.* Vancouver: Douglas & McIntyre, 1992.

Pengelly, Marianne, and Eldon Oja. *West Coast Marine Weather Hazards Manual: A Guide to Local Forecasts and Conditions.* 2nd Edition. Vancouver: Gordon Soules Publishing/Environment Canada, 1992.

Poole, Michael. *Ragged Islands: A Journey by Canoe through the Inside Passage.* Vancouver: Douglas & McIntyre, 1991.

Rasmussen, Greg, et al. *Kayaking in Paradise: Journeys through the Inside Passage.* Vancouver: Whitecap Books, 1997.

Renner, Jeff. *Northwest Marine Weather: From the Columbia River to Cape Scott.* Seattle: The Mountaineers, 1993.

Rogers, Joel. *The Hidden Coast: Kayak Exploration from Alaska to Mexico.* Anchorage: Alaska Northwest Books, 1991.

Russell, Charles. *Spirit Bear.* Toronto: Key Porter Books, 1994.

Schimelpfenig, Tod, and Linda Lindsey. *National Outdoor Leadership School Wilderness First Aid.* Lander, WY: NOLS, 1991.

Seidman, David. *The Essential Sea Kayaker.* Camden, Maine: Ragged Mountain Press, 1992.

Snively, Gloria. *Exploring the Seashore in B.C., Washington and Oregon.* Vancouver: Gordon Soules, 1995.

Snowden, Mary Ann. *Island Paddling: A Paddler's Gude to the Gulf Islands and Barkley Sound.* Victoria: Orca Books, 1997.

Stoltmann, Randy. *Written by the Wind.* Victoria: Orca Books, 1993.

Walbran, John. *British Columbia Coast Names.* Vancouver: Douglas & McIntyre, 1991.

Washburne, Randel. *The Coastal Kayaker: Kayak Camping on the Alaska and B.C. Coast.* Seattle: Pacific Search Press, 1983.

———. *Kayak Trips in Puget Sound and the San Juan Islands.* Seattle: Pacific Search Press, 1986.

Wertheim, Anne. *The Intertidal Wilderness.* San Francisco: Sierra Club Books, 1984.

White, Charlie. *Living Off the Sea.* Surrey: Heritage House Publishing, 1991.

Periodicals

Sea Kayaker, 135-7001 Seaview Ave. NW, Seattle, WA 98117-6059. Tel. (206) 789-9536, fax (206) 781-1141. Webpage: www.seakayakermag.com/.

Wave-Length Paddling Magazine, RR #1, S-17, C-49, Gabriola Island, B.C., V0R 1X0. Tel./fax (250) 247-9789. Webpage: www.island.net/~wavenet/.

Jamie Boulding first experienced boating in Nootka Sound as a child in the 1960s and has been coming back ever since. He is the owner of Strathcona Park Lodge and the Canadian Outdoor Leadership Training School (COLTS) through which he is able to introduce hundreds of people to paddling every year. Jamie, the lodge and the school all operate with the belief that training people to travel safely and experience wilderness by themselves is healthier for both people and the land.

Frank Brown is a member of the Heiltsuk Nation and a tourism operator in Bella Bella. He and his wife Cathy own and operate SeeQuest Adventures, which includes an interpretive centre at McLoughlin Bay, a water taxi service for kayakers and traditional canoe adventures. Active in the resurgence of canoe building and paddling, Frank helped make history organizing the voyage of a traditional canoe from Bella Bella to Expo 86 in Vancouver. Frank has a degree in outdoor recreation from Capilano College.

Michele Deakin has worked for Parks Canada since 1985. She started in Ontario and moved westward until she reached Haida Gwaii in 1991. She has paddled Gwaii Haanas for pleasure and for business and believes strongly that the rawness and power of the area must be protected for future generations. Gwaii Haanas contributions to this book were based on information developed over the years by many staff. Thanks also to Meredith Reeve, Pauline Scott and the Archipelago Management Board for their assistance.

Bodhi and Dorothy Drope have been paddling in British Columbia for 15 years. They make their home on the Sunshine Coast and know that area most intimately.

In 1991, they established Sunshine Kayaking in Gibsons, offering kayak classes, day tours, extended tours and rentals. The luscious natural environment of coastal B.C. gives inspiration for the painting, drawing, fabric work and writing that occupies them during the off season.

Bonny Glambeck has lived and kayaked in Tofino since 1988 and is active in the movement to save Clayoquot Sound. She is an avid expedition kayaker and has been guiding and teaching professionally since 1995. Her special passion is sharing paddling skills with other women, so they can enjoy wilderness travel as much as she does.

Liz Hicks is the owner operator of Tyee Resort in Bamfield on Vancouver Island. She has lived on the West Coast all her life, never too far from the ocean, on boats, islands, float homes and small villages. She has been kayaking for over 20 years, has travelled all over the world on expeditions and now offers accommodation, fishing, hiking and kayak tours at her resort. She is also actively involved with the Loyal Bamfield Kayak Club and a member of the Auxillary Coast Guard.

Edwin Hubert is a marine biologist and kayak guide who has been operating Seabird Kayaking out of Bamfield for the last three years. The company runs small, customized day and multi-day trips that focus on environmental and cultural aspects of Bamfield Harbour and the nearby Deer Group. Edwin also has a strong historical interest in the coastal town and recently authored a self-guided historical walking tour of the Bamfield boardwalk on behalf of the Bamfield Preservation and Development Society.

Fran Hunt-Jinnouchi and Marc Jinnouchi own and operate North Island Kayak Rentals. They offer the "Ancient Voices" Native Cultural Kayak Expedition, along with other unique trips, such as an Ethnobotonay Tour and a children's Summer Science Kayak Trip. North Island Kayak Rentals has outlets in Port Hardy, Alder Bay and will soon be expanding into Telegraph Cove. Fran is Kwakwaka'wakw First Nation and has a great love for her ancestral home of Quatsino Sound. Both Fran and Marc are active in their community.

Darryl Jensen is a graphic designer who has worked with the B.C. Marine Trail Association on various projects, including the maps to this guidebook. Although he grew up in northern Saskatchewan where he paddled canoes with his family, Darryl hasn't looked back since he first saw the B.C. coast from a kayak. When he isn't paddling rivers and oceans, Darryl can be found running ODIN Graffix in Abbotsford.

Charles Justice is a nurse, president of the Prince Rupert Kayak Club and northern coordinator for the B.C. Marine Trail Association. He has kayaked extensively throughout the north coast and occasionally teaches sea kayaking. The last we heard from Charles, he was heading north to Alaska.

Ralph Keller has been exploring Desolation Sound and the Coast Mountains since he and his wife Lannie settled on Read Island 17 years ago. Ralph is knowledgeable in homestead and alternative energy technologies and is an active environmentalist with a keen interest in forest biology. As the owners of Coast Mountain Expeditions, Ralph and Lannie take great pleasure in sharing their remote island lifestyle and the natural beauty of their home at the edge of the mountains.

Dan Lewis started sea kayaking in 1978 and has been teaching kayaking professionally since 1980. He was a founder of the Ecomarine Coastal Kayaking School in 1984, designing courses and teaching there until 1991. His 1990 circumnavigation of Vancouver Island led him to become a strong advocate for wildland protection. He lives and teaches kayaking in Tofino, where he enjoys paddling year round.

Peter McGee has been paddling for over 15 years and has guided in B.C., Alaska and Mexico. In 1993, following a trip that covered much of the B.C. coast, he founded the B.C. Marine Trail Association as a means of preserving and caring for areas that are critical to the paddling community. Pete was executive director of the association until 1997.

Bill McIntyre has been Chief Naturalist at Pacific Rim National Park Reserve for 15 years and currently works there as an Outreach and Environmental Education Coordinator. He has also worked and volunteered in research, sailing and coastal expeditions and tours in Alaska, the Queen Charlottes, the Gulf Islands and Vancouver Island. Bill makes his home in Ucluelet, on the edge of Barkley Sound—an area he has travelled extensively since 1973.

John Nelson Over the years, John has worked with B.C. Wild, the Steelhead Society of B.C. and the Sierra Club of B.C. on numerous conservation issues. In the fall of 1996 his passion for paddling brought him in contact with the B.C. Marine Trail Association, and in 1997 he became executive director.

Allen Palmer   An outdoors enthusiast, Allen was first introduced to the paddling wonders of Puget Sound over 10 years ago and has been exploring its nooks and crannies ever since. Allen has been involved in the Washington Water Trails Association since the early 1990s and sat on the board until 1996.

Tessa van Scheik has been kayaking for many years, both river and ocean; she also competed as a runner in the Olympics for her mother country, South Africa. Although involved in many outdoor sports such as wind surfing, her passion is kayaking. Tessa worked as a kayak guide for North Island Kayak Rentals for three years before returning to South Africa.

Catrin Webb is a Capilano College Outdoor Recreation graduate who is both a canoe and kayak instructor and guide. During the summer she is the assistant manager at Deep Cove Canoe and Kayak Centre, a full-service kayak rental operation located on Indian Arm that also offers instruction and tours. When the weather turns cold, Catrin heads to the mountains where she works at the Northshore Outdoor School.

Alan Wilson is managing editor of *Wave-Length Paddling Magazine* and coordinator of the Annual Ocean Kayak Festival. He was born on the West Coast and has lived in the Gulf Islands for many years, writing, publishing and paddling.

Rupert Wong is a professional biologist who works primarily in the Kyuquot area. He works with First Nations, local industry and governments to restore watershed habitat and volunteers as warden for the Checleset Bay Ecological Reserve. Rupert is the owner of West Coast Expeditions, an educational nature tour company. He was 11 years old when he first visited Kyuquot.

Howard Zatwarnitski has been a canoe and kayak enthusiast for the past 20 years and is the owner and operator of Natural West Coast Adventures. Based out of White Rock, Natural West Coast Adventures runs tours in and around Vancouver as well as in Hotham Sound. After 12 years working in the mental health and social services profession, Howard has found a means to combine business and pleasure.

Sources

Books

Chappell, John. *Cruising Beyond Desolation Sound: Channels and Anchorages from the Yuculta Rapids to Cape Caution.* Surrey: Naikoon Marine, 1987.

Coull, Cheryl. *A Traveller's Guide to Aboriginal B.C.* Vancouver: Whitecap Books, 1996.

Dowd, John. *Sea Kayaking: A Manual for Long-Distance Touring.* Vancouver: Greystone Books/Douglas & McIntyre, 1997.

Drope, Bodhi, and Dorothy Drope. *Paddling the Sunshine Coast.* Madeira Park, B.C.: Harbour Publishing, 1997.

Duff, Wilson and Michael Kew. *Ninstints.* Victoria: Report of the Provincial Museum, 1957.

Dalzell, Kathleen E. *The Queen Charlotte Islands—Places and Names, Vol. 2.* Prince Rupert: Cove Press, 1973.

Gardner, Julia E. *Pressure Group Politics and the Campaign to Protect South Moresby Island.* Vancouver: UBC Press, 1990.

Hendrickson, Robert. *The Ocean Almanac.* Toronto: Doubleday, 1984.

Ince, John, and Hedi Kottner: *Sea Kayaking Canada's West Coast.* Vancouver: Raxas Books, 1982.

Macdonald, Bruce. *Vancouver: A Visual History.* Vancouver: Talonbooks, 1992.

MacDonald, George F. *Haida Monumental Art: Villages of the Queen Charlotte Islands.* Vancouver: UBC Press, 1983.

MacFarlane, J.M. et al. *Official Guide to Pacific Rim National Park Reserve.* Blackbird Naturgraphics, 1996.

Maine Island Trail Association. *The Maine Island Trail Guidebook.* Portland, ME: MITA, 1996.

May, Elizabeth. *Paradise Won: The Struggle for South Moresby.* Toronto: McClelland & Stewart, 1990.

National Outdoor Leadership School. *Leave No Trace: Temperate Coastal Zones.* Lander, WY: NOLS, 1996.

Pengelly, Marianne, and Eldon Oja. *Marine Weather Hazards Manual: A Guide to Local Forecasts and Conditions.* 2nd ed. Ottawa: Environment Canada, 1990.

Renner, Jeff. *Northwest Marine Weather: From the Columbia River to Cape Scott.* Seattle: The Mountaineers, 1993.

Rogers, Joel. *The Hidden Coast: Kayak Exploration from Alaska to Mexico.* Anchorage: Alaska Northwest Books, 1991.

Snowden, Mary Ann. *Island Paddling: A Paddler's Guide to the Gulf Islands and Barkley Sound.* Victoria: Orca Books, 1997.

Walbran, John T. *British Columbia Coast Names.* Vancouver: Douglas & McIntyre, 1991.

Washington Water Trails Association. *A Guide to*

the *Cascadia Marine Trail System.* Port
Orchard, WA: Pack and Paddle Publishing,
1994.

Wilson, Ian R. et al. *Cultural Heritage
Background Study.* Victoria: Clayoquot Sound
Sustainable Development Strategy, 1991.

Wolferstan, Bill. *Cruising Guide to British
Columbia Vol. 2: Desolation Sound and the
Discovery Islands.* Vancouver: Whitecap
Books, 1987.

Other

BC Parks. "The Legend of Princess Louisa Inlet."
Victoria: Queens Printer, 1992.

Ecomarine Ocean Kayaking Centre. "Cultural

Impacts." Vancouver: Ecomarine, 1997.

Energy, Mines and Resources Canada. "The
Geology of Howe Sound." Vancouver: EMR
Canada.

Ministry of Forests. "A Safety Guide to Bears in
the Wild." Victoria: MOF, 1997.

Ministry of Small Business, Tourism and Culture.
"Middens." Victoria: MSBTC, 1997.

Outdoor Recreation Council. "Back Country
Sanitation: Protecting Yourself Against
Water-Borne Disease." Vancouver: ORC,
1996.

———. "A Wilderness Code of Ethics."
Vancouver: ORC, 1996.

Schroeder, Bob. "Routes to Jedediah Island."

Index